I0200178

Manu V. Devadevan

A Prehistory of Hinduism

Manu V. Devadevan

A Prehistory of Hinduism

Managing Editor: Katarzyna Tempczyk

Series Editor: Ishita Banerjee-Dube

Language Editor: Wayne Smith

Open Access
Hinduism

DE GRUYTER
OPEN

ISBN: 978-3-11-051736-1
e-ISBN: 978-3-11-051737-8

(cc) BY-NC-ND

This work is licensed under the Creative Commons Attribution-NonCommercial-NoDerivs 3.0 License.
For details go to http://creativecommons.org/licenses/by-nc-nd/3.0/.

© 2016 Manu V. Devadevan
Published by De Gruyter Open Ltd, Warsaw/Berlin
Part of Walter de Gruyter GmbH, Berlin/Boston
The book is published with open access at www.degruyter.com.

Library of Congress Cataloging-in-Publication Data
A CIP catalog record for this book has been applied for at the Library of Congress.

Managing Editor: Katarzyna Tempczyk
Series Editor:Ishita Banerjee-Dube
Language Editor: Wayne Smith

www.degruyteropen.com

Cover illustration: © Manu V. Devadevan

In memory of U. R. Ananthamurthy

Contents

Acknowledgements

My parents, Kanakambika Antherjanam and Vishnu Namboodiri, were my first teachers. From them, I learnt to persevere, and to stay detached. This book would not have been possible without these fundamental lessons.

I was introduced to the traditions discussed in this work through the poems and plays of the leading Kannada playwright, H.S. Shivaprakash. Discussions with him, and with three other prominent Kannada litterateurs, the late U.R. Ananthamurthy, the late Shantarasa, and Keshava Malagi, have provided insights that were otherwise not available in most academic studies on religious life in South Asia. Although their thoughts were framed by the popular academic equations of religion, caste, class, political authority, the ascetic ideal, and the ethical life, they brought to bear upon their understanding, the significant questions of creativity and performance, which presented these traditions in an altogether different light. I owe them a debt of gratitude.

No less rewarding were my engagements with many a saint of our times. Svami Vinaya Chaitanya, Guru Nirmalananda, Shaikh Riyaz-ud-din Chisti, and Svami Vimala Sarasvati enriched my thoughts with their strikingly original assessment of *vedantic*, Sufi and Buddhist cosmologies, and their sympathetic appreciation of modern European thought from Descartes and Spinoza to Wittgenstein and Bergson. I must also record my debt, although intellectually less rewarding, to the late Fakira Channavira Svami IV and Fakira Siddharama Svami V of the Shirahatti Matha, the late Puttaraja Gavayi of the Viresvara Punyasrama in Gadaga, Sivalingesvara Kumarendra Svami of the Savalagi Matha, Sivaratri Desikendra Svami of the Sutturu Matha, Sivamurti Murugha Sarana of the Murugharajendra Matha, Chitradurga, Bharati Tirtha Svami, the Sankaracharya of Sringeri, Visvesa Tirtha Svami of the Pejavara Matha, Udupi, Virabhadra Channamalla Svami of the Nidumamidi Matha, Bagepalli, and Saranabasavappa Appa of the Saranabasavesvara Matha, Kalaburagi.

Much of what I have to say about the political economy in the pages that follow springs from stimulating discussions I had with Y. Subbarayalu, with whom I often agree, and K.N. Ganesh, whose positions I all too often don't share. For a long time, my understanding of religious traditions and practices in Karnataka was primitive and dogmatic, due, in large part, to the influence of counter-intuitive theories of religion propounded by a range of scholars from James George Frazer and William James to Clifford Geertz and Talal Asad. The late M.M. Kalburgi drew me out of the slumber of theory, threw me into the rather-hostile terrain which this book explores, and helped me acclimatize to this brave old world. Conversations with Romila Thapar, Bhairabi Prasad Sahu, the late Ram Sharan Sharma, Uma Chakravarti, Vijaya Ramaswamy, Rajan Gurukkal, S. Settar, M.G.S. Narayanan, B. Surendra Rao, Kumkum Roy, and Chetan Singh, at various times, have been of considerable help. More personal, although no-less intellectual, are my debts to Kunal Chakrabarti, who has always been encouraging, and R. Mahalakshmi and Shonaleeka Kaul, constant sources of inspiration. I have also benefitted from the conversations I had with Surya Prakash Upadhyaya and Ashok Kumar M., colleagues at the Institute where I teach.

I have not had the privilege of meeting Sheldon Pollock, but the email conversations which we shared have opened up for me new and stimulating ways of engaging with premodern South Asia; nor have I had the privilege of meeting David Shulman (although we are working together on a joint project!). My telephone and Skype conversations with him and the exchange of emails have enabled me to think beyond the accepted frontiers of my discipline. I regret that I have known him only for two and a half years.

As usual, it was Kesavan Veluthat and Abhilash Malayil who had to bear the burden of prolonged discussions on almost every theme discussed in this book. They listened to me with patience for hours and hours every week, and made interventions that were crucial in developing my arguments. They have been my greatest teachers in history (although the latter is now masquerading as my student).

Although this book was in the cards for a long time, I sat down in earnest to work on it only after Ishita Banerjee-Dube urged me to do so on more than one occasion. But for her, this work would have remained in cold storage for many more years. Thank you very much, Ishita-di.

Thanks also to Katarzyna Tempczyk, Managing Editor of Theology and Religious Studies in De Gruyter Open, who waited for the manuscript with kind patience, when I failed to meet the deadline; and to Wayne Smith, the Language Editor, whose efforts have enhanced the book's readability to a substantial degree.

The innocent questions of H.G. Rajesh have been the most difficult to answer. I am indebted to him. I also thank him for accompanying me on a 3000-kilometre tour of Karnataka and southern Maharashtra in early August 2015, when I set out to have one last glimpse of the great landscapes and centres of monasticism discussed in this work, before sending it to print. A similar journey with Gil Ben-Herut in late June 2014 is unforgettable not only for the discoveries we jointly made, but also for the stimulating discussions that we had as we travelled from Bīdara, Basavakalyāṇa and Kalaburagi to Kāginele, Abbalūru and Harihara.

Part of the research that went into the making of this book was carried out with fellowships from the Department of Culture, Government of India (in 2005), and the India Foundation for the Arts, Bangalore (in 2006), and a joint research project, funded by the University Grants Commission of India and the Israel Science Foundation (in 2014). I thank these funding agencies. S.K. Aruni and Sangappa Karjagi of the Indian Council of Historical Research, Southern Regional Centre, Bangalore, Vasanta Gowda of Mythic Society Library, Bangalore, and R.F. Desai of Basava Samithi Library, Bangalore, were always helpful, when I approached them for books, books and more books.

M.S. Pramod and K.P. Pradip Kumar have been great sources of encouragement for the last two decades. Manorama Tripathy, Gayatri Deshpande, and Prabodh Kumar have stood by me in times of need. Aneish P. Rajan, Ameet Parameswaran,

Arathi P.M., Sreejith Divakaran, Ancy Bay, Divya K., and K.D. Pradeep have been great pillars of support. The warmth of Shail Shankar, Kavita Pandey, and Suman has been invaluable in my life as a teacher in a sleepy town in the Himalayas. Shail and Kavita provided the much-needed respites, and the smile of their wonderful little son, three-year old Cheeku (Akshat Mishra), added colours to it that I can scarcely forget.

This book was completed at 8:30 am on 30 August 2015 in Bhubaneswar. Fifteen minutes later, at Dharwad in northwestern Karnataka, two young men shot dead Professor M.M. Kalburgi, the greatest authority of our times on premodern religion, language, and literature in Karnataka. It was as if he stood by me like a guardian angel while the book was being written, and left immediately after the work was accomplished. I weep in silence.

A Guide to Pronunciation of Diacritical Marks

In order to ensure uniformity, the diacritical marks used in this book follow the Dravidian convention even for Sanskrit, Persian, Arabic, and other non-Dravidian languages. Thus, Hāveri and *kevalajñāna* will be written as Hāvēri and *kēvalajñāna*, Gurshāsp and Shāh as Gurśāsp and Śāh.

Vowels

a as *o* in *mother*
ā as *a* in *park*
i as *i* in *bill*
ī as *ee* in *week*
u as *oo* in *book*
ū as *oo* in *root*
ṛ as *r* in *crystal*
e as *e* in *men*
ē as *a* in *sage*
ai as *y* in *cry*
o as *o* in *robust*
ō as *o* in *smoke*
au as *ou* in *ground*

Semi-labial

ṃ as *m* in *empire*

Semi-aspirate

ḥ as *ah* in the exclamation, *yeah*, but with mild aspiration

Guttural or Velar Consonants

k as *c* in *country*
kh as *kh* in *ask her*
g as *g* in *wagon*
gh as *gh* in *big hunch*
ṅ as *n* in *monk*

Palatal Consonants

c as *ch* in *charity*
ch as *chh* in *witch hunt*
j as *j* in *jungle*
jh as *geh* in *challenge him*
ñ as *n* in *bench*

Retroflex or Cerebral or Lingual Consonants

ṭ as *t* in *talk*, but uttered with tongue bent upwards to touch the hard palate
ṭh as *th* in *boat house*, but uttered with tongue bent upwards to touch the hard palate
ḍ as *d* in *rod*, but uttered with tongue bent upwards to touch the hard palate
ḍh as *dh* in *god head*, but uttered with tongue bent upwards to touch the hard palate
ṇ as *n* in the American pronunciation of *horn*, but uttered with tongue bent upwards to touch the hard palate

Dental Consonants

t as *th* in *three*, but without aspiration
th as *th* in *think*
d as *th* in *other*
dh as *theh* in *bathe her*
n as *n* in *native*

Labial Consonants

p as *p* in *province*
ph as *ph* in *stop him*
b as *b* in *beach*
bh as *bh* in *abhor*
m as *m* in *master*

Liquids

y as *y* in *young*
r as *r* in *aroma*
l as *l* in *love*
v as *w* in *wheat*

Sibilants

ś as *sh* in *ash*
ṣ as *sh* in *wash*, but with tongue bent slightly upwards
s as *s* in *secret*

Aspirate

h as *h* in *host*

Dravidian liquids

ṟ as *r* in *ring*, but uttered with tongue slightly bent upwards to touch the hard palate

Dravidian retroflex liquids

ḷ as *l* in *blow*, but uttered with tongue bent upwards to touch the hard palate
ḻ as *r* in the American pronunciation of *practice*

1 Introduction

In the first half of the nineteenth century, a new religious consciousness began to take shape in the Indian subcontinent. This was the great Hindu consciousness. It was a phenomenon that was at once passionate and compassionate, egalitarian and divisive, benevolent and virile. With a checkered, sensitive history, it has pervaded religious life in India ever since, integrating and dividing millions of Indians in its own ambivalent ways. Historians trace the origins of the Hindu consciousness to the late eighteenth century, when the scholarly study of Indian religious texts such as the Vēdas, the Upaniṣads, and the *Bhagavadgīta* commenced under the aegis of the Asiatic Society, established in Calcutta by Sir William Jones in 1784, but it was not until the early decades of the nineteenth century that it was used as a marker of identity. Raja Rammohan Roy is credited with the use of the word 'Hinduism' for the first time. Roy used the word in one of his writings in 1816, and again, in 1817.[1] It came into circulation almost immediately. At least one use of the word is known from 1818, and one from 1820, the latter in the *Asiatick Researches*.[2] By 1839, the word had already appeared in the title of a book, Alexander Duff's *India and Indian Missions: Sketches of the Gigantic System of Hinduism Both in Theory and Practice*.[3] Duff spoke, among other things, of the theory of Hinduism,[4] the origin of Hinduism,[5] the system of Hinduism,[6] and even the territory of Hinduism.[7] In fact, the use of the word 'Hindu' as a marker of identity was already known by the time Rammohan Roy spoke of 'Hinduism' as a religion. In the first volume of *the History of British India*, published in 1817, James Mill used phrases such as the Hindu religion,[8] the Hindu system,[9] Hindu expressions and beliefs,[10] Hindu ideas,[11] the Hindu doctrine,[12] the Hindu character,[13] the Hindu law[14] and the Hindu society,[15] – all expressions in which the notion of Hinduism as an identity was manifestly embedded. However, for many years, the reach of the expressions Hindu and Hinduism was limited to scholarly debates

1 Lorenzen 2006: 3.
2 Ibid.
3 Ibid., 4.
4 Duff 1840: 144.
5 Ibid., 297.
6 Ibid.
7 Ibid., 603.
8 Mill 2010: 264.
9 Ibid., 171; 470.
10 Ibid., 198.
11 Ibid., 215.
12 Ibid., 243.
13 Ibid., 304.
14 Ibid., 141, 156.
15 Ibid., 171, 429.

and descriptions. Their scope as markers of identity was only feebly felt. Those who identified themselves as practicing Hindus were few in number. As the later half of the nineteenth century progressed, literate men and women in the leading metropolises of India were beginning, in increasing numbers, to speak of a religion called Hinduism to which they belonged. By the turn of the century, it had evolved into one of the most compelling historical realities of our times. So captivating was its impact that when the first World's Parliament of Religions was held in Chicago in 1893, its organizers identified Hinduism as one of the religions to be offered a platform. By this time, Hinduism was already being represented as the oldest religion in the world. Among its representatives at the Parliament in Chicago was the redoubtable Swami Vivekananda. On 11 September 1893, he thanked the "Sisters and Brothers of America" for the warm and cordial welcome they had accorded, and said: "I thank you in the name of the most ancient order of monks in the world; I thank you in the name of the mother of religions".[16] On 19 September, he opined in his address to the Parliament that Hinduism was one of the three religions of the world that have come down from prehistoric times, the other two being Zoroastrianism and Judaism.[17] Things evolved very quickly in the following years. In 1906, a Hindu Sahayak Sabha was formed in Lahore. On 4 August that year, Lala Lajpat Rai, Shadi Lal, Harkrishna Lal, Raja Narendra Nath, Ram Saran Das, Ruchi Ram Sahini, Ram Bhaj Datta, and Lala Hans Raj established a Hindu Sabha in the same city.[18] In 1915, an 'All India' organization called the Sarvadeshak Hindu Mahasabha was launched to protect the interest of the Hindus. The organization was renamed Akhil Bharatiya Hindu Mahasabha in 1921.[19] The trajectory of evolution was rather spectacular.

How was Hinduism produced in the nineteenth century? Much ink has been expended in addressing this question over the last three decades. Attempts to explain Hinduism's emergence in the late eighteenth and the nineteenth centuries are regarded as constructionist, as they proceed from the premise that Hinduism was constructed during the colonial period under British influence, if not under British patronage or supervision. Constructionism encapsulates several different positions. Some of them deny the very existence of Hinduism. Robert E. Frykenberg, for instance, holds that "there has never been any such thing as a single 'Hinduism' or any single 'Hindu community' for all of India".[20] More scathing is John Stratton Hawley's observation that Hinduism "is a notoriously illegitimate child".[21] It is worth quoting Hawley at some length as it exemplifies this strand of constructionism.

16 Paranjape 2015: 3.
17 Ibid., 5.
18 Bapu 2013: 16. Note that the All India Muslim League was formed in December 1906, four months after the establishment of the Hindu Sabha.
19 On the Hindu Mahasabha, see Bapu 2013. Also see Gordon 1975.
20 Frykenberg 1989: 29.
21 Hawley 1991: 20.

> Hinduism—the word, and perhaps the reality too—was born in the 19th century, a notoriously illegitimate child. The father was middle-class and British, and the mother, of course, was India. The circumstances of the conception are not altogether clear. One heard of the "goodly habits and observances of Hindooism" in a Bengali-English grammar written in 1829, and the Reverend William Tennant had spoken of "the Hindoo system" in a book on Indian manners and history written at the beginning of the century. Yet it was not until the inexpensive handbook *Hinduism* was published by the Society for Promoting Christian Knowledge in 1877 that the term came into general English usage.[22]

Other positions are more cautions; thus, Christopher John Fuller writes:

> "Hinduism" as a term for that indigenous religion, became current in English in the early nineteenth century and was coined to label an "ism" that was itself partly a product of western orientalist thought, which (mis)constructed Hinduism on the model of occidental religions, particularly Christianity.... That linguistic development significantly reflects the impact of modern Hindu reformist thought and the Hindus' own search for an identifiable, unitary system of religious belief and practice. Nonetheless, "Hinduism" does translate any premodern Indian word without serious semantic distortion, and it still does not correspond to any concept or category that belongs to the thinking of a large proportion of the ordinary people.... Yet that is not a decisive objection against employment of the term.... That "Hinduism" is not a traditional, indigenous category, concept, or "cultural reality"—albeit an important negative fact—in no way nullifies an analysis that demonstrates that Hinduism is a relatively coherent and distinctive religious system founded on common structures of relationships.[23]

More often than not, the constructionist position has held that Hinduism was invented by the British in the nineteenth century. J. Laine, an early constructionist, does not share this position fully. Writes Laine:

> the concepts 'Hinduism' and 'religion' were part of the intellectual baggage packed off to India with the eighteenth century British, and with their introduction into Indian thought, Indians themselves used these terms in their efforts at self-definition and understanding *vis-à-vis* the alien Englishmen. Even if the categories did not quite fit, the process of cultural translation thus sparked by the need for self-understanding necessitated their use.[24]

Arguments against the British invention thesis are also made by Brian K. Pennington, who holds that it "grants altogether too much power to colonialism; it both mystifies and magnifies colonial means of domination and erases Hindu agency and creativity".[25] Pennington also rejects the view that the construction of Hinduism was carried out by reformers like Raja Rammohan Roy. In his view, popular Hinduism was 'manufactured' by initiatives that were opposed to both the colonial and the reformist projects. The early nineteenth-century Bengali newspaper, *Samācār Candrikā*,

22 Ibid, 20-21.
23 Fuller 2004: 10.
24 Laine 1983: 165.
25 Pennington 2005: 5.

is identified as one such initiative. As far as the likes of the *Samācār Candrikā* are concerned,

> the phrase ("construction of Hinduism") has broader implications, describing not only representational practices but also the manipulations of ritual, belief, and their rationale that helped produce a cohesive Hinduism in tune with its multiethnic, multireligious colonial environment.... Manufacturing this Hinduism proved to be an act less of promoting particular items of doctrine or sites of authority—a strategy pursued especially by the Hindu reformer Rammohan Roy and is religious organization the Brahmo Samaj—and more of patterning a general structure for Hindu action, social and ritual.[26]

The constructionist position has not gone unchallenged. The absence of the word Hinduism before the nineteenth century, it is argued, is no proof of the absence of what the word might represent. In David N. Lorenzen's assessment, "the claim that Hinduism was invented or constructed by European colonizers, mostly British, sometime after 1800 is false"[27] because "textual evidence against this claim is so overwhelming".[28]

> Major historical changes in the economic and political institutions of India during the Turco-Afghan conquest, the Mughal invasion, the consolidation of the Mughal polity, and the establishment of the British colonial regime undoubtedly effected important changes in the religious traditions of India, but the rapid changes of early colonial times never had such an overwhelming impact that they led to the construction or invention of Hinduism. Hinduism wasn't invented sometime after 1800, or even around the time of the establishment of the Delhi Sultanate. What did happen during the centuries of rule by dynasties led by Muslim Sultans and Emperors was that Hindus developed a consciousness of a shared religious identity based on the loose family resemblances of variegated beliefs and practices of Hindus, whatever their sect, caste, chosen deity, or theological school.[29]

We may call this the primordialist position, although this view is by no means oblivious to the changes brought about by historical developments of the nineteenth and the twentieth centuries. While acknowledging the extensive nature of the changes that Hinduism underwent during the colonial period, it argues that Hinduism existed in India long before the arrival of the British. Thus, according to Thomas R. Trautmann,

> there are a number of good reasons to be wary of saying that the British invented Hinduism. Many of the elements of the way in which Hinduism is constructed by the British in the period of Indomania derive from Indians and Indian sources.... The very (Persian) word *Hindu* for an inhabitant of India and follower of a certain religion shows that the conception predated British contacts with India. In any case the British conception of Hinduism as the religion of the natives

26 Ibid., 140.
27 Lorenzen 2006: 2.
28 Ibid., 24.
29 Ibid., 36.

> of India is well along in its development in the seventeenth century, when Henry Lord wrote an account of what we would recognize as Hinduism.... To adopt the view that the British had no conception of Hinduism before the new Orientalism...would be to fall in with the propaganda of its own authority claims.[30]

A leading Indologist who shares the primordialist thesis on Hinduism is Wendy Doniger. Her unjustly controversial work, *The Hindus: An Alternative History*, which gives an account of the 'the Hindus', begins the story thus:

> Once upon a time, about 50 million years ago, a triangular plate of land, moving fast (for a continent), broke off from Madagascar (a large island lying off the southeastern coast of Africa) and, "adrift on the earth's mantle," sailed across the Indian Ocean and smashed into the belly of Central Asia with such force that it squeezed the earth five miles up into the skies to form the Himalayan range and fused with Central Asia to become the India subcontinent.... This prehistoric episode will serve us simultaneously as a metaphor for the way that Hinduism through the ages constantly absorbed immigrant people and ideas and as the first historical instance of such an actual immigration.[31]

The section where these words occur is entitled "Origins: Out of Africa". If the present writer was to attempt a history of the landmass we now call India, it would in all likelihood commence on a similar note. Only that it would not be called a history of the Hindus. Doniger makes her views clear in the opening piece of an anthology of essays "on Hinduism" in premodern India. "For the past few decades", writes she,

> scholars have raised several and strong objections to the use of any single term to denote one of the world's major and most ancient faiths. The name 'Hinduism' that we now use is of recent and European construction. But it is Eurocentric to assume that when Europeans made the name they made the game. 'Hinduism' (dare I use the 'H' word, and may I stop holding up my hands for mercy with quotation marks?) is, like the armadillo, part hedgehog, part tortoise. Yet there *are* armadillos, and they were there before they had names. I would like to suggest some ways in which the disparate parts of what we call Hinduism have in fact existed for centuries, cheek by jowl, in a kind of fluid suspension.[32]

She goes on to note:

> It is true that before the British began to categorize communities strictly by religion, few people in India defined themselves exclusively through their religious beliefs; their identities were segmented on the basis of locality, language, caste, occupation and sect. Even today...most people in the country would define themselves by allegiances other than their religion. There is, after all, no Hindu canon; ideas about all the major issues of faith and lifestyle—vegetarianism, nonviolence, belief in rebirth, even caste—are subjects of debate, not dogma. And yet, if we look carefully, there are shared ideas, practices and rituals that not only connect the diverse people

30 Trautmann 1997: 67-68.
31 These are the opening lines of chapter 2, Doniger 2009.
32 Doniger 2013: 3.

> generally called 'Hindus' today, but also link the people who composed and lived by the Vedas in northwest India around 1500 BCE with the Hare Krishna converts dancing in the streets of twenty-first-century New York.[33]

This, certainly, is not a piece of history a modern practitioner of the craft is expected to produce. The *vaidic* people who lived "in northwest India around 1500 BCE" were still not familiar with the use of iron, while the group of ill-informed dancers "in the streets of twenty-first-century New York" live at a time when a manned mission to Mars is being worked out. The nature of the relationship which the two share is by no means obvious. One wonders if this is a piece of 'connected history' writ large?[34] As far as tracing the antiquity of Hinduism is concerned, this understanding of Hinduism is not qualitatively different from Zaehner's 1962 work, which the *Guardian* praised as "the best short introduction to Hinduism in existence".[35] Zaehner's Hinduism consisted of the Vēdas, Brahman, *mōkṣa* or liberation, god, *dharma*, and *bhakti*. It was, in other words, more of an intellectual history. Doniger's concerns are almost altogether different, as she engages with a wide range of topics such as gods and goddesses, women and ogresses, violence and sacrifice, devotion and sex. In her 'alternative' history, which is richer in details, sharper in analysis, and oftentimes illuminating for its raw insights, even dogs, monkeys, and talking animals find respectful space. This is, truly, a story coming from a gifted chronicler of times at the height of her powers. Nevertheless, her Hinduism and that of Zaehner share the same template of primordialism.

Most studies on Hinduism accept the fact that the term is hard to define. There are no prophets and no books acceptable to everyone, no single common deity worshipped by all practitioners. Yet, it is claimed that some essential features of Hinduism can indeed be identified 'if we look carefully'. Exemplifying this position are these words of Gavin D. Flood:

> while it might not be possible to arrive at a watertight definition of Hinduism, this does not mean that the term is empty. There are clearly some kinds of practices, texts and beliefs which are central to the concept of being a 'Hindu', and there are others which are on the edges of Hinduism.... 'Hinduism' is not a category in the classical sense of an essence defined by certain properties, there are nevertheless prototypical forms of Hindu practice and belief.[36]

The differences between the constructionists and the primordialists have produced a body of writings that is rich in documentation and spirited in arguments. Yet, the cumulative light it sheds on how Hinduism was constructed, or transformed, is by no

33 Ibid., 3-4.

34 The phrase 'connected history' is used here sarcastically and should not be mistaken for the idea made popular in South Asian historiography by the two-volume Subrahmanyam 2004a and 2004b.

35 Zaehner 1962.

36 Flood 1996: 7.

means remarkable. This is due in large to the fact that both groups approach Hinduism with an essentialist bent of mind. The 'illegitimate child' thesis of the constructionists seems to be suggesting that other religions like Islam and Christianity were not constructed, or that the construction would have been legitimate had it happened several centuries before the coming of the British (or the Muslims). It also naively presumes that a religion like Hinduism can be constructed with the help of a body of writings produced in the nineteenth century by the British, or by Indian reformers, or by counter-manoeuvres like the one the *Samācār Candrikā* has represented. In other words, it bestows undue determinism and autonomy on discourse. If it was discourse that created Hinduism, all we would need in order to undo it in our day is a counter-discourse. The world, unfortunately, is ontological, not discursively constituted, as the present study will demonstrate.

The primordialist position, on the other hand, is often apologetic, and expressed in the form of statements that are easy to falsify.[37] Its arguments are based largely on the fact that beliefs, practices, and texts identified as Hindu in the nineteenth century existed for several centuries before the arrival of the British. The occasional occurrence of the word Hindu, at least after the fourteenth century, in Indian sources is also taken as evidence for the existence of Hinduism before the colonial era. But the primordialists have failed to produce evidence to the effect that a Hindu universe was imagined before the nineteenth century in the same way as, for example, Christendom, the Islamicate, or the respective Buddhist, Jaina, Sikh, and Jewish worlds were imagined.

The essentialist approach of the constructionists and the primordialists takes religion as an always-already formed entity, with an essential core of its own. Changes caused by political, economic, and other factors are of course acknowledged and extensively discussed. That most aspects of religion, ranging from the institutional to the ritual, are subjected to transformation is also accepted. Even so, the insistence that there is an identifiable set of features inherent in a religion tends to essentialize the phenomenon. Essentialism, per se, is by no means undesirable. In fact, the identification of common traits, and their classification and categorization, constitutes one of the methods through which information is processed for the purpose of knowledge production. Essentialism is central to this mode of information processing.[38] It is through this imperative that the structuring of knowledge, and the process of conceptualization through definitions and taxonomies, become possible. Thus, essentialism is characteristic of at least some forms of knowledge production. The problem with it begins to manifest when the approach is generalized in order to

37 One wonders if falsification is what authenticates their claims to the status of knowledge (in the Popperian sense).

38 However, such an exercise does not in itself constitute knowledge, as the early Jaina theorists of South Asia very clearly understood.

essentialize everything. This is also true of the urge to theorize that informs so much of our contemporary academic pursuits.

Today, it is more-or-less an accepted maxim that theorizing is the only way of producing valid knowledge about the human world. The validity of the maxim itself has never been tested. It is assumed, for no sustainable reason, that knowledge production is contingent upon the production of theory. "Theories," according to one definition, "are nets cast to catch what we call 'the world'."[39] It has "promised the relief of new problems and new interests."[40] These are sober views, more in the nature of an apology rather than an argument for theory. Less temperate views exist. One of them, for instance, tells us that a theory enables us to "decide whether or not some newly discovered entity belongs to its domain", and to assign domains through arbitration when such decision-making involves a conflict.[41] Well? This means that theory is all about distinguishing an apple from an orange, an aircraft from a submarine, a Hindu from a Muslim, a Brahmin from a Dalit. Theory, then, is all about segregation, placing objects of inquiry in distinct, unique, and well-demarcated domains, where there are no possibilities of overlaps, exchanges, similarities or spillovers of any kind. Ensuring distinction and difference in their pristine forms is what this approach to theory is aimed at.

The urge to theorize every object of inquiry is in fact driven by the desire to endow everything with distinct and unalterable attributes of its own. It is a *universal* desire to *particularize*, to *differentiate*, to *break up*, and *dismantle*, and to assign to every object its own space or domain. When brought to the level of human beings, the message it sends out is too unambiguous to be missed. There are no shared experiences or shared histories, no common hopes and dreams, no common destinies either, no possibilities of realization, transformation, forgiveness, or redemption. It affirms and celebrates a life of self-assertion and chauvinism that nurtures indifference—if not intolerance and hatred—for the rest of the world.

The essentialism that lurks behind the theory-bug is not free from the effects of reification. It has its parallels in the unique-in-itself logic of the commodity produced by the capitalist praxis of production, and is, clearly, a classic instance of reification of the commodity logic. More dangerously, it is also in reified harmony with the rhetoric of ethnicity, caste, religion, separatism, hatred-nationalism, fundamentalism, and clash of civilizations, which are all governed by the same logic of uniqueness and ontological difference from the rest. What we see here is the infamous we-cannot-live-together mentality in a thoroughly reified, and therefore unconscious, form. It

39 Popper 2002: 37.

40 Jameson 1991: 182.

41 Balagangadhara 2005: 246.

reminds us of Octavio Paz's Mexican who "shuts himself off from the world: from life and from death."[42]

We are not suggesting that difference is evil or that there are no differences in the world. The existence of difference is what necessitates theory in the first place. But the belief that theory alone can make knowledge possible results in either affirming difference where they may not really exist, or in undermining the presence or possibility of similarities, exchanges, interfaces, and overlaps between different objects. A theory of the market, as different from a theory of language or a theory of renunciation is understandable. But a theory of the market, distinct from a theory of money, commodity, trade, and inflation, can only offer us a tunnel vision of the market.

The moral of the above discussion is plain and simple: the production of knowledge is not at the mercy of theory. Theorizing as an academic enterprise has its palpable limits. Its possibilities are not endless or extendable to every object of inquiry. At the same time, these limits by no means exhaust the possibility of generating valid knowledge about the human world. Inquiries that do not culminate in a theory can be as fruitful, or even more meaningful, than the ones that do. The desire to theorize everything is not found to be springing from an examination of the possibility or otherwise of theorizing. It is an *a priori* position, governed by the processes of reification in the capitalist world of generalized commodity production. Its logic of uniqueness, distinction, and difference is also the one that informs the marketing of cars, cellphones, chocolates, and cigarettes on the one hand, and the passions that drive the rhetoric of ethnicities, religious fundamentalism, and clash of civilizations an the other.

Karl Marx theorized capital. Ferdinand de Saussure and Sigmund Freud produced theories of language and the unconscious respectively, no matter how unconvincing they were. Not all objects of inquiry enjoy similar advantages. It is too early to say whether religion is open to theorizing or not. It follows, then, that the question of identifying the essential core of Hinduism—or any religion, for that matter—has not arisen.

This study is an attempt to trace a prehistory of Hinduism. The geographical limits and the select traditions chosen for analysis presuppose that it is *a* prehistory, and not *the* prehistory of Hinduism. Many such prehistories are possible, which differ in varying degrees in their details. The larger trajectory of historical development, though, is likely to be similar, if not identical, as it is intricately entwined with the trajectory of the political economy.

Our study proceeds from the presumption that Hinduism was imagined and brought into existence in the course of the nineteenth century. To that extent, it shares

42 Paz 1961: 64.

one of the central premises of the constructionists that Hinduism is a new religion. Our starting point springs from the following historical considerations.

We have already noticed that the word Hinduism, or its variants in any Indian language, did not exist before the year 1816. Far more compelling is the fact brought to light by an analysis of the context in which the word Hindu figured in the sources before the nineteenth century. Let us look at two instances of the use of the expression occurring in sources from the region taken up for study in this work. One is from the corpus of Vijayanagara inscriptions. Here, the king of Haṃpi is identified as 'Hindūrāya Suratrāṇa' or 'Hindūrāya Suratāḷu'. The expression may be roughly translated as "a Sultān among Hindu kings".[43] It is noteworthy that the word Hindu is placed in juxtaposition with an Islamic term, Sultān. It is not an autonomous or internally constituted marker of identity. In other words, the referent is elusive. A religious identity—like all identities—is by definition, relational, and therefore not altogether self-constituted. However, it has always been possible for Buddhism, Jainism, Judaism, Christianity, and Islam to produce self-descriptions without invoking the other. Such is not the case with the use of 'Hindu' in the Vijayanagara inscriptions. The second instance is from the *Nandiyāgamalīle*, the hagiography of the saint Koḍēkallu Basava that we will take up for discussion in chapter 4. Hindu occurs twice in this text. Both figure in the same scene of action, and in both cases, the word is placed in contradistinction with Musalmāna, i.e., Muslim. Koḍēkallu Basava has set out on a long journey, wearing a 'Hindu' footwear on one leg and a 'Muslim' footwear on the other. Towards the last leg of his journey in northern India, a group of curious interlocutors ask him why he wore different footwear on each leg. To this, the saint offers an explanation which they find convincing.[44] The point to be noted is that Hindu has no independent or self constituted reference in this case too. It is a term that occurs as a relational expression, *vis-à-vis* Muslim. What the word contained or signified is, therefore, not clear to us in retrospect. Nowhere else in the text is Koḍēkallu Basava identified as a Hindu.

These two instances capture in a nutshell the manner in which Hindu as a marker of identity was deployed in the Deccan region before the nineteenth century. The use of the term from other parts of the Indian subcontinent follows this broad pattern. It occurs in a situation that warrants comparison with Islam. Where this is not the case, the expression signifies India as a geographical entity. The identification of Islam as a religion centered on the *Koran* and the Prophet, and as characterized by monotheism and opposition to idol worship, recurs constantly in the sources. This is clearly a self-definition of Islam, although practitioners consistently deviated from these norms by incorporating the worship of non-Islamic deities, polytheism, and adherence to tomb-worship into their everyday practices. Scholarly discussions are not duty-bound

43 See Wagoner 1996 for a lively discussion. Also see Wagoner 2000.
44 *Nandiyāgamalīle*, 13.44 and 13.51.

to accept such a self-definition as the essential constituent of Islam; for scholarly engagements are professionally obliged to ask why such self-definitions were arrived at, and not to take them at face value. Inasmuch as such self-definitions of Hinduism were never formulated before the nineteenth century, there arises the question why they were never attempted. Genuine scholarship must raise this question, rather than decrying the recent 'invention' of Hinduism, or making apologetic statements concerning the absence of Hinduism as a clearly-defined category before the nineteenth century.

An attempt is made in this study to understand a set of religious processes that unfurled between the eleventh and the nineteenth centuries in the Deccan region, especially in the present-day Karnataka, and partly, southern Maharashtra. The study is set against the backdrop of the changing nature of the political economy over these centuries, and how religious processes were constitutive of, or responded to, these changes. The foregrounding of class relations is central to this enterprise. Although it is now fashionable among a section of the academia to underrate the effects of class in the Indian context, and to foreground caste in its stead, our study will demonstrate why this view is misplaced.

It is generally presumed that religious identity is an essential component of the human world.[45] Thus, discussions on early Indian religion use expressions like Buddhist, Jaina, *vaidic* or Brāhmaṇical, and so on, rather uncritically to refer to the religion of the communities concerned. Chapter 2 of this study demonstrates why this presumption is historically unfounded. It shows, through an examination of texts and inscriptions from the Deccan region, that religious identities were created as a result of formidable historical processes during the eleventh and the twelfth centuries. Chapter 3 discusses how a new religious orthodoxy emerged between the twelfth and the fifteenth centuries in the Deccan region. This orthodoxy commenced in the early twelfth century with Rāmānuja, who offered an ingenious interpretation of *vēdānta* in his scheme of qualified monism (*viśiṣṭādvaita*). Rāmānuja's system was profoundly influential, and its impress was felt in the systems developed by the pioneering dualist (*dvaita*) saint, Ānanda Tīrtha, and the leading exponent of monism (*advaita*), Vidyāraṇya. New religious forces in the fifteenth century, who were opposed to the tenets of *advaita*, *dvaita*, and *viśiṣṭādvaita*, were nonetheless influenced by them, and produced a rich body of exegetical works in the court of the Vijayanagara king, Dēvarāya II. Chapter 4 explores how these fifteenth-century projects and the changing class structure of the period paved way for innovative religious practices in the region by way of pioneering the establishment of new monastic institutions that were fundamentally different from the monasteries of the preceding centuries. It also examines how the new monasteries underwent further transformations in the course of the seventeenth and the eighteenth centuries. Chapter 5 explores a great divergence

45 See Balagangadhara 1994 for a poorly-informed critique of this position.

in the practices of renunciation that began to unfold from the late fifteenth century. It explains how the divergence was governed by two diametrically opposite ethical paradigms produced by the political economy, one centering on the ethic of enterprise, and the other, on the ethic of complacency. Sainthood underwent tremendous transformations in the eighteenth and the nineteenth centuries, paving way for the rise of stand-alone saints, who neither built monasteries nor were affiliated with any religious lineages. At the same time, existing monasteries expanded their portfolio to include a set of new initiatives that were crucial vis-à-vis programmes of the Christian missionaries. These processes are taken up for examination in chapter 6. The study concludes with an epilogue, which offers a prolegomenon for a fresh assessment of that great phenomenon of the nineteenth and twentieth-century religious history, called Hinduism.

2 Indumauḷi's Grief and the Making of Religious Identities

Sometime towards the end of eleventh century, a devotee of Śiva pulled down a Jaina temple (*basadi*) in Puligeṟe—the present-day Lakṣmēśvara in the Gadaga district of Karnataka—and installed an image of Sōmanātha in its place. He was a merchant, and came from Saurāṣṭra. We do not know his name. Kannada sources call him Ādayya, which seems to be an unlikely name for a Saurāṣṭran merchant. The event seems to have caused great unrest in the region, perhaps even bloodshed, if later day accounts are to be believed. It certainly captured the Śaivite imagination, and over the centuries, it has been recounted several times, mostly in 'Vīraśaiva' hagiographies.[46]

Over half a century after the destruction of the *basadi* at Puligeṟe, a similar incident took place at Abbalūru—in the neighbouring Hāvēri district—in which Jainas apparently tried to desecrate the Brahmēśvara temple. Ēkānta Rāmayya, a devotee of Śiva, prevented the desecration by performing a miracle. He severed his own head, and put it back again after seven days, to the consternation of the Jainas assembled there.[47] This was an act for which he was allegedly honoured by the Kaḷacūri king, Bijjaḷa II. Like the merchant from Saurāṣṭra, the saviour of Abbalūru has attained a pride of place in hagiographic literature.[48]

Devotees of Śiva, like Ādayya and Ēkānta Rāmayya, were known as *śaraṇa*s in the Kannada-speaking region. Harihara (ca. 1175), one of the greatest ever poets of

---

46 This account need not be accepted in its entirety. The Sōmanātha temple at Lakṣmēśvara shows few signs of destruction or rebuilding. On the other hand, the Śaṅkha *basadi* of the town is of greater antiquity and carries extensive signs of rebuilding. This *basadi* is likely to have been the scene of action, but it was not converted into a Śiva temple. A parallel tradition credits a certain Sōmaṇṇa with installing the Śiva image in the *basadi*. This is recorded in works like the *Basavapurāṇa*, the *Cannabasavapurāṇa*, the *Vīraśaivāmṛtapurāṇa*, the *Gururājacāritra*, the *Pālkurike Sōmēśvarapurāṇa*, etc. For a comparative discussion of the evidence, see Kalburgi 2010 Vol.1: 322-332.

47 *Ēkāntarāmitandegaḷa Ragaḷe*, 231-380. On Rāmayya, see Ben-Herut 2012.

48 These are not rare instances from this period. A number of temples are known to have been destroyed in sectarian conflicts in the region. For an overview, see Kalburgi 2010 Vol. 3: 36-51.

the Deccan region, was their first hagiographer.[49] He was a junior contemporary of many *śaraṇa*s like Basava, Allama Prabhu, Cannabasava, Akkamahādēvi, Maḍivāḷa Mācayya, and so on, who are known for the *vacana*s they composed.[50] According to Harihara, the *śaraṇa*s were part of Śiva's entourage (*gaṇa*) in his abode, Kailāsa. Indumauḷi (Śiva) was aggrieved by their sensual lapses, and sent them to earth to live a life of carnal fulfillment. They also had a religious mission to accomplish, and the incidents at Puligeṟe and Abbalūru were part of this mission. But later day narratives, mostly from the fifteenth and the sixteenth centuries, have attempted to sanitize the lives of the *śaraṇa*s, as the *śaraṇa*s were believed to be too infallible to fall prey to sensual calls. The authors of these works held that Indumauḷi's grief was caused by

---

49 There is no consensus on the date of Harihara, although most scholars tend to place him in the early thirteenth century. Our suggestion of an earlier date is borne out by the following considerations. Verses from his *Girijākalyāṇaṃ* figure in Mallikārjuna's anthology, the *Sūktisudhārṇavaṃ*, which was completed in 1245. A date later than 1245 for Harihara is therefore ruled out. An inscription from Dāvaṇagere, dated 1224, states that Pōlāḷva Daṇḍanātha had composed the *Haricāritra* in the *ṣaṭpadi* metre. Now, according to tradition and modern scholarly consensus, the use of full-length *kāvya*s in *ṣaṭpadi* was an innovation made by Rāghavāṅka. Tradition identified him as "the master who established *ṣaṭpadi*" (*ṣaṭpadīsaṃsthāpanācārya*). We must therefore place Rāghavāṅka's works before 1224. Thus, a date of 1175 is reasonable for Harihara, Rāghavāṅka's maternal uncle. Besides, we also have the evidence of the *Padmarājapurāṇa* of Padmaṇāṅka (ca. 1400), which is a hagiographic account of Harihara's contemporary, Kereya Padmarasa. Harihara and Padmarasa lived in the Hoysaḷa court of Narasiṃha Ballāḷa (i.e., Narasiṃha I, r. 1152-1173) at Dōrasamudraṃ. Padmaṇānka was a ninth-generation descendent of Padmarasa, which places Padmarasa (and therefore, Harihara) in the late twelfth century. A further piece of evidence is that Padmarasa was the grandson of Sakalēśa Mādarasa, a senior contemporary of Basava (d. 1167). If a birth date between ca. 1080 and ca. 1100 is accepted for Mādarasa, then it can be safely held that the young Padmarasa and Harihara entered the service of Narasiṃha I between ca. 1160 and ca. 1170, and that Harihara, who retired to Haṃpi after serving at the Hoysaḷa court for a few years, was active as a Śaiva poet in ca. 1175.

50 The word *vacana* can mean many things, from 'speech' to 'a promise kept'. But in the eleventh and twelfth century literary context, it was used to mean 'prose' in the dominant *caṃpu* (Sanskrit *caṃpū*) works, which deployed a mix of prose and poetry. Early hagiographers like Harihara speak of these compositions as *gīta*, 'songs'. Instances include *Basavarājadēvara Ragaḷe*, 9.195-207; Ibid., 10, *sūcane*; and *Mahādēviyakkana Ragaḷe*, 7.196. But the use of the word *vacana* for these compositions was not unknown. Harihara's nephew Rāghavāṅka refers to it in *Siddharāmacāritra*, 9.20; 9.27; 9.38. The word attained popularity in the course of the compilation of the *vacana*s in the fifteenth century, wherein they were embedded into narrative texts in the form of dialogues between the *śaraṇa*s. Each *vacana* in the narrative was preceded by the statement that when so-and-so happened or when *Śaraṇa* A made a statement, *Śaraṇa* B uttered the following *vacana*, literally 'words'. The repeated use of this expression on hundreds of occasion within these texts doubtless played a major role in transforming the expression *vacana* into a genre. Ramanujan 1973 and Shivaprakash 2010 are accessible English translations of select *vacana*s.

the destruction of *dharma* on earth, and that it was the mission of the *śaraṇa*s to restore the lost world.[51] Ādayya and Rāmayya were participants in this sacred mission.

Ādayya might have been the subject of legends by the time Harihara composed a poem on him. Nearly a century separates the merchant from the poet. Rāmayya on the other hand was closer in time to the poet. It is likely that Harihara was already born when the Abbalūru incident occurred. He might also have had access to firsthand, eyewitness accounts of it. Harihara composed numerous hagiographic poems of varying length on the lives of the Nāyanārs[52] of Tamilnadu and the *śaraṇa*s of Karnataka in the rhythmic *raghaṭa* metres in what is called the *ragaḷe* genre.[53] The *ragaḷe*s on the *śaraṇa*s were original, while those on the Nāyanārs were based on legends circulating in the temple networks and centres of pilgrimage. Cēkkiḻār's *Periyapurāṇaṃ* in Tamil (c. 1140), which contain hagiographies of the Nāyanārs, was also based on these legends. 108 *ragaḷe*s of Harihara are now extant. A significant number of them have been identified by modern scholarship as spurious. The *Ādayyana Ragaḷe* on Ādayya and the *Ēkānta Rāmitandeya Ragaḷe* on Ēkānta Rāmayya are regarded as actual work of Harihara's.[54]

The Puligeṟe and Abbalūru incidents have been recounted in numerous later day literary works in Kannada where they have assumed metonymic proportions, exemplifying the triumph of Śaivism over Jainism. The story of Rāmayya is also recorded in an undated inscription.[55] While his life had inspired an entire hagiographic *kāvya* composed in the mid-seventeenth century by Śānta Nirañjana, a similar account of Ādayya's journey to Puligeṟe was written in the late twelfth century by no-less a figure than Rāghavāṅka, a redoubtable presence in the region's history of letters, who served his literary apprentice under the great Harihara, his maternal

51 The expression 'from Indumauḷi's grief' (*indumauḷiya besanadinda*) occurs in Bhīma's *Basavapurāṇa*, 2.56. The idea of Śiva being in grief seems to have been generally accepted (although the narratives present Śiva in a pleasant mood with no signs of grief as such). We come across 'Indudhara's grief' (*indudharana besanaṃ*) in Rāghavāṅka's *Sōmanāthacāritra*, 1, *sūcane*, and 'Hara's grief' (*harana besanaṃ*) in Harihara's *Basavarājadēvara Ragaḷe*, 2.

52 Sundaramūrtti, the ninth century Śaiva saint of Tamilnadu, identified sixty-three Śaiva saints—who lived between the sixth and the ninth centuries in the region—as Nāyanārs, perhaps in response to the identification and canonization of sixty-three holy men as *śalākapuruṣa*s by the Jainas. Intriguingly though, the greatest of Tamil Śaiva saint poets, Māṇikyavācagar, does not figure in this list of Nāyanārs. The hagiographies of the Nāyanārs are compiled in Cēkkiḻār's *Periyapurāṇaṃ*.

53 The use of *ragaḷe* was found in the early *caṃpu* works of tenth-century poets like Paṃpa, as well as in inscriptions, like the eleventh-century *praśasti* of the Jaina monk Indrakīrti (Hagaribommanahaḷḷi 15, *Kannada University Epigraphical Series*, Vol. 1). However, Harihara was the first to use *ragaḷe* to compose full-length poems.

54 See Ben-Herut 2015 for a discussion on the cross-influences and connections across regions and languages, through which the legends were circulated.

55 *Epigraphia Indica* V, pp. 213-265.

uncle. In fact, the seventeenth-century poet, Siddhanañjēśa, composed a full-length hagiographic *kāvya* on the poet: the *Rāghavāṅkacarite* (1672).

There is an interesting episode in Rāghavāṅka's *Sōmanāthacāritra*. Ādayya hails from a prosperous mercantile family in Saurāṣṭra. Soon after his marriage, he leaves home on a trading tour of the south. During his sojourn at Puligeṟe, he meets a girl called Padmāvati.[56] Her bewitching beauty mesmerizes him. The girl is also drawn towards our hero by his charisma. They fall in love at once, and in no time Padmāvati's friends arrange for the two to make love. The lovers spend many days in intense lovemaking. One day, braced by his intention to marry Padmāvati, Ādayya asks whose daughter she was, and of which family (*kula*), and of what faith (*samaya*) she belongs. Padmāvati replies that she belongs to the Jaina faith (*jainamata*). Ādayya is shocked by this reply. It throws him into a state of deep shame and sorrow, for he had unwittingly fallen in love with a girl who was not only a non-devotee (*bhavi*, literally 'worldly'), but also of another faith (*parasamaye*). To have a wife who professed by another faith is not merely unthinkable, but it is, for the merchant, a very act of sin. He decides to desert Padmāvati, and plans to cunningly sneak out of Puligeṟe, but the girl learns of his designs. She falls at his feet crying, "I can't live [without you]; kill me of take me with you." Ādayya concedes eventually, but not before convincing her to become a Śaiva. The girl agrees. She marries Ādayya after embracing Śaivism under the counsel of the Ācārya of Hōjēśvara. Padmāvati's parents are scandalized. Her father Pārisaseṭṭi cries: "[N]o one in our line (*anvaya*) had ever become a *bhakta*.... [Our] daughter has killed [and] brought disgrace on the glorious Jaina faith (*haduḷirda jinasamaya*)."[57]

This is an average story, the kinds of which are the staple of romances. There is much to be desired of it, as far as shedding light on the human condition with its perennial desires and denouements is concerned. However, no mediocrity is forever deprived of redemption. The story of Ādayya's marriage to Padmāvati had the fortune of reaching the hands of Rāghavāṅka, a giant of high-mimetic poetry and one of the greatest poets that ever wrote in Kannada. With a forceful centering of the trope of

56 Note that Padmāvati is the name of a major Jaina deity. A Jaina image of Padmāvati is found in Kendhūḷi near Bhuvanēśvar in Odisha, believed to be the place where Jayadēva (of the *Gītagōvinda* fame) was born. The image seems to have been appropriated by the Vaiṣṇavas after the decline of Jainism in the region. Jayadēva perhaps worshipped Padmāvati, which is hinted in the prologue to the *Gītagōvinda*: *vāgdēvatā carita citrita cittasadmā / padmāvatī caraṇacāraṇa cakravartī*, but legends from a later date regard Padmāvati as Jayadēva's wife. So the story goes, Jayadēva composed the *Gītagōvinda* in the temple of Jagannātha in Puri (about sixty kilometres from Kendhūḷi), and Padmāvati, a brāhmaṇa *dēvadāsī* whom he had married, danced to its tunes. The name Padmāvati figuring in the Ādayya legend may have a similar dimension.

57 *Sōmanāthacāritra*, 2.46-61.

valour,[58] Rāghavāṅka transformed the story into a *tour de force* of chivalrous piety. This, however, does not alter the fact that the story, in its bear essentials, has nothing special to offer: a man falls in love with a girl from another faith, and marries her after converting her to his own faith. Can there be something less intellectually rewarding?

Things cease to be as plain and simple once the historian's gaze falls upon it. The historian is professionally obligated to compare and contrast things in relation to time, to ask if it was possible for a man in India to marry a woman after converting her to his faith in, say, the fourth century, or the sixth century, or the ninth century. The sources of information, available for scrutiny, are not reassuring on this count. No such instances are recorded in any South Asian texts or documents before the twelfth century—not once, to be sure. How, then, did this become possible in the twelfth century? It is in enabling us to ask this question that Rāghavāṅka's account becomes significant, as far as the purposes of the present study are concerned.

The story of Ādayya and Padmāvati brings to light a momentous transformation in the nature of religious identities that occurred during this period. It enables us to raise a set of fundamental questions concerning such identities in particular, and religious practices in general. The episode narrated above is compelling, because it presents the historian with a drastically different picture of religious identities in the Indian subcontinent when contrasted to earlier times. Padmāvati's statement that she is a Jaina is one of the earliest instances from the subcontinent's literature where a layperson is identified as belonging to a particular religion without being initiated into it either as a renouncer of worldly life or as a listener/worshipper (*śrāvaka*/*upāsaka*), but by the mere fact of being born to parents who profess by that faith. Such identities were hitherto unknown in the subcontinent's history. They were altogether new in ethic, substance, and modes of representation. As a matter of fact, the only known pre-Rāghavāṅka references to the uninitiated lot being identified by their religion did not antedate the poet by more that half a century. Literary instances include those found in some of the *ragaḷe*s of Harihara: the reference to Nāraṇakramita, Saurabhaṭṭa, and Viṣṇupeddi, the Kaḷacūri king Bijjaḷa II's ministers, as Vaiṣṇavas in the *Basavarājadēvara Ragaḷe*,[59] and a similar allusion to an unnamed Cōḻa king in the *Rēvaṇasiddhēśvarana Ragaḷe*.[60] Besides, there are not more than half a dozen references to Vaiṣṇavas in epigraphic records, none of them older than the twelfth

58 Bharata's *Nāṭyaśāstra* identified eight emotions or 'essences' (*rasa*) as central to an understanding of drama. The *vīra-rasa*, i.e., the emotion of valour, is one of them. Udbhaṭa added a ninth emotion, *śānta*, the tranquil, to the list in the late eighth/early ninth century. The *rasa* model was later extended to poetry, and informed poetics and literary practices for several centuries in premodern India. On the *rasa* theory, see Raghavan 1940.

59 *Basavarājadēvara Ragaḷe*, 8.

60 *Rēvaṇasiddhēśvara Ragaḷe*, 1.113.

century.[61] A clearly discernable transformation in the structure of religious identities had occurred by the early decades of the twelfth century. The *ragaḷe*s of Harihara and the *Periyapurāṇaṃ* of Cēkkiḻar exemplify this transformation. In Pārisaseṭṭi's lament, that "our daughter has brought disgrace on our faith", we have one of the earliest instances of a family being identified by its religious persuasion. A religious identity is now being inherited by a family of believers. For the first time, Rāghavāṅka narrates the story of a man who finds himself at fault for having fallen in love with a woman, and decides to desert her, because and only because she belonged to a rival faith. Never was such a story told before his time. And for the first time in the subcontinent's history, Rāghavāṅka speaks of conversion from one faith to another.[62]

The historicity of the episode need not detain us here. Suffice it to say that such a narrative would have appeared outlandish, if not impossible, two centuries and a half before Rāghavāṅka's time, when the great Paṃpa lived. Paṃpa's *Ādipurāṇaṃ* (CE 941) recounts the life-cycles (*bhava*s) of Ādinātha until his accumulated *karma*s wither away and he attains *kēvalajñāna* to become the first Jaina *tīrthaṅkara*. It also gives an account of the lives of Ādinātha's sons, Bharata and Bāhubali. The battle between the two brothers is celebrated in Jaina lore. Bāhubali, as is well known, emerges victorious in it, but he is overwhelmed with grief and remorse for having fought his own brother, merely to acquire worldly fortune. He decides to renounce the world, obtains *jainadīkṣa* (initiation into *Jainism*), and leaves for the forests.[63] This last point is of no mean consequence for our analysis. Bāhubali becomes a Jaina by being initiated by a preceptor. He is not born a Jaina, although he is the son of the first *tīrthaṅkara*. Paṃpa was rendering into Kannada a work composed in Sanskrit a century earlier (CE 837)—the *Pūrvapurāṇa* of Ācārya Jinasēna II. The Ācārya, too,

---

61 At about the same time (ca. 1200), a hagiography of Nārōpa (1016-1100)—the Mantrayāna Buddhist and the disciple of Tilōpa—written in Tibet by iHa'i btsun-pa Rin-chen rnam-rgyal of Brag-dkar recounted a similar incident. Jñānacakṣumanta, the minister of Śāntivarman, the chief of Śrīnagara in Bengal, seeks the hands of Vimalā, the daughter of Tiśya for his master's son Samantabhadra (Nārōpa). Tiśya initially refuses saying: "Your king belongs no doubt to an excellent family, but we are high caste brāhmaṇas and not Buddhists. Since you are Buddhists I cannot give my daughter." But the villagers persuade Tiśya and he concedes. This is another early instance where a person (Śāntivarman) is identified as belonging to a faith by virtue of birth and not by initiation, and where a proposal for marriage is turned down on religious grounds. See Guenther 1995: 16-17.

62 We come across instances of conversion in Cēkkiḻar's *Periyapurāṇaṃ*, like the ones in the legend of Tirunāvukkarasar (Appar). By the time Cēkkiḻar produced his work, the historical transformation we are alluding to had already begun to unfold, and given the structure of religion in his time, it is obvious that what he had in mind was conversion from one faith to another. But from the historian's hindsight, it needs to be pointed out that these were, historically speaking, not conversions as Cēkkiḻar believed, but initiations (*dīkṣā*) into the order. What makes Rāghavāṅka's reference to Padmāvati's conversion the first known instance of its kind is the fact that he was speaking of a contemporary reality in contemporary terms, even if the historicity of the event itself may be open to question.

63 *Ādipurāṇa*, 14.139.v

did not fail to make this point.[64] Even the son of the first *tīrthaṅkara* had to *become* a Jaina. He could not be *born* as one.[65]

An examination of the nature of religious identities before the eleventh century points to an order of things that confirms this picture. Religious identities were restricted to the renouncer, and often centered on the monastery. Forsaking worldly life and becoming a renouncer after formal initiation were prerequisites for assuming religious identities like Jaina, Bauddha, Pāśupata, Kāḷāmukha, Mahāvrati, Ājīvika etc. Thus, these identities turned out to be the exclusive preserve of saints and renouncers.

It must be noted that many of the lay devotees, who generally patronized the Order, were also initiated. They were, however, never identified as Jaina or Bauddha or Mahāvrati. They were only listeners (*śrāvaka*) or worshippers (*upāsaka*).[66] There were also many layers of lay devotees, depending upon their importance and proximity to the monasteries. Romila Thapar invokes a beautiful metaphor to identify this layering as a "rippling out of the degrees of support."[67] Not all lay devotees warranted initiation. Yet, it is remarkable that text after text referred to religious identities only in the context of monks and nuns, their monasteries, and the listeners and worshippers who patronized them, and never to a human collective outside the monastic order. In the *Cilappadigāraṃ*, for instance, it was only Kavundi, the Buddhist nun, who bore a religious identity. No other character in the text—Kaṇṇagi, Kōvalan, Mādhavi, Mānāygan, Mācāttuvan, Kauśikan, Mādari, the Pāṇḍya king, the goldsmith, Ceṅguṭṭuvan, Iḷaṅgō Veṇmāḷ—assumed any such appellation. There were no religious identities outside the monastery or beyond the world of the wandering ascetics. Worshipping a deity was simply a part of everyday life, not a marker of identity. Just as eating rice did not enable a person to be identified as a rice-eater, and just as wearing cotton clothes, residing in a thatched hut or making love never produced identities like cotton-wearer, thatched-hut-dweller or love-maker, so also the worshipping of Śiva or Viṣṇu or the Jina did not confer identities like Śaiva, Vaiṣṇava or Jaina. Thus, the famous Anāthapiṇḍika, Āmrapālī, and Aśōka were only patrons of Buddhism, not Buddhists. Those identified as Buddhist—or *bhikku*s, as they were called—were essentially renouncers: Ānanda, Upāli, Mahākāśyapa, Śāriputra, Maudgalyāyana, Aniruddha. There were, therefore, no religious conversions either, before the eleventh century. Although historians have often written about 'religious conversions' in early India—the conversion of Aśōka and Nāgārjuna to Buddhism, and Mahēndravarman to Śaivism, for instance—these were not conversions, as we understand them today,

---

64 *Pūrvapurāṇa*, 36.105-106.

65 For a broad introduction to Paṃpa, see Thimmappayya 1977.

66 We do not know if lay devotees of Kṛṣṇa, identifying themselves as Bhāgavatas and Paramabhāgavatas, were formally initiated to this status of laity-hood. What is certain, though, is that they did not constitute a self-conscious and self-representing community outside the monastic fold.

67 Thapar 2000b: 902.

but initiations into the order by a preceptor, either as an ascetic or a renouncer, or as a listener/worshipper.

A dominant trend in contemporary South Asian Studies would argue—although such argument has not been made specifically in the context of religious identities—that it was 'Enlightenment epistemology' or 'colonial discourse' that made us believe in religious identities as a given and constituent condition of the human collective.[68] This argument appears banal in the light of the evidence on hand. The Indian subcontinent has been living with such identities at least since the (late) eleventh century. Besides, there is nothing in the modes of thought scandalously labeled 'Enlightenment epistemology' or 'colonial discourse' to suggest that such positions were nineteenth century inventions. Nonetheless, modern scholarship has, in large measure, failed to appreciate, or at least state in categorical terms, that religious identities are not an *a priori* constituent of human existence, and that they were historically brought into existence through practices that were deeply entrenched within the larger set of changes and transformations in the political economy. In the last two hundred years, histories of religion have only characterized religious identities as being subject to change and transformation. There has been scant focus on the historical emergence of such identities. Much has been written on religious 'communities' in history, although what these communities consisted of in substance, and how they differed from other forms of communities, is not clearly brought out. Most studies presume 'community' to be a category obvious in itself, while some manage with functional definitions that are not valid in other historical situations, and many a time ambiguous even within the milieu under examination.

The above discussion leads us to two obvious questions: first, in what ways were the practices of renunciation adopted by those who assumed religious identities through initiation into a chosen Order different from the everyday practice of worshipping a deity?; second, what in the eleventh and the twelfth centuries led to the historical emergence of religious identities based on birth and familial affiliations, and not on practices of renunciation, of which the Padmāvati of the *Sōmanāthacāritra* is an early representative? In other words, how were religious identities configured before the great transformation of the eleventh and the twelfth centuries? Why and how did the great transformation occur, altering these configurations? What follows in this chapter is an attempt to address these two questions.

At least four distinct expressions were used in premodern India to designate religion: *samaya*, *darśana*, *mata*, and *dharma*. These call for explanation, as they shed invaluable light on the question of what the practices of renunciation before the eleventh century actually involved.

---

68 See Dirks 2001; Pandey 1990; and Inden 1990. Also see Asad 1993 and King 1999. Balagangadhara 1994 takes a controversial position that religion itself was alien to most "heathen" traditions.

Whatever compelled men and women to forsake mundane lives and take to renunciation may be a difficult question to answer in the present status of knowledge. One of the pedestrian notions, widely held but never systematically investigated, is that they were driven by a quest for truth. Truth, in this understanding, is not reality or facticity, but the supreme, transcendental determinant of the universe. At least two authorities in recent times, Wilfred Cantwell Smith and Clifford Geertz, have tried to reaffirm a place for truth in the sphere of religion. Smith distinguishes between personal and impersonal truths, and tries to make a case for the former, arguing that the latter "handles the natural world well, but comprehends the human world ineptly". He goes on to write:

> Pilate's unanswered question, What is Truth? whether expressed or latent, haunts every civilisation, and finally, I guess, every man, woman and child. We may hope that our society will not cease to wrestle with it earnestly and nobly. In such wrestling, even if we be maimed by it, there may surely be a blessing.[69]

While Smith's wrestling session differs from the perspective of Mircea Eliade in its approach to religion on many counts, it shares with the latter the emphasis on subjective experiences and their inaccessibility to empirical research. This, then, becomes an easy ground from which claims about truth and its relationship with subjective experiences can be made, and arguments concerning the personal and the inner world of emotions put forward, without finding it necessary to critically explore them. In a very different vein, Geertz writes:[70]

> A man can indeed be said to be "religious" about golf, but not merely if he pursues it with passion and plays it on Sundays: he must also see it as symbolic of some *transcendent truths* (emphasis added).

Notions like these are Semitic in origin. That God and the world He created are characterized by transcendental truths that must be known is an idea that springs from the foundations upon which Semitic religious traditions are generally based. In saying so, we are certainly not proposing to identify an entity called Semiticism or essentialize it by disregarding complexities and diversities, for the Semitic traditions also produced the Sūfis and the Gnostic authors of what survives in the form of the Nāg Hammādi library. Our purpose, rather, is to argue that the notion of truth is not an essential component of religion. Truth as a transcendental category was rarely

69 Smith 1997: 119.
70 Geertz 1973: 98.

invoked in early Indian thought, or in practices of asceticism and renunciation.[71] The word for truth, *satya*, had different meanings in different contexts. In the four noble truths (*chattari ariya sacchani*) of the Buddha, the word signified reality, or a fact about everyday life, that the world is full of suffering, that suffering is caused by (carnal) desire, that suffering can be overcome by overcoming (carnal) desire, and that it was possible to accomplish this through an eight-fold path. Truth as facticity also informed the ontologies of Nāgārjuna and Śaṅkara, as suggested in the latter's case by the distinction made between *vyāvahārika sat* and *pāramārtthika sat*. But in *satyaṃ vada* (speak the truth), the well-known maxim from the *Taittirīya Upaniṣad* of the *Yajurvēda*, it was employed as an ethical principle in opposition to *asatya*, lie. Here, the word revolved around the idea of righteousness. Elsewhere, as in the story of Hariścandra, and in the famous declaration of the *Chāndōgya Upaniṣad* that truth alone triumphs (*satyamēva jayatē*), it was used in the sense of adherence to a normative order that was considered moral, even if at times it violated larger ethical concerns. In the *Muṇḍakōpaniṣad*, truth (*tad ētat satyaṃ*) was seen as the possibility of realizing Brahman and in turn becoming Brahman oneself. *Satya* assumed sublime connotations in some traditions like those of the Nāthas, the Viraktas, and the Ārūḍhas. Here, it often referred to that which was not affected by the past, the present, and the future. But, it was not an appellation for permanence. It only meant that the thing being referred to as *satya* was not affected by the vagaries of time. It could, however, be brought into existence, sustained or destroyed by forces other than time. That which was permanent was at times juxtaposed with *satya*. It was called *nitya*. These meanings do not qualify to be regarded as signifying a transcendental truth free from or beyond the grasp of ethical, moral, creative, or logical reasoning and imagination. We, then, need to look elsewhere to find an answer.

The problem we are trying to grapple with has occupied some of the finest minds of our times. A satisfactory consensus is yet to emerge.[72] Ours is an attempt to offer

---

71 In the interest of conceptual clarity, we propose to make a distinction (after Thapar 2010a) between the ascetic and the renouncer, although it is not of consequence to the present study. Writes Thapar: "The renouncer is identified not necessarily with a religious sect but with an order constituting an alternative life-style, in many ways contradictory to that of his original social group. Thus he cannot observe caste rules, he must be celebate, he cannot own property, he must carry the distinctive outward symbols of his order and he may be required to break various food tabus. The ascetic on the other hand lived in isolation, observed the food tabus by subsisting on what was naturally available in the forest, stressed the fact of his brahmanhood (where he was, as was often the case, a *brāhmaṇa*) by the austerities which he undertook. A further and fundamental distinction between the two was that whereas the ascetics were figures of loneliness working out their salvation each one for himself, the renouncer was concerned about other people and this concern was expressed in his desire to lead others along the path which he had found." (Thapar 2010a: 877).

72 Thapar 2010a: 876-913 makes the interesting suggestion that renunciation involved dissent, which she however notes, was articulated rather ambiguously. The renouncer, according to this view, was trying to establish 'a parallel society' or 'a counter-culture'. See also Dumont 1960.

an empirically verifiable description, drawing upon the proposition that asceticism, renunciation, and religious practices need not be—and cannot always be—understood in terms of truth. We need a cause that is more compelling, more consistent, and more convincing, one that does not yield to the rhetoric of subjective experiences and their inaccessibility. Is suffering one such cause? Perhaps yes. Our emphasis, though, is on *perhaps*, not on *yes*. In the current state of knowledge, we cannot be firm like Friedrich Nietzsche, who in one of his later writings observed, rather emphatically: "You have no feeling for the fact that prophetic human beings are afflicted with a great deal of suffering; you merely suppose that they have been granted a beautiful "gift," and you would even like to have it yourself."[73]

A survey of the literature of various early religious traditions from the subcontinent tells us that the question of suffering was one of their major preoccupations. The first of the four noble truths attributed to the Buddha held that the world was full of suffering, caused by (carnal) desire. The *Kathōpaniṣad* of the *Yajurvēda* also declared that those who chose the course of desire were destined to be drowned in it,[74] and that the destruction of desire alone could transform mortals (*martya*) into immortals (*amṛta*).[75] It was through knowledge that the *Kaṭhōpaniṣad* sought to overcome the world of desire. The *Muṇḍakōpaniṣad* also emphasized knowledge (*brahmavidyā*) as the means to overcome suffering, although, unlike the *Kaṭhōpaniṣad* or the Buddhist thought, it did not seek to establish a relationship between suffering and desire. In the Upaniṣadic scheme of things, the pursuit of knowledge was intimately associated with the resolve to transcend suffering. The nature of suffering formed one of the major preoccupations of *Suhṛllēkhā*, an anonymous Buddhist text.[76] Īśvarakṛṣṇa's *Sāṅkhyākārikā* began by stating that the assault of the three forms of suffering generates curiosity to learn how it can be mitigated.[77] The question of suffering and the means of overcoming it were among the central concerns of the Jaina writer Kundakunda too. In his *Pravacanasāra*, he asked: "Of what avail is [the distinction between] the auspicious and inauspicious activities of the soul, if humans, dwellers of hell, sub-humans and gods suffer miseries attendant on the body?"[78] "A saint," Kundakunda said, "should, to the extent possible, aid his fellow saint suffering from disease, hunger, thirst or exhaustion."[79] Time and again, religious traditions in India took recourse to metaphors like ocean (*sāgara*) and shackles (*bandhana*) to describe worldly existence marked by suffering (*bhava* or *saṃsāra*). There is enough evidence

---

73 No. 316, Nietzsche 1974.
74 *Kaṭhōpaniṣad*, 2.3.
75 Ibid., 6.14.
76 *Suhṛllēkhā*, 41-114. Tradition holds that this was a letter written by Nāgārjuna to his friend and the Sātavāhana king, (Gautamīputra?) Sātakarṇi.
77 *Sāṅkhyākārikā*, 1.
78 *Pravacanasāra*, 72.
79 Ibid., 252.

to argue on the lines of Jeffery Moussaieff Masson that the ideational justification behind the emergence of renunciation in India was the desire to overcome pain.[80]

Renunciation or asceticism was the means through which these traditions sought to overcome suffering. Traditions differed from one another on the question of what caused suffering. They also differed on the ways and means through which it could be overcome. There was only one ideal, though, which was unanimously accepted. It was believed that as long as one was in a state of worldly awareness, i.e., a state of mind for carrying out the mundane chores of life, one was condemned to live a life of suffering. The only way out was to attain a state of awareness that offered an altered vision of the world and one's relationship to it. Such a vision had to be conceptualized in advance. The practices of renunciation were meant to transform the mind from its present state of awareness to the altered state. This shift was gradual and evenly configured, and took a long period to accomplish. This movement of the mind from one state of awareness to another was called *samaya* (*sam* + *aya*, even/measured movement) and the altered image of the world obtained at the end of long periods of practice was *darśana* (vision). Practices of renunciation, aimed at attaining the chosen vision, were perhaps as old as the Vēdas. Yāska declared in his *Nirukta* that one became a sage by virtue of having attained the vision.[81] The views held by different traditions concerning the viability of different practices and the ethicality of the ultimate vision and the practices leading to it, often resulted in polemical debates among their proponents. These views were called *mata* (opinion). The logical stand arrived at in the course of these polemics was a description and vindication of the chosen vision. *Mata* was, therefore, the validation and justification of the vision. And the word *dharma*—which of course had various other meanings in different mundane contexts—referred to unswerving adherence to the chosen *samaya* and *darśana*. The state of awareness considered the ultimate goal differed from tradition to tradition and depended upon the ways in which vision (*darśana*) and the practice leading to it were conceptualized. The Buddhists referred to this state as *nirvāṇa*. The Jainas called it *kēvalajñāna*. The Vīraśaivas conceptualized a scheme of six stages of progression (*ṣaṭsthala*s) and the attainment of the sixth stage (*aikyasthala*) as their ideal. The goal set by other traditions included transcending the six circles (*ṣaṭcakra*) visualized as existing in the spinal column of the body, and reaching the seventh circle—*sahasrāra*—beyond the body. Also imagined was the attainment of states like *vajrakāya*, *mōkṣa*, *mukti*, *jīvanmukti* etc. The practices prescribed for reaching these goals ranged from moderate ones like the meditation-centered middle-path of the Hīnayāna (Thēravāda) Buddhists, the knowledge-centered approach of the Advaitis, and the devotional capitulation and trance-driven inaction of some schools of the Vaiṣṇavas, to extreme forms like the *pañca-makāra-siddhi* of the Kāpālikas (indulging

80 Masson 1980.
81 *Nirukta*, 2.11.

in the five Ms: *matsya*, *māṃsa*, *madya*, *mudra*, and *maithuna*, i.e. fish, meat, alcohol, money, and sexual orgy), consumption of urine and human excreta by the Kaulas, and human sacrifice and partaking of human flesh by the Aghōris. In the Jaina scheme of things, the ultimate goal—*kēvalajñāna*—was not possible as long as the soul resided in the body. The soul had to find release by 'wiping out' the body (*sallēkhana*). Theories of inviting and embracing death were, therefore, of special interest to the Jainas.[82]

Modern scholarship has generally referred to these states as freedom or salvation. Particularly striking is the reference to the Buddhist state of *nirvāṇa* as "Enlightenment." That the Buddha attained Enlightenment is one of the most uncritically accepted facts, repeated for over two centuries as if by rote.[83] What does it mean to say that a human being attained Enlightenment is a question scholars of our times have shied away from asking. The Enlightenment theory is a direct outcome of the relationship between religion and truth, which modern scholarship has tried to forge. The word Enlightenment, as used in scholarly discussions on Buddhism, presumes the existence of a transcendental truth and that through *nirvāṇa*, the Buddha gained privileged and perpetual access to it. But once the presumption that truth as a transcendental ideal is a necessary component of religion is called into question, the Enlightenment theory has to make way for an understanding that is richer and grounded in verifiable forms of certitude.

We must pause here to clarify that the mitigation of suffering, which preoccupies so much of the religious literature from the subcontinent, was an ideal that had found wide acceptance in the contemporary milieu. However, it does not explain why monks and nuns chose to organize themselves into monasteries and Orders, and institutionalize the practice of renunciation.[84] "Fundamental to renunciation," notes Alex Mckay in what is a matter-of-fact statement, "is the need for economic support, without which a renunciate lifestyle cannot be sustained".[85] A great measure of reciprocity between the renouncer and the laity was therefore essential for the institutionalization of renunciation. We have said little in the above discussion on the structure, meaning, and complexity of these relationships of reciprocity, or on their historical implications. Neither have we dwelt upon the political, economic, and other secular functions of the renouncer. These were, historically speaking, more important for contemporary religious life than the ideal of mitigating suffering.[86]

---

82 For an account of the Jaina theories of death, see Settar 1986 and 1990.

83 Collins 1998 offers a different explanation of *nirvāṇa*, laying emphasis on its narrative aspects. But "Enlightenment" remains important in his scheme of things too, and he uses the term almost as uncritically.

84 This critique, directed at Masson 1980, is made in Thapar 2000c: 918-919.

85 Mckay 2015: 112.

86 Representative studies in this regard include Thapar 2000b & 2000c; Chakravarti 1987; Ray 1986; Ray 1994; Sen 2004; Champakalakshmi 2011.

Back to the story. Before the eleventh century, religious identities remained the preserve of renouncers or ascetics who chose the attainment of altered states of vision—*nirvāṇa, kēvalajñāna, vajrakāya, jīvanmukti*—as their goal. We have suggested that they were driven by the proverbial desire to transcend desire, the hotbed of all sufferings. The old practices of initiation did not come to an end, though. They have continued well into our times. Hundreds of men and women continue to be initiated as practitioners year after year. While the practices have continued, the identities they conferred, and the meanings they generated, underwent a major transformation in the eleventh and the twelfth centuries. How did this transformation take place?

One of the most significant changes in religious practices that occurred towards the turn of the millennium was the inundation of the agrarian landscape with temples, and the new forms of worship they brought into existence. Temple-building was known in the region for over five hundred years before the eleventh century. The seventh century temple complexes of the Caḷukyas at Bādāmi, Aihoḷe, and Paṭṭadakallu, and the Kailāsanātha temple of the Rāṣṭrakūṭas at Ellōra, have attracted great attention in our times, especially due to their grand architecture. The Pallava temples of Mahābalipuraṃ and Kāñcīpuraṃ are also well known. A good number of these temples were rock-cut complexes meant for housing the renouncers and their Order. The four caves carved out on the Bādāmi hill, and the Rāvaḷaphaḍi and Jaina caves in Aihoḷe, are instances. Structural temples were also built in large numbers, and were beginning to replace the construction of rock-cut temples. Nevertheless, temple-building and temple-centered worship do not seem to have been well-entrenched local practices until the end of the tenth century, when temples began to dot the Deccan country in great and hitherto unprecedented numbers. Town after town, and village after village, took to frenzied temple-building. Temples were established in hundreds of places by rulers and chiefs, merchants, peasant proprietors, and other elites. The practice of worshipping a deity would henceforth gravitate towards this new institution.

The feverish pace at which temples were built during this period can hardly be overstated. Most *basadi*s in Śravaṇabeḷagoḷa, the foremost Jaina centre of South India, belong to the twelfth century. The Candragupta Basadi on the Candragiri hill was perhaps built some time around the year 900. The Cāvuṇḍarāya Basadi was built in the early decades of the eleventh century, and the Nēminātha Basadi on its rooftop, shortly after. The remaining eleven *basadi*s on Candragiri appeared in the twelfth century: the Śāntinātha Basadi, the Supārśvanātha Basadi, the Candraprabhā Basadi, the Kattale Basadi, the Śāsana Basadi, the Pārśvanātha Basadi, the Majjigaṇṇana Basadi, the Eraḍukaṭṭe Basadi, the Savatigandhavāraṇa Basadi, the Śāntīśvara Basadi, and the Tērina Basadi. Of the six *basadi*s in the town, five—the Nakhara Jinālaya, the Bhaṇḍāri Basadi, the Dānaśāle Basadi, the Siddhānta Basadi, and the Akkana Basadi—were built in the twelfth century and one—the Māṅgāyi Basadi—in the fourteenth. There were no *basadi*s in the town before the twelfth century.[87]

87 See the second revised edition of *Epigraphia Carnatica*, Volume 2, and Settar 1986.

Bhālki in the Bīdara district, which is the northern-most tālūk of the present-day state of Karnataka, produced its first temple in the late tenth century, but between 1000 and 1200 CE, twelve temples came to be built in the tālūk (Table 1):

Table 1. Temples built in the Bhālki tālūk of Bīdara district between 1000 and 1200 CE[88]

Sl. No.	Temple	Place
1.	the Traipuruṣa temple	Bhālki
2.	the Kapilēśvara temple	Bhālki
3.	the Uttarēśvara temple	Bhālki
4.	the Bhalluṅkēśvara temple	Bhālki
5.	the Vīradēva temple	Bhātaṃbra
6.	the Uttarēśvara temple	Gōraciñcoḷi
7.	the Bhōgēśvara temple	Candāpura
8.	the Kēśava temple	Koṭagyāla
9.	the Dhōrēśvara temple	Iñcūru
10.	xx (name lost)	Lañjavāḍa
11.	Jaina *basadi*	Halasi
12.	Jaina *basadi*	Dhannūru

Meanwhile, the adjoining Basavakalyāṇa tālūk, where there were no temples till the end of tenth century, produced thirty-three temples in the two hundred years that followed (Table 2).

These figures from the northern end of Karnataka are comparable with the ones coming from the south. The earliest known temples of the southern-most tālūk, Guṇḍlupēṭe in the Cāmarājanagara district, belong to the late tenth century: the Sōmēśvara temple of Bendavāḍi (now Haḷḷada Mādahaḷḷi) and an image of Sūrya now found at the Cauḍēśvari temple in Kelasūru. In the eleventh and the twelfth centuries, nine new temples appeared in the tālūk (Table 3).

A temple appeared in the mid eighth century at Homma in the neighbouring Cāmarājanagara tālūk during the reign of the Gaṅga king Śrīpuruṣa, while what is today the Rāmēśvara temple was built at Heggoṭhāra in the ninth century by Cāvuṇḍabbe, the daughter of Jōgabbe, a concubine of one of Śrīpuruṣa's successors. The late tenth century witnessed the construction of three more temples in the taluk: the Hammēśvara temple at Āladūru, the Bhujaṅgēśvara temple at Bāgaḷi, and the Aikēśvara temple at Hoṅganūru. But in the two centuries that followed, fifteen temples came up in the tālūk (Table 4).

88 Source: Culled from *Kannada University Epigraphical Series*, Volume VIII.

Table 2. Temples built in the Basavakalyāṇa tālūk of Bīdara district between 1000 and 1200 CE[89]

Sl. No.	Temple	Place
1.	the Brahmadēva temple	Basavakalyāṇa
2.	the Malayavati temple	Basavakalyāṇa
3.	the Bhīmēśvara temple	Basavakalyāṇa
4.	the Svayambhu Hāṭakēśvara temple	Basavakalyāṇa
5.	the Mahādēva temple	Basavakalyāṇa
6.	the Koppēśvara temple	Basavakalyāṇa
7.	the Vināyaka temple	Basavakalyāṇa
8.	the Kēśava temple	Basavakalyāṇa
9.	the Sōmēśvara temple	Basavakalyāṇa
10.	the Nārāyaṇa temple	Basavakalyāṇa
11.	a second Nārāyaṇa temple	Basavakalyāṇa
12.	the Candraprabha Jinālaya	Basavakalyāṇa
13.	xx (name lost)	Basavakalyāṇa
14.	the Mahādēva temple	Nārāyaṇapura
15.	the Kēśava temple	Nārāyaṇapura
16.	the Mūlasthāna Dévarasa temple	Nārāyaṇapura
17.	the Kōdaṇḍa temple,	Nārāyaṇapura
18.	a goddess temple (name lost),	Nārāyaṇapura
19.	temple in the Harimūla Gāhaṇṇa street	Nārāyaṇapura
20.	the Kuṃbhēśvara temple	Gōrṭā
21.	the Nagarēśvara temple	Gōrṭā
22.	the Mallēśvara temple	Gōrṭā
23.	the Rudrēśvara temple	Gōrṭā
24.	a second Rudrēśvara temple	Gōrṭā
25.	Jaina temple of Padmāvati	Gōrṭā
26.	the Gōhilēśvara temple	Gaura
27.	the Kēśavadēva temple	Gaura
28.	the Rāmēśvara temple	Mucaḷaṃba
29.	the Sōmēśvara temple	Mōrkhaṇḍi
30.	the Tripurāntaka temple	Tripurāntaka
31.	the Paṃpēśvara temple	Haḷḷi
32.	xx (name lost)	Sōḷadābaka
33.	a Jaina *basadi* (name lost)	Ujjaḷaṃ

89 Source: Culled from Ibid.

Table 3. Temples built in the Guṇḍlupēṭe tālūk of Cāmarājanagara district between 1000 and 1200 CE[90]

Sl. No.	Temple	Place
1.	the Rāmanātha temple	Śītaḷavāri (now Beḷacalavāḍi)
2.	the Vāsudēva temple	Niṭre
3.	the Mādhava temple	Haḷḷada Mādahaḷḷi
4.	the Vīranārāyaṇa temple	Kallahaḷḷi
5.	the Sōmēśvara temple	Kandāgāla
6.	xx (name lost)	Saṃpigepura
7.	a Jaina *basadi* (names lost)	Saṃpigepura
8.	the Biṭṭi Jinālaya	Tuppūru
9.	the Sarvalōkāśraya Basadi	Kelasūru

Table 4. Temples built in the Cāmarājanagara tālūk of the same district between 1000 and 1200 CE[91]

Sl. No.	Temple	Place
1.	the Trikūṭa (now Pārśvanātha) Basadi	Cāmarājanagara
2.	the Rāmēśvara (now Śaṃbhuliṅgēśvara) temple	Ādalūru
3.	the Mallikārjuna temple	Marahaḷḷi
4.	the Mūlasthāna temple	Maṅgala
5.	the Mūlasthāna temple	Siṅganapura
6.	the Mūlasthāna temple	Homma
7.	the Mūlasthāna temple	Haḷē Ālūru
8.	the Arkēśvara temple	Haḷē Ālūru
9.	the Kēśavēśvara (now Janārdana Svāmi) temple	Haraḷukōṭe
10.	the Sōmēśvara temple	Tammaḍihaḷḷi
11.	Pārśvanātha Basadi	Maleyūru
12.	the Vāsudēva (now Balavāsudēva) temple	Kulagāṇa
13.	a Caityālaya (name lost)	Kallipusūru
14.	xx (name lost)	Puṇajūru
15.	xx (name lost)	Dēvaḷāpura

The inscription, which mentions the Trikūṭa Basadi of Cāmarājanagara, also alludes to many other *basadi*s at Arakōttara without naming any.

The spectrum found at the northern and southern ends of Karnataka was not unique, but representative of what was occurring in the rest of the region. Two tālūks each from the Rāyacūru district in the Kṛṣṇa valley and the Maṇḍya district in the Kāvēri valley may be examined as representative samples from northern and southern Karnataka respectively.

90 Source: Culled from *Epigraphia Carnatica* (revised edition), Volume 3.
91 Source: Culled from *Epigraphia Carnatica* (revised edition), Volume 4.

The Dēvadurga tālūk of the Rāyacūru district, which had no temples before the eleventh century, came up with thirty-five temples between 1000 and 1200 (Table 5). Twenty-seven of them were constructed at Gabbūru alone.

Table 5. Temples built in the Dēvadurga tālūk of Rāyacūru district between 1000 and 1200 CE[92]

Sl. No.	Temple	Place
1.	the Mahādēva temple	Gabbūru
2.	the Mēḷēśvara (now Mēl Śaṅkara) temple	Gabbūru
3.	the Tripurāntaka temple	Gabbūru
4.	the Gavarēśvara temple	Gabbūru
5.	the Kēśava (now Veṅkaṭēśvara) temple	Gabbūru
6.	the Hariharēśvara temple	Gabbūru
7.	the Siddha Sōmanātha temple	Gabbūru
8.	the Śaṅkara temple	Gabbūru
9.	the Prasanna Kēśava temple	Gabbūru
10.	the Prasanna Rājēśvara temple	Gabbūru
11.	the Rāmēśvara temple	Gabbūru
12.	the Nāgabhūṣaṇa temple	Gabbūru
13.	the Brahma (or Nagara) Jinālaya	Gabbūru
14.	the Gojjēśvara temple	Gabbūru
15.	the Rāmanātha temple	Gabbūru
16.	the Vināyaka temple	Gabbūru
17.	the Viṣṇu temple	Gabbūru
18.	the Gaṇapati temple	Gabbūru
19.	the Sarasvatī temple	Gabbūru
20.	the Sūrya temple	Gabbūru
21.	the Umā Mahēśvara temple	Gabbūru
22.	the Sōmēśvara temple	Gabbūru
23.	the Jēḍēśvara temple	Gabbūru
24.	the Mallikārjuna temple	Gabbūru
25.	the Jinēśvara temple	Gabbūru
26.	the Kalidēvasvāmi temple	Gabbūru
27.	xx (name lost)	Gabbūru
28.	the Īśvara temple	Hirērāyakumpi
29.	the Bhōgēśvara temple	Bāgūru
30.	the Kapālēśvara temple	Vīragōṭa
31.	the Sōmēśvara temple	Gaṇajāli
32.	the Mallikārjuna temple	Nilavañji
33.	the Toreya Śaṅkaradēva temple	Nilavañji
34.	the Mallikārjuna temple	Candanakēri
35.	the Hemmēśvara temple	Candanakēri

92 Source: Culled from *Kannada University Epigraphical Series*, Volume VII.

Temple-building was also widespread in the eleventh and the twelfth centuries in the neighbouring Sindhanūru tālūk too. We learn from an inscription at Diddigi that there were seven temples in and around the village in the early tenth century: the Viṣṇu, the Subrahmaṇya, the Rāmēśvara, the Sōmēśvara, the Bikēśvara, the Baḷari Mārakabbe, and the Baḷari Piriyakabbe. But in the eleventh and the twelfth centuries, twenty-four new temples rose in the tālūk (Table 6):

Table 6. Temples built in the Sindhanūru taluk of Rāyacūru district between 1000 and 1200 CE[93]

Sl. No.	Temple	Place
1.	the Karṇēśvara temple	Rauḍakunde
2.	the Kālēśvara (now Kālakālēśvara) temple	Sālagunde
3.	the Nāgēśvara temple	Sālagunde
4.	the Kēśava (now Murahari) temple	Mukkundi
5.	the Bācēśvara temple	Mukkundi
6.	the Viṣṇu temple	Mukkundi
7.	the Kalidēva temple	Mukkundi
8.	the Kapālēśvara (now Pāpanāśēśvara) temple	Mukkundi
9.	xx (name lost)	Mukkundi
10.	xx (name lost)[94]	Mukkundi
11.	the Bīcēśvara temple	Jālihāḷu
12.	the Svyaṃbhu Kalidēva (now Kallēśvara) temple	Hirēberige
13.	the Huliyamēśvara temple	Dēvaraguḍi
14.	the Viṣṇudēva temple	Koḷabāḷu
15.	the Agastyadēva temple	Baḷagānūru
16.	the Amṛtaliṅga temple	Baḷagānūru
17.	the Nakarēśvara temple	Baḷagānūru
18.	the Manōhara temple	Baḷagānūru
19.	the Cannakēśava temple	Baḷagānūru
20.	the Lakṣmīnārāyaṇa temple	Baḷagānūru
21.	the Mūlasthāna temple	Oḷabaḷḷāri
22.	the Bālabhāskara temple	Oḷabaḷḷāri
23.	the Kēsaradēva temple	Oḷabaḷḷāri
24.	xx (name lost)	Māḍaśiravāra

The figures from the Maṇḍya district tell a similar story. In the year 776, Kuṇḍacci, the daughter of Māruvarma of the Sagara family, obtained a generous grant from Śrīpuruṣa through a request made by her husband Paramagūḷa, and constructed the Lōkatilaka Basadi at Śrīpura. The town was perhaps named after the king. This was

93 Source: Culled from Ibid.
94 Perhaps the present-day Sōmaliṅgēśvara temple.

the first temple to come up in the Nāgamaṅgala tālūk of the Maṇḍya district. Another record from the early tenth century mentions a grant made for the maintenance of a tank as part of a *dēvabhōga*, which suggests that there stood a temple near the tank during this period. These were the only two temples known from the tālūk till the end of the tenth century. But between 1000 and 1200, as many as twenty-one temples appeared in the tālūk (Table 7). Besides, a *Śivaliṅga* was set up at Mūḍigere in the twelfth century, and named as Garañjēśvara Liṅga.

Table 7. Temples built in the Nāgamaṅgala tālūk of Maṇḍya district between 1000 and 1200 CE[95]

Sl. No.	Temple	Place
1.	the Saumyakēśava temple	Nāgamaṅgala
2.	the Bhuvanēśvari temple	Nāgamaṅgala
3.	the Pārśvanātha Basadi	Kaṃbadahaḷḷi
4.	the Śāntīśvara Basadi	Kaṃbadahaḷḷi
5.	the Mallikārjuna (now Īśvara) temple	Lālanakere
6.	the Madhukēśvara (now Mādēśvara) temple	Lālanakere
7.	the Pārśvanātha Basadi	Yallādahaḷḷi
8.	Jaina *basadi* (name lost)	Daḍaga
9.	Another Jaina *basadi* (name lost)	Daḍaga
10.	Another Jaina *basadi* (name lost)	Daḍaga
11.	Another Jaina *basadi* (name lost)	Daḍaga
12.	Another Jaina *basadi* (name lost)	Daḍaga
13.	Another Jaina *basadi* (name lost)	Aḷīsandra
14.	Another Jaina *basadi* (name lost)	Cākēyanahaḷḷi
15.	Another Jaina *basadi* (name lost)	Elēkoppa
16.	the Pañcakēśvara temple	Beḷḷūru
17.	the Maṇḍalēśvara (now Gaurēśvara) temple	Beḷḷūru
18.	the Hēmēśvara (now Īśvara) temple	Doḍḍa Jaṭaka
19.	the Kalidēva (now Kallēśvara) temple	Kasalagere
20.	the Pārśvanātha (also called Ekkōṭi) Basadi	Kasalagere
21.	the Śrīkaraṇa Jinālaya	Bōgādi

To the southwest of the Nāgamaṅgala tālūk is the Kṛṣṇarājapēṭe tālūk. Records from here support our proposition. While no temples are known to have come up in the tālūk during or before the tenth century, twenty-one temples appeared in the eleventh and the twelfth centuries (Table 8):

95 Source: Culled from inscriptions in *Epigraphia Carnatica* (revised edition), Volume 7.

Table 8. Temples built in the Kṛṣṇarājapēṭe tālūk of Maṇḍya district between 1000 and 1200 CE[96]

Sl. No.	Temple	Place
1.	the Trikūṭa Jinālaya	Hosahoḷalu
2.	the Koṅgaḷēśvara (now Koṅkaṇēśvara) temple	Akkihebbāḷu
3.	the Brahmēśvara temple	Kikkēri
4.	the Mallēśvara temple	Kikkēri
5.	the Pañcaliṅgēśvara temple	Gōvindanahaḷḷi
6.	the Hoysaḷēśvara (now Īśvara) temple	Teṅginaghaṭṭa
7.	xx (name lost)	Teṅginaghaṭṭa
8.	the Aṅkakāradēva temple	Toṇaci
9.	the Nagarīśvara temple	Toṇaci
10.	the Karidēva temple	Toṇaci
11.	the Mariyadēva temple	Toṇaci
12.	the Mahādēva (now Basavēśvara) temple	Toṇaci
13.	the Bhōgēśvara temple	Sāsalu
14.	the Mahādēva (Mallēśvara) temple	Nāgaraghaṭṭa
15.	the Mākēśvara temple	Hubbanahaḷḷi
16.	the Karmaṭēśvara (now Īśvara) temple	Māḷagūru
17.	the Svayaṃbhu Aṅkakāradēva (now Basava) temple	Hirēkaḷale
18.	the Lakṣmīnārāyaṇa temple	Sindhaghaṭṭa
19.	the Saṅgamēśvara temple	Sindhaghaṭṭa
20.	the Jannēśvara temple	Sindhaghaṭṭa
21.	the Hoysaḷa Jinālaya (now Jinnēdēvara Basadi) at Basti.	Basti

Karnataka has more than two hundred taluks. We have examined only eight of them, which alone have yielded information about 170 temples built during the eleventh and the twelfth centuries. These statistics are telling in their own right.[97] They cry out for explanation. But no attempts have been made to explain them yet. Studies on temples have almost exclusively been directed towards grand and sprawling temple complexes, their focus being primarily on the structure and semantics of architecture, its relationship to the sacred, and questions concerning polity, the economy, and at times, gender. The changes effected by the mushrooming of small and medium-sized

96 Source: Culled from inscriptions in *Epigraphia Carnatica* (revised edition), Volume 6.
97 The enumeration is based on tālūk-wise distribution of inscriptions, which do not however correspond to the localities or administrative units of the period under examination. Also, the figures do not represent the exact number of temples built during the eleventh and the twelfth century, but only to the numbers made available to us by the corpus of published inscriptions based upon what has survived. It is likely that important temples are left uncounted, as they are not referred to in the inscriptions, although fieldwork by the present author confirms that such instances do not exist in these *tālūks*.

temples across the lengths and labyrinths of the region in the eleventh and the twelfth centuries have not attracted the attention it richly deserves.[98]

If our statistics are to be believed, the emergence of temple-centered religious practices was the single most important religious phenomenon to have swept over Karnataka in the eleventh and the twelfth centuries. Forms of worship also evolved into well-organized conventions. Inscriptions tell us that rituals like *nityābhiṣēka* (the everyday anointing), *aṣṭavidhārcane* (the eight-fold offering), and *amṛtapaḍi* (the rice-and-milk offering) were extensively observed after this period. Practices like setting up the *nandādīpa* (perpetual lamp), making gifts like oil, milk, rice, and gold to the temples, and setting up idols, lamp-posts, pillars, and *maṇṭapa*s (platforms) as part of offering worship to the deities, were widespread in the region. Some of these practices were new. Others drew upon practices known in earlier times when rock-cut cave temples were being built. Reference to the perpetual lamp is found as early as in the Vākāṭaka records of the fifth century, and in Pallava records of the eighth century.[99] This was now expanding exponentially, while the making of gifts—known in early historical Buddhist sites like Sāñcī and in the cave complexes of western Deccan[100]—became pervasive, leading to far-reaching historical consequences.

It is in this transformed historical setting that Rāghavāṅka narrates the story of Padmāvati who identifies herself as a Jaina without finding it necessary to join an order of renouncers either as a nun or as a listener. And as we have seen, she was also able to discard the Jaina faith and embrace Śaivism, without affiliating herself to any monastic Order as a renouncer.

Even as Rāghavāṅka was composing his works like the *Sōmanāthacāritra* and the *Siddharāmacāritra* to uphold the cause of Śaivism, one of his Śaiva contemporaries, Brahmaśiva, found his faith less fulfilling, and embraced Jainism. Shortly thereafter, he wrote the *Samayaparīkṣe*, the first text of its kind from the subcontinent, in which he launched a hardhearted tirade against all major faiths (*samaya*) of his time, concluding that Jainism was the greatest of all faiths. Critiques of rival traditions were not unknown in pre-twelfth century India. But they were significantly different from Brahmaśiva's project. More often than not, they took the form of critical engagements with the logical foundations of the vision and the stipulated practices of the rivals, and were more in the nature of systematically argued debates. By Brahmaśiva's time, religious identities outside the monastic Order were firmly in place. The clash was now between human collectives who chose to identify themselves by their religion, not between monastic groups for whom the phenomenological primacy of their *darśana*

---

98 Recent attempts to study the temples of Karnataka from within the architectural perspective include Foekema 2003a and 2003b; Hardy 2001 and 2007; Michell 2002 and 2011; Sinha 1996. Also see Settar 2012.

99 No. 97, Mahalingam 1988.

100 Roy 2010a; Kosambi 1955.

was of utmost importance. The Puligeṟe and the Abbalūru incidents, with which we began, were inevitable fallouts of this great transformation. Like the destruction of the Babri Masjid and the Bamiyan Buddha in our own times, the razing of temples was certainly not a demanding task in the twelfth century. What was indeed difficult was to defend one's own faith in a manner that Brahmaśiva found apposite, no matter how poorly it was accomplished. It took over a century and a half for the *advaita* school to produce a similar vindication of their faith—the *Sarvadarśanasaṅgraha* of Vidyāraṇya—and for the Jainas to produce another *parīkṣe*—the *Dharmaparīkṣe* of Vṛttivilāsa. Many a temple had been desecrated by this time.

It was the emergence of temple-centered forms of worship that eventually led to the transformation of religious identities in the Deccan region during the eleventh and the twelfth centuries. It is then pertinent that this discussion concludes with an attempt to account for the rise of temples.

The Deccan region witnessed a rapid phase of urbanization from the mid-ninth century. This was a period of urbanization in most parts of the subcontinent. After the pan-Indian decay of urban centres in the second and third centuries,[101] cities began to reappear across South Asia in the sixth century. The urban decay of the second and third centuries was contingent upon agrarian expansion, the genesis of shorter and more effective trading networks as opposed to the erstwhile long-distance *sārttavāha* trade, and the role played by the new regional elites in exploiting newer resources and creating a sustainable surplus base at the local level.[102] It was in this context that the earliest states like the ones founded by the Kadaṃbas and the Gaṅgas made their appearance in the region. By the sixth century, agrarian expansion had considerably advanced, facilitating the advent of urban centres and the revival of long-distance trade. By the early seventh century a strong monarchy—the Caḷukyas of Bādāmi—was able to reign over these upcoming cities. The surplus appropriation machinery in this milieu was effectively organized around distinct agrarian localities, transformed into chiefdoms called *viṣaya* or *nāḍu*.[103] These chiefdoms came to be placed in a set of hierarchical positions vis-à-vis the king, whose centrality then enabled him to claim the status of a *cakravarti* or *vijigīṣu*, as modelled in the *Dharmaśāstras*.[104] Sēndraka Viṣaya, Vaḷḷāvi Viṣaya, Teggattūru Viṣaya, Tagare Viṣaya, Paruvi Viṣaya, Vanne Viṣaya, Kovaḷāla Viṣaya, Sinda Viṣaya, Kaivara Viṣaya, Marukara Viṣaya, Korikunda Viṣaya, Hoḍali Viṣaya, Nīrggunda Nāḍu, Eḍetoṟe Nāḍu, Kuluṅgijya Nāḍu, Morasa Nāḍu, Pudal Nāḍu, Gañje Nāḍu, Badagere Nāḍu, Puṟamalai Nāḍu, and Beḷvola Nāḍu were

101 On the great urban decay, see Sharma 1987. See also Chattopadhyaya 1994: 130-154 and Kaul 2010: 9-12 for a critique of the urban decay thesis, and Devadevan 2009c: 11-12 for a reassessment.

102 Devadevan 2009c: 11-12.

103 For a discussion of *nāḍu*, see Subbarayalu 1973; Veluthat 1990; and Ganesh 2009. Also see Stein 1980 and Adiga 2006.

104 That the *dharmaśāstras* provided the model for kingship is a thesis persuasively argued in Veluthat 2012: 47-85 (i.e., chapter 1).

among the flourishing localities of Karnataka. These localities were complex fields of conflict over resource appropriation. They also opened up avenues for vertical political mobility and geopolitical integration.

As early as the fifth century, the royal elites had resorted to the use of *praśasti*s (eulogies) in their inscriptions in the Deccan region. The Tāḷagunda pillar inscription, containing a *praśasti* of the Kadaṃba king Mayūraśarman, is one such instance.[105] The Guḍnāpura inscription of Ravivarman is another.[106] Royal titles like Mahārājādhirāja, Paramēśvara, and Pṛthvīvallabha were increasingly used after the seventh century. Besides, titles specific to the dynasties concerned were also invented. The Caḷukyas of Bādāmi used Raṇarāga (lover of war) and Raṇavikrama (triumphant in war) as titles.

The situation began to change from the early ninth century onwards, when a far more consequential phase of urbanization swept over the subcontinent, expanding and altering trade relations, producing newer classes such as traders who formed their own corporations, artisan groups organized around relations of kinship, and provincial administrators whose control over the resources of their region had rendered subversive tendencies more prescient, and usurpations, much easier. The remarkable increase in the number of inscriptions found after the ninth century points to these historical shifts, but this profusion also seems to have taken the regality away from the inscribed letter. Grants made by kings became fewer in number, while the agrarian elites, locality chiefs, and royal functionaries became more involved in making grants. Recording land transactions, and commemorating heroic and ritual deaths (*vīragallu* and *niśidhi* respectively) increased substantially.[107] But the milieu was already inventing newer forms of political expression. Genealogies were being forged, tracing family origins to the solar and the lunar lines. Newer dynastic titles were being invented. The Gaṅgas used Satyavākya (of truthful speech) and Nītimārga (of righteous path) as titles, while the Rāṣṭrakūṭas invoked the idea of rain-maker by using titles with *varṣa* (rain) as suffix, as in Amōghavarṣa, Akālavarṣa, Nirupamavarṣa, Dhārāvarṣa, and Suvarṇavarṣa. They also used *tuṅga* (summit) as a title. Prominent examples were Nṛpatuṅga, Śaratuṅga, and Jagattuṅga. Their successors, the Cāḷukyas of Kalyāṇa, went a step further to become the Lords of the Three World (Tribhuvanamalla or Trailōkyamalla), and the Sole Lords of the World (Bhuvanaikamalla and Jagadēkamalla).

At the same time, the affluence generated by urbanization could afford the invention of alternate forms of expression dearer than the setting up of inscriptions. One of them centered on literary traditions that called for a deep knowledge of

---

105 No. 4 in Gopal 1985.
106 No. 23, Ibid.
107 On memorial stones, see Settar and Sontheimer 1982.

language, grammar, metres, and prosody, and a class of urban connoisseurs with their refined tastes. The other, and more influential practice, was temple-building.[108]

Temple-building was perhaps an expression of munificence or piety. But, it was politically significant for another reason. Statecraft in peninsular India had turned increasingly to the praxis of divine kingship after the seventh century, and more pronouncedly, after the ninth century. The king was often equated with Viṣṇu. The title Pṛthvīvallabha, by a double entendre, signified the king as the lord of the earth, and also as Viṣṇu, the husband of the earth. Most Caḷukya rulers were Pṛthvīvallabhas. Even in the early sixth century, the Kadaṃba king Ravivarman had identified himself on similar lines as Bhūvadhūtilaka (the vermillion mark of the earth bride) and Bhūmīśvara (lord of the earth).[109] By the eighth century, Śrī, which is another name of Viṣṇu's wife Lakṣmī, was being invoked. The Gaṅga king Paṭṭāṇi Eṟeyan, who succeeded Śivamāra I in the early eighth century, used Śrīpuruṣa (the Husband of Śrī) as his personal name. The first three stanzas of the *Kavirājamārga* (ca. 850), which is the earliest extent literary text in Kannada, carries a eulogy of Viṣṇu with the play of double entendre making it, simultaneously, a eulogy of its patron, the Rāṣṭrakūṭa king Amōghavarṣa I Nṛpatuṅga.[110]

The praxis of divine kingship was a praxis, and not merely a flourish of rhetoric occurring in inscriptions and literary texts. This is borne out by a number of considerations. There was no distinction between the temple and the palace in this scheme of things, as a temple-complex functioned as the headquarters of the king. The *Mānasāra*, a text on architecture, assigns positions to the deity, the king, his ministers, and his entourage within the temple-complex. The structure hosting the deity was called *dēvaharmya* and the one housing the king, the *rājaharmya*.[111] The features and dimensions of the throne meant for the deities and the king were mentioned,[112] and a hierarchy of thrones identified. The throne of Śiva and Viṣṇu was called *padmāsana*, the other gods and the wheel-turning sovereign (*cakravarti*) occupied the *padmakēsara*. The overlord (*adhirāja*) below the wheel-turning sovereign was assigned *padmabhadra*. The other thrones were *śrībhadra* for *adhirāja* and *narēndra*, *śrīvilāsa* for *narēndra* and *pārṣṇika*, *śrībandha* for *pārṣṇika* and *paṭṭadhara*, *śrīmukha* for *maṇḍalēśa*, *bhadrāsana* for *paṭṭabhāga*, *padmabandha* for *prākāra*, *pādabandha* for *astragāha*, and subordinate thrones (*upapīṭha*) for all other lower rulers.[113] Similar hierarchical descriptions occur in the *Mānasāra* for the *kalpa* tree,[114] hairstyle,[115] and

108 Devadevan 2009a: 75-77.
109 No. 23, Gopal 1985.
110 *Kavirājamārga*, 1.1-3.
111 *Mānasāra*, 19.
112 Ibid., 45.1.
113 Ibid., 45.59-93.
114 Ibid., 48.1, *passim*.
115 Ibid., 49.4, *passim*.

grooming.[116] What this prescriptive text indicates is that kingship was imagined as being part of a divine hierarchy. It is for this reason that the word *prāsāda* in Sanskrit signified both temple and palace, and the words *dēva*, *ṭhakkura*, and *bhaṭṭāraka*, both the deity and the king.[117]

The rituals for the king were also not different from the services to the deity in the temple. The five great instruments (*pañcamahāśabda*) assigned to the lords under the king (i.e., *māṇḍalika* or *maṇḍalēśvara*) were used in the temple, and survives in the form of *pañcavādyaṃ* in the present-day temples of Kerala.[118] The daily services, including the anointing (*abhiṣēka*), followed a similar pattern.

Divine kingship found its most energetic expression in Tamilnadu under the Cōḻa kings, Rājarāja I and Rājēndra I, who both were identified with Śiva. The deity at the Bṛhadīśvara temple at Tañjāvūr was called *Uḍaiyār Rājārājadēvar*, which was also the name of the king. It has been observed that "*uḍaiyār* or *perumāḷ* meant both the king and the deity, *kōil* meant both the temple and the palace and the day-to-day routine of services in the temple followed, to the last detail, the services in the palace".[119]

The growing power of the locality chiefs and landed elites in the tenth, the eleventh, and the twelfth centuries posed a serious challenge to the practice of divine kingship. This began with many a chief claiming divinity. In his *Vikramārjunavijayaṃ*, Paṃpa narrated the story of the *Mahābhārata*, equating his patron Arikēsari of the Vēmulavāḍa Cāḷukya line with Arjuna. Similarly, Ranna equated his patron Satyāśraya with Bhīma in his version of the *Mahābhārata*, entitled *Sāhasabhīmavijayaṃ* (also called *Gadāyuddhaṃ*). Satyāśraya was not yet a king at this time, but a *maṇḍalēśvara* under his father and the founder of the Kalyāṇa Cāḷukya state, Taila II. A third chief who commissioned a work of this kind was Śaṅkaragaṇḍa, who bore the title Bhuvanaikarāma. Ponna wrote the *Bhuvanaikarāmābhyudayaṃ* in his honour. This work narrated the *Rāmāyaṇa* by equating the exploits of Śaṅkaragaṇḍa with that of Rāma.[120] Resonance of this literary innovation in Kannada was felt in the distant Bengal in the early twelfth century, when the Pāla king Rāmapāla commissioned Sandhyākara Nandi to write the Sanskrit *Rāmacaritaṃ*. This work, based on the *Rāmāyaṇa*, narrated how Rāma had lost Sītā and eventually succeeded in winning her back. It was also the story of how Rāmapāla lost and regained *sītā* (furrow, and by a metonymic extension, land or kingdom).[121]

By the eleventh century, landed elites were beginning to build temples on a large scale, and tacitly making claims to divinity. Temples were built in which the deity was

116 Ibid., 50.1, *passim*.
117 The word *ṭhakkura* survives today in the name Ṭhākur, which has come to signify both a chief and a deity.
118 Devadevan 2009a: 52.
119 Veluthat 2009: 67.
120 The *Bhuvanaikarāmābhyudayaṃ* seems to be lost, as no surviving manuscripts are known.
121 On the *Rāmacaritaṃ*, see Roy 2010b.

named after the patrons. The builders of the temple placed themselves in a mirror-image relationship with their deities, as if suggesting that *I am the reflection of god on earth*, without altogether ruling out the reverse possibility that *god is indeed a reflection of my personality*. This development was to strike at the very heart of divine kingship as a political praxis.

Three of the *basadi*s which came up on the Candragiri hill in Śravaṇabeḷagoḷa in the twelfth century were identified with their patrons. While the *basadi*s built by Cāvuṇḍarāya and Majjigaṇṇa bore their name, the one built by the Hoysaḷa queen Śāntala came to be known after one of her titles as the Savatigandhavāraṇa Basadi. Likewise, three of the *basadi*s built in the town were also identified after their patrons. The *basadi* built by Hullarāja, the Hoysaḷa *bhaṇḍāri* (treasurer) was called Bhaṇḍāra Basadi, and the one built by Āciyakka, the wife of the Hoysaḷa minister Candramauḷi, the Akkana Basadi. A trader called Nāgadēva built a *basadi* for his *nakhara* (corporate group of traders). It went by the name of Nakhara Jinālaya.[122]

Numerous Jaina temples build during the eleventh and twelfth centuries were named after their patrons. But Śaiva temples often had the deity itself bearing the builder's name. Temples built by *nakhara*s (trading corporations), *gavare*s (roving merchants), *telliga*s (oil-pressers), and those who worked in the *kammaṭa*s (mints) often named the deities in their temples as Nakharēśvara, Gavarēśvara, Telligēśvara, and Kammaṭēśvara, respectively.

The Bhōgēśvara temple at Chandapura was built by Lakṣmīdhara Caṭṭōpādhyāya in memory of his father Bhōgadēva. The Dhōrēśvara temple at Iñcūru, and the Gojjēśvara and Jēḍēśvara temples at Gabbūru also seem to be named after their builders. The Kalidēvasvāmi temple of Gabbūru was named after Kallapayya, who commissioned it. The Hemmēśvara temple of Chandanakēri was set up by Hemmaḍi Dēvarasa. The Kālēśvara temple of Sālagunda was built by Nāca Daṇḍanātha in his father Kalidāsa's memory, while Bācarasa built the Bācēśvara temple at Mukkundi, and Bịcagāvuṇḍa, the Bīcēśvara temple at Jālihāḷu. The Huḷiyamēśvara temple of Dēvaraguḍi also appears to have derived its name from its patron.[123] Unlike the setting up of inscriptions, the building of temple commanded greater respect and was symbolically better privileged in the race for vertical political mobility. The catalytic role it played in marshalling popular support and gaining greater access to resources through the new temple-centered redistributive machinery can hardly be overstated.

Table 9 gives a list of Śaiva temples from the localities around Baḷḷigāve where deities were named after the patron. These localities were spread over the present-day Śikāripura and Soraba tālūks of the Śivamogga district, and Hirēkērūru tālūk of the Hāvēri district.

---

122 See related inscriptions in *Epigraphia Carnatica* Vol 2.
123 See related inscriptions in Vol. VIII and VII of *Kannada University Epigraphical Series.*

Table 9. Śaiva Temples and Their Builders in the Localities Around Baḷḷigāve, CE 1000-1250[124]

Sl. No.	Date	Place	Deity	Builder	Background
1.	1033	Kuppagadde	Ālēśvara	Ālayya	Local chief
2.	1054	Baḷḷigāve	Sōmēśvara	Sōviseṭṭi	Merchant
3.	n.d.	Baḷḷigāve	Kēdārēśara	Kēdāraśakti	Saint
4.	1090	Baḷḷigāve	Mañjēśvara	Mañjeyanāyaka	Guard
5.	1096	Baḷḷigāve	Sarvēśvara	Sarvadēva	Local chief
6.	1098	Baḷḷigāve	Lōkēśvara	Lōkarasa	Local chief
7.	1098	Baḷḷigāve	Jōgēśvara	Jōgarasa	Local chief
8.	1104	Abbalūru	Brahmēśvara	Bommagāvuṇḍa	Village chief
9.	1145	Udri	Boppēśvara	Boppādēvi	*Nāḍu* Queen
10.	1155	Cikkakereyūru	Biyapēśvara	Biyapaseṭṭi	Merchant
11.	1159	Baḷḷigāve	Vīra Kēśava	Kēśirāja	General
12.	1159	Baḷḷigāve	Jagadēkamallēśvara	Jagadēkamalla	Emperor
13.	1163	Bandaḷike	Sōmēśvara	Sōvidēva	*Nāḍu* chief
14.	1167	Māyitammana Mucaḍi	Jagadēkamallēśvara	Jagadēkamalla	Emperor
15.	1174	Bandaḷike	Boppēśvara	Boppadēva	*Nāḍu* chief
16.	1184	Kuppagadde	Rāmēśvara	Rāmayya	Brāhmaṇa
17.	1209	Huraḷi	Kalidēvēśvara	Kaligāvuṇḍa	Village chief
18.	1239	Tiḷuvaḷḷi	Sāvantēśvara	Kalidēvaṭhakkura	*Sāmanta*
19.	1248	Giṇivāla	Nēnēśvara	Nēnasidēva	Local chief

These were the historical processes that foreshadowed and determined the rise of religious identities outside the monastery. More dramatically perhaps, the idea that sainthood involved renunciation came to be called into question. A large number of men and women were initiated into Śaiva sainthood, but continued with their worldly pursuits. These were the *śaraṇa*s, the forebears of Vīraśaivism. Some leading saints such as Allama Prabhu, Akkamahādēvi, and Siddharāma took to renunciation, but most others emphasized the significance of labour (*kāyaka*) and held to their professions. Monastic life was not of any significance to them, as they believed that true renunciation was possible even without renouncing worldly life. Basava, who was the most influential among them, became a saint while retaining the office of the treasurer of the Kaḷacūri king, Bijjaḷa II. Dēvara Dāsimayya remained a weaver, practiced his profession, worshipped Śiva in his form as Rāmanātha, and attained renown as a saint. In the same way, Maḍivāḷa Mācayya remained a washer man, Nageya Mārayya a clown, Kannada Mārayya a burgler, Mādāra Cannayya and Mādāra Dhūḷayya cobblers, Aṃbigara Cauḍayya a ferryman, Heṇḍada Mārayya a toddy tapper, Bahurūpi Cauḍayya a performer, Haḍapada Appaṇṇa a betel leaf carrier, Mēdara Kētayya a cane weaver, Mōḷige Mārayya a woodcutter, Nuliya Candayya a rope maker, Āydakki Mārayya a rice gatherer, Vaidya Saṅgaṇṇa a physician, Turugāhi Rāmaṇṇa a cowherd, Kannaḍi

124 Source: Hegde 2003: 92.

Kāyakada Remmayya a barber, Eccarike Kāyakada Muktināthayya a watchman, and so on. Note than most *śaraṇa*s had their profession prefixed to their names, although this was not seen in some instances, like Urilingadēva, Urilingapeddi, and Ghaṭṭivāḷayya. In contrast, female saints were not always associated with their profession. We learn of Sūḷe Saṅkavva (a sex worker), Mōḷige Mahādēvi (a woodcutter), and Āydakki Lakkamma (a rice gatherer), which are exceptions. The female saints were, in general, known by their given names: Gaṅgāṃbike, Nīlāṃbike, Bonthādēvi, Goggavve, Remmavve. In several instances, they were identified as the wife (*puṇyastrī*, literally 'sacred woman') of a *śaraṇa*. Thus, Lakkamma the *puṇyastrī* of Āydakki Mārayya, Kētaladēvi the *puṇyastrī* of Guṇḍayya, Liṅgamma the *puṇyastrī* of Haḍapada Appaṇṇa, and Guḍḍavve the *puṇyastrī* of Bāci Basavayya.

Most *śaraṇa*s came from the labouring classes. The more affluent among them were associated with temples, Basava with the temple in Kūḍalasaṅgama, Allama Prabhu with the temple in Baḷḷigāve, and Akkamahādēvi and Siddharāma with the temple in Śrīśailaṃ. Siddharāma also built a temple in Sonnalige or Sonnalāpura (now Sōlāpur). Maḍivāḷa Mācayya was the washer man of the Tripurāntaka temple of Kalyāṇa. There were occasions when the association with the temple turned out to be violent, and caused bloodshed in places like Puligeṟe and Abbalūru.[125] Generations to come would valorize these acts of incandescent terror and make sparkling pieces of poetry of them, oblivious that what it ultimately involved was the choice of pyre or pyre, to be redeemed from fire by fire. But the greater majority of the *śaraṇa*s had no temples to look up to, nor the means to cause carnage and bring down a rival shrine. At a time when rulers, landed elites, and merchant corporations were building temples in large numbers, the ferrymen, cobblers, toddy tappers, cane weavers, cowherds, and rice gatherers could ill afford to emulate them. They could at best name the deities of their choice after them. Nageya Mārayya chose to worship Mārēśvara, Mādāra Dhūḷayya prayed to Dhūḷēśvara, Gajēśa Masaṇayya gave himself up to Mahaliṅga Gajēśvara. The less fortunate *śaraṇa*s perhaps believed that their body was the temple, their legs the pillars, and their head the golden capstone, and that they were simply moving temples, in a manner of speaking. Basava gave voice to them in one of his *vacana*s:

> The rich build temple for Śiva.
>   What shall I do, lord, poor that I am?
>
> My legs are pillars,
>   Body, the shrine,
>   My head, my lord, is the golden capstone.

125 The dimension of violence in the Abbalūru incident, often downplayed in modern scholarly accounts, is discussed in Ben-Herut 2012.

Kūḍalasaṅgamadēvā,
The standing will perish,
The moving will not pass away.[126]

The poor built no temples. But the rich did, and in great numbers, as we have seen. This was occasioned by a momentous process of transformation in the political economy of the region, which involved the assertion of their political presence by the locality chiefs, landlords, merchants, and other elites. By the late twelfth century, the scope and meaning of political action and relationships had undergone considerable pluralization. In this milieu rife with subversion and insubordination, the emergent elites forged newer forms of loyalty, association, and ties of dependence and reciprocation. Our discussion has shown that the making of lineage groups and communities based on religious identities were inevitable fallouts of this great historical process. By the end of the twelfth century, forms of religious affiliation, hitherto unknown, had come into being.

It was towards the consolidation of the new groups, communities, identities, and affiliations that religious processes in the Deccan region would, in the coming centuries, gravitate.

126 No. 820, Basavanal 1968 (translation mine).

3 Forests of Learning and the Invention of Religious Traditions

A series of important political developments took place in the Deccan region in the fourteenth century, with which the evolution of sainthood and its ideology in the coming centuries was deeply interlaced. It had a long history. An overview of this history will be instructive, as it will enable us to place the subsequent discussions in a fruitful perspective.

The Cāḷukyas of Kalyāṇa (ca. 973-1200) were in control of large parts of the Deccan region in the eleventh and the twelfth centuries.[127] When their power began to decline in the mid twelfth century, the Kaḷacūris of Maṅgaḷavāḍa (now Maṅgalvēḍhā) began to assert themselves. The Kaḷacūri chief Permāḍi had earlier entered into a matrimonial alliance with the Cāḷukyas, which had enabled his family to exercise greater influence in the affairs of the state. The agrarian infrastructure that he commanded from his headquarters at Maṅgaḷavāda on the riparian belt of the Bhīma was among the most formidable in the region. His son, Bijjaḷa II, began to assert his independence in the wake of a conflict over succession between Sōmēśvara III's sons, Jagadēkamalla II and Mallikārjuna. Under Jagadēkamalla II's successor Taila III, the Cāḷukyan forces suffered serious setbacks following attacks from the Kākatīya chief, Prōla. Taking advantage of this situation, Bijjaḷa II usurped the throne in 1162. Taila III tried to retain a foothold, but was killed by his Hoysaḷa subordinate, Narasiṃha I (r. ca. 1152-1173), perhaps in 1163. Bijjaḷa II's was not a successful entreprise, though. His rule came to an end in 1167 following what seems to have been a case of regicide. The killer, whom legends identify as Jagadēva, was apparently faithful to the Cāḷukyas, and continued to espouse their cause, if evidence from epigraphy is to be believed. Owing to the fact that Bijjaḷa II's relationship with his treasurer Basava had turned into friction towards the end of his life, later Vīraśaiva accounts have appropriated Jagadēva's act by identifying him as a devotee of Basava. In subsequent accounts, the killing was jointly attributed to Jagadēva and Mallibomma, both allegedly Basava's followers. Bijjaḷa II was succeeded by his son Sōvidēva who ruled up to 1176. What followed was sheer confusion. Between the years 1176 and 1184, the throne was occupied by at least five rulers, Maiḷugi, Saṅkama, Āhavamalla, Kannara, and Siṅghaṇa.[128] The Cāḷukyas returned to power briefly under Sōmēśvara IV, but by this time, their realm had come to be parceled out between three prominent warlord families, the Sēvuṇas of Dēvagiri, the Kākatīyas of Vāraṅgallu, and the Hoysaḷas of Dōrasamudraṃ (Haḷēbīḍu), who carved out spheres of influences in the Marathi, Telugu, and Kannada speaking regions, respectively. They represented the great dryland polities, which contrasted in

---

127 For a history of the Kalyāṇa Cāḷukyas, see Gopal 1981.
128 On the Kalacūris, see Desai 1968. Also, Gopal 1981.

many ways with the Cōḻas of Tañjāvūr, the Cēras of Mahōdayapuraṃ, and the eastern Cāḷukya chiefs of Veṅgi, who were rooted in wetland regions, although their sway extended over dryland belts as well. By the early decades of the fourteenth century, these successor states had also weakened considerably.

Between the ninth and the thirteenth centuries, powerful peasant proprietors and warlords had been enlisted into the service of the state across much of peninsular India in various capacities, but mostly as revenue farmers commanding militias of their own. Wetland polities also appropriated mercantile groups for extracting revenue. This was most prominently seen among the Cōḻas[129] and, to a lesser extent, among the Cēras.[130] According to Kesavan Veluthat, the corporate body of merchants, called *nagaraṃ*, "is shown to have been held collectively responsible for the collection of land revenues from its domain and to have handled its internal assessments and collections in a manner as it saw fit".[131] Kenneth R. Hall identifies the *nagaraṃ* as an administrative institution,[132] stresses its role in collecting revenue on behalf of the Cōḻa state,[133] and notes that its "right to tax was distinct from its private right over land".[134] But merchants did not figure in a similar capacity in the dryland polities. In fact, the data made available by inscriptions show that some of these states shared a difficult relationship with the powerful merchant syndicates of the day. The Cannakēśava temple of Belūru, built in the early twelfth century by the Hoysaḷa king Viṣṇuvardhana, received grants, gifts, and donations from a number of people. Not one of them was a merchant before the fifteenth century.[135] At Śravaṇabeḷagoḷa, merchants were more active on the big hill, whereas their presence was almost negligible on the small hill, where functionaries of the Hoysaḷa state dominated.[136] Hoysaḷa relationship with the mercantile classes was anything but cordial.

In the dryland belts of southern Karnataka, peasant proprietors who gained greater access to state revenue succeeded in the course of the eleventh, the twelfth, and the thirteenth centuries in developing and controlling rural markets. A certain Ādigavuṇḍa obtained control of a (weekly?) fair and, with the help of his brothers and

---

129 Hall 1980.

130 The Syrian Christian (Tarisāpaḷḷi) copperplates and the Jewish copperplates exemplify this. For the text of the Jewish copperplates, see No. 39, Ramachandran 2007. It was believed for a long time that there were two sets of Syrian Christian copperplates, recording two different grants. M.R. Raghavavarier and Kesavan Veluthat have recently shown that the so-called second set of plates is only a continuation of the first set. In effect, therefore, there is only one set of plates. See Raghavavarier and Veluthat 2013 for a revised text and a reassessment of the plates.

131 Veluthat 2012: 220.

132 Hall 1980: 51-63 (i.e., chapter 3).

133 Ibid., 58-59, *passim*.

134 Ibid., 62.

135 Cf. Bl. 1-93, *Epigraphia Carnatica*, (revised edition), Vol. 9.

136 Cf. inscriptions in *Epigraphia Carnatica*, (second revised edition), Vol. 2.

sons, built a village from its proceeds in 1182, after clearing the forests.[137] An earlier case of obtaining the revenue of a fair comes from Tekkalakōṭe in the Baḷḷāri district from the year 1020.[138] Peasant proprietors were beginning to gain a firm foothold over rural markets in the south and in the Tuṅgabhadra valley. Inscriptions from this period mention a large number of merchants, i.e., *seṭṭis*, in southern Karnataka, which, one might argue, goes against our proposition that peasant magnates controlled the rural markets. But there is evidence to show that these merchants belonged to peasant proprietor families. An inscription from the time of Ballāḷa II speaks of a Seṭṭigauṇḍa. That he was a peasant magnate is underscored by the expression *gauṇḍa* (originally *gāvuṇḍa* from the Sanskrit *grāmavṛddha*, now *gauḍa*). But he had *seṭṭi*, 'trader', as a personal name. His two sons swore allegiance to the king, which is indicated by the stock expression, *tatpādapadmōpajīvi*, 'who lives by that lotus feet'. One of them, Taḷāṟa Suṅkada Mahadēvaṇṇa, controlled the transit toll on the movement of goods (*suṅka*). The other, Būciya Boppaseṭṭi, was a merchant. Mahadevaṇṇa's son-in-law was Kētamalla Heggaḍe, and as his title suggests, he maintained village records. Elsewhere, he is referred to as Taḷāṟa Suṅkada Kētamalla, suggesting that he inherited the rights to transit toll from his father-in-law.[139] Until recent times, Seṭṭigauḍa was a common name in the Hāsana district and adjoining areas of southern Karnataka. A thirteenth century inscription from Sōmavārapēṭe in Koḍagu district refers to several peasant proprietors (*gauḍugaḷu*) as constituting the *nāḍu-nakhara*.[140] This compound expression is revealing: *nāḍu* (Sanskrit *viṣaya*) is a peasant locality,[141] and *nakhara*, the corporate body of local merchants. A group of peasant proprietors, who managed the agrarian affairs of a locality, were also in control of its mercantile initiatives.

By the twelfth century, individual merchants had emerged in southern as well as northern Karnataka, who operated in their own capacity without being aligned to any of the great merchant syndicates. This was the outcome of a historically far-reaching development that took place after the tenth century, and which has for some reason continued to elude the historian's gaze, viz., the practice of making gift of money or gold as endowment to temples and religious establishment in lieu of land grant, by the merchant syndicates. This birth of interest-bearing capital gradually percolated into the realms of agrarian production in the form of usury. The potentials that credit was imbued with led to individual mercantile and moneylending initiatives. Ādayya, with whose story we commenced this study, was one such merchant. Pārisaseṭṭi, the father of Padmāvati whom Ādayya married, was another. Neither of them was affiliated to

---

137 Bl. 240, *Epigraphia Carnatica*, (revised edition), Vol. 9.
138 Siraguppa 55, *Kannada University Epigraphical Series*, Vol. 1. Tekkalakōṭe was among the most prominent of neolithic settlements in the Deccan region.
139 Bl. 373, *Epigraphia Carnatica*, (revised edition), Vol. 9.
140 No. 60, *Epigraphia Carnatica*, (revised edition), Vol. 1.
141 On the *nāḍus* of Tamilnadu, see Subbarayalu 1973 and Veluthat 1990. Adiga 2006 offers a discussion in the context of Karnataka. Also see Ganesh 2010 for *nāḍus* in Kerala.

any merchant syndicate of the day. The growing power on the one hand of peasant proprietors and the supralocal alliances they were successful in forging, and on the other of the individual merchants who began to develop systems of agrarian credit, led to the decline of organized mercantile groups. Great syndicates of the preceding centuries such as the Ayyāvoḷe Ainūrvar or the Diśai Āyiratti Aiññūṟṟuvar, the Maṇigrāmaṃ, the Hañjamāna (Anjuman?), the Vaḷañjiyar, and many itinerant groups called Nānādēśi, withered away, as did local merchant groups like the *nakhara*s or the *nagarams*.[142] By the late thirteenth century, their presence had become too feeble to be recorded, and by the close of the fifteenth century, the last of the *nakhara*s and the Hañjamānas, who unlike the other groups seem to have resisted dissolution, had also vanished from the scene completely.

The major peasant magnates were also in control of military bands that were placed at the service of the state as and when called upon to do so. With the increasing autonomy of the market-controlling peasant proprietors, it became possible for rival powers to buy their loyalties. The individual merchant represented a centrifugal tendency that was hard for the state to contain. This was all the more so because, the northern peasantry was gradually coming under the spell of the private moneylender, and was serving his cause at the expense of the services it hitherto rendered as mercenary troops to the state and its functionaries. This situation of precarious loyalties weakened the Sēvuṇas, the Kākatīyas, and the Hoysaḷas to a considerable extent. Beginning 1296, a series of invasions by the Khalji and the Tughlak Saltanats of Dilli laid bare the vulnerability of these states.

Alā-ud-dīn Khalji was the first of the Sultāns of Dilli to raid the Deccan. As early as 1293, when his uncle Jalāl-ud-dīn Khalji held the throne, he carried out a campaign in central India around the areas centering on Bhilsa. In 1296, he invaded Dēvagiri without the Sultān's knowledge, defeated the Sēvuṇa king Rāmacandra, and returned with rich booty. The Sultān was assassinated shortly thereafter, on 21 July 1296, and Alā-ud-dīn enthroned. In the first few years of his reign, Alā-ud-dīn was engaged in consolidating his hold over north India. He ordered a campaign against Vāraṅgallu in 1302, but his forces were defeated by the fierce troops of the Kākatīya king, Pratāparudra II, in 1303. Three years later, in 1306, he ordered a campaign against Dēvagiri. Alā-ud-dīn's trusted eunuch general, Malik Kāfūr, led this campaign, and returned after reducing Rāmacandra to submission. Malik was sent again to the south late in 1309. With Rāmacandra offering military assistance, Malik came to command a formidable army. Rāmacandra died shortly thereafter. Malik's campaign was extensive. It lasted

---

142 The Ayyāvoḷe 500 and Maṇigrāmaṃ syndicates are discussed at length in Abraham 1988. Also see Hall 1980; Champakalakshmi 1996: 311-326 (i.e., chapter 5); Veluthat 2012: 218-222. The Hañjamāna was active in coastal Karnataka even in the late fourteenth century (No. 350, *South Indian Inscriptions*, Vol. 7, record dated 1399) and the early fifteenth century (No. 349, *South Indian Inscriptions*, Vol. 7, record dated 1406), but vanished by the end of the fifteenth century.

up to 1311. Malik reduced Vāraṅgallu with the help of the deceased Rāmacandra's forces, and coerced Pratāparudra II to acquiesce. The Hoysaḷa king Ballāḷa III, and the Pāṇḍyan brothers of Madurai, Sundara Pāṇḍyan and Vīra Pāṇḍyan, were defeated and forced to sue for peace. These victories were made possible due to the support Malik Kāfūr was able to marshal from Pratāparudra II.[143] Two years later, in 1313, he marched again against Dēvagiri to rein in Rāmacandra's son and successor, Siṅghaṇa III, who was hostile to Dilli. Alā-ud-dīn died on the fourth day of the year 1316. Half and three months later and after a number of intrigues, his son Mubārak ascended throne on 18 April. Three years later, in 1319, he attacked Dēvagiri. It was Mubārak who for the first time commissioned governors in his conquered territory in the Deccan, thereby departing from Alā-ud-dīn's policy of subjugation for tribute. Yaklakhī was appointed the governor of Dēvagiri, which brought an end to the Sēvuṇa state. Mubarak had similar plans to annex the Kākatīya region. He asked his trusted homosexual partner Hassan, upon whom he had conferred the title of Khusrau Khān, to invade Vāraṅgallu. Khusrau Khān was an influential figure in the early fourteenth-century politics of Dilli. He succeeded in killing Mubārak in 1320, and rose to the throne as Nāsir-ud-dīn. But Khusrau's rule lasted only for two months. He was killed by his opponent Ghāzi Malik, who held Dīpālpur at the time. Ghāzi Malik succeeded Khusrau to the Dilli throne as Ghiyās-ud-dīn Tughlak. Thus commenced the Tughlak rule.

In the following year, 1321, Ghiyās sent his son Fakhr-ud-Dīn Jauna, who now carried the title Ulugh Khān, to invade Vāraṅgallu and collect tributes. Jauna had other plans. Instead of reducing Vāraṅgallu to a tributary status, he wished to annex it to Dilli. But the campaign turned out to be a disaster. Two years later, in 1323, Jauna invaded Vāraṅgallu again. This time around, he succeeded in annexing it. Vāraṅgallu was renamed Sultānpur, the Svayaṃbhu Śiva temple of the city razed, a mosque built in the vicinity of the old temple, and a mint established to utter Tughlak coins.[144] A century and a half of Kākatīya rule was thus brought to an end. Ghiyās died in 1325. Jauna succeeded him, adopting the name Muhammad bin Tughlak. Muhammad aspired to bring much of the Deccan under Dilli's control, and evolved a number of strategies to this effect. The first of these was to appoint governors in the region. This turned out to be an unsuccessful measure after his cousin Bahā-ud-dīn Gurśāsp, the governor of Sagara, rebelled against him in 1326. Soon thereafter, in 1327, Muhammad decided to move the capital of the Saltanat from Dilli to Dēvagiri in order to contain recalcitrant tendencies among the governors. In 1328, he ordered the people of Dilli to move to the new capital, which was renamed Daulatābād. The project turned out to be a disaster. Thousands died during the journey. Most migrants returned back to Dilli by 1335. Jalāl-ud-dīn Ahsān Khān, the Tughlak governor of Madurai, declared

143 Talbot 2001: 135.
144 Eaton 2005: 20-21.

his independence and founded the Saltanat of Madurai in 1335. Muhammad's control over the Deccan became tenuous in the coming years, and when he died on 20 March 1351, the region was effectively out of Dilli's reach.

Among the numerous acts of insubordination that led to the collapse of Dilli's authority in the Deccan, two were especially significant. The first of these came from a recalcitrant Tughlak military official, Hassan Gaṅgu, who held the title Zafar Khān. He occupied Daulatābad, and declared his independence in 1345. Hassan assumed a regal name, Alā-ud-dīn Hassan Bahman Śāh. In 1347, he moved to Kalaburagi,[145] where the wheels of the Bahmani state were fully set in motion. The second act was less rebellious in nature. It came from Harihara I, Bukka I, Kaṃpaṇa I, Muddappa, and Mārappa, the five sons of a certain Saṅgama. They had served their political apprentice under the Hoysaḷas.[146] The Hoysaḷa state had weakened to a great extent following repeated raids from Dilli, but its territory was still not lost. Unlike Dēvagiri, Vāraṅgallu, and Madurai, which were placed under governors after overthrowing the Sēvuṇa, the Kākatīya, and the Pāṇḍya states, respectively, Dilli had not succeeded in eliminating the Hoysaḷas. The Saṅgama brothers were thus able to take advantage of the vacuum created by the decline in Hoysaḷa influence, without engaging in confrontation with Dilli. Harihara I seems to have commenced his independent rule in or shortly before 1346, an act that is likely to have been inspired by Hassan Gaṅgu's defiance of Dilli a year ago. In his early years, he ruled from the Hoysaḷa heartland. By the late 1350s, he had consolidated his position around Haṃpi, known variously at the time as Hosapaṭṭaṇa, Vijayavirūpākṣapura, and Virūpākṣapaṭṭaṇa, and since 1357, as Vijayanagara. The great initiative that commenced with Harihara I and his four brothers was to have a lasting impression on the praxis of statecraft in the region.

Like their immediate predecessors, both the Vijayanagara and the Bahmani states were dryland polities. Burton Stein has gone to the extent of saying that "Vijayanagara was to prove the grand apotheosis" of dryland political formations.[147] But contrary to Stein's view, the Vijayanagara kings were also in control of the riparian belts,[148] as irrigation in the Vijayanagara heartland was mainly tank-fed, and had to depend upon the great tank watershed networks replenished through thousands of channels drawn from the perennial rivers. Under this geopolitical dispensation, peasant proprietors constituted the most dominant class that controlled the economy of the region.

---

145 Gulbarga, as renamed by the Government of Karnataka in 2014.

146 This is confirmed by contemporary inscriptions, although literary sources from a later date at times speak of the Saṅgamas as serving the Kākatīyas. See Kulke 1993: 208-239 (i.e., chapter 11) for a discussion.

147 Stein 1989: 21.

148 Ibid.

There were intrinsic differences in the economy controlled by the Bahmanis and the Vijayanagara rulers. The Bahmanis held sway over the areas to the north of the Kṛṣṇa, and oftentimes, to the north of the Tuṅgabhadra. The Vijayanagara rule on the other hand was concentrated to the south of these rivers. The north was a black-soil belt, parts of which fell within the basaltic Deccan trap. There were considerable stretches of plains too, although the general alignment of the land was towards the east. The plains, and their great rivers like the Gōdāvari, the Bhīma, the Kṛṣṇa, and the Malaprabha, played key roles in the evolution of the peasantry in this region. As early as the first and second centuries CE, the north was able to support petty chiefdoms and impressive Buddhist establishments like the ones found in Sannati and Vaḍagāv-Mādhavapura (Beḷagāvi). It was in this region that the most important states of the Deccan, like the Bādāmi Caḷukyas, the Rāṣṭrakūṭas, and the Kalyāṇa Cāḷukyas, arose. In sharp contrast, the south had an undulating topography. Lowlands merged into the plains, hills skirted the lowlands, fertile pieces of land lie scattered in the midst of granite outcrops. Agriculture was extensively dependent on tank irrigation. The production of grain surplus was less impressive, compared to the north. As a result, an entrenched class of peasantry was slow to emerge in the areas to the south of the Tuṅgabhadra. Few attempts were made to establish states here. Fewer were actually successful.

One consequence of this difference was that the modes of surplus extraction between the north and the south were substantially different from each other. In the north, peasant localities called *nāḍu* were larger in size, fewer in number, and managed more effectively through assessments and extraction of taxes and rents by locality chiefs and peasant proprietors, who worked closely with the state. Unlike the Cōḻa heartland, where the countless distributaries of the Kāvēri, a perennial river, enabled the development of extensive tank watersheds and the parcelling of agrarian land among numerous claimants due to the availability of irrigation water in spite of poor monsoon rains, which in turn paved way for the rise of hundreds of *nāḍu*s, the dryland belts to the north of the Tuṅgabhadra and the Kṛṣṇa suffered from want of irrigation. The general eastward tilt of the land made the construction of tank networks difficult, and at times, impossible. As a result, tanks were built less frequently in the north. Incentives from smaller holdings were therefore less attractive, although the fertility of the soil was impressive. Consequently, holdings tended to be huge. As opposed to this, *nāḍu*s flourished in the south even when state control was tenuous. This was because in the absence of extensive plain-land, small pieces of land were upturned for cultivation. These were under the control of local peasant magnates. Scarcity—both potential and real—forced the peasantry into raids and brigandage. This is testified by the hundreds of hero-stones found in the south, recording the death of 'heroes' in cattle-lifting adventures. Under these geographical constraints, large holdings were not easily forthcoming. The number of *nāḍu*s was therefore greater in the south, and their size, smaller. And owing to the unevenness of the terrain, which threw up numerous natural depressions and made the eastward tilt of the land less prominent, it was possible to build tanks in great numbers. Correspondingly, and in consequence, the number of peasant proprietors was also larger. This made systematic assessments and collection of revenue a tricky affair for the state. The ideal solution to the problem was to establish tributary relationships with the big men of the localities.

The invaders from Dilli seem to have clearly understood this difference between the north and the south. In a recent study, Richard M. Eaton and Phillip B. Wagoner have observed that the Tughlaks assigned *iktās* or revenue assignments to the erstwhile chiefs under the Sēvuṇas and the Kākatīyas to the north of the Kṛṣṇa. The *iktādārs* turned into instruments of regular tax collection in these areas. To the south, however, the autonomy of the former chiefs was recognized. These chiefs were identified as *amīrs*. They paid tributes to the Tughlak state.[149] Thus, the agrarian structure—which depended upon the geography of the region—determined the nature of surplus appropriation in the Deccan. The Bahmani state spread out its reach over the areas where the Tughlaks had established *iktādāri*. The authority of the Vijayanagara state extended over the landscape of the *amīrs*. This distinction is crucial for the purposes of our study.

Very early in their existence, the Vijayanagara kings forged an alliance with the maṭha of Śṛṅgēri. There is a popular legend, often presented as history, which attributes the founding of the Vijayanagara state to Vidyāraṇya, the pontiff of the Śṛṅgēri maṭha. This, nevertheless, is not borne out by contemporary evidence. It is a story promoted by the Śṛṅgēri maṭha only in the sixteenth century when the Saṅgama state, which supported them, was not in existence any more, and the Tuḷuva rulers, who swore by Vaiṣṇavism, promoted the cause of the Veṅkaṭēśvara temple of Tirupati.[150] According to Joan-Pau Rubiés, the Vidyāraṇya legend was meant to provide dharmic legitimation to the new dynasty.[151] Although the legend was from a later date, the relationship between the maṭha and the Saṅgama brothers was not. As early as 1346, the five brothers celebrated a *vijayōtsava* at Śṛṅgēri, during which Harihara I granted nine villages to the pontiff, Bhāratī Tīrtha.[152] Ten years later, in 1356, Bukka I visited Śṛṅgēri, and made an endowment to Vidyā Tīrtha.[153] It was in 1375 that Vidyāraṇya received a grant.[154] He was the pontiff at the time. Considering the fact that Bhāratī Tīrtha died in 1374, it is reasonable to suggest that Vidyāraṇya rose to become pontiff that year. The role he played in making the Śṛṅgēri maṭha an

149 Eaton and Wagoner 2014: 27.
150 Kulke 1993: 212-213.
151 Rubiés 2000: 262. It is, however, not clear why the early founders of Vijayanagara did not resort to seek 'legitimacy' through such legends. The theory of legitimacy has been called into question in recent years. See Pollock 2007: 511-524.
152 Kulke 1993: 226-227.
153 Ibid., p. 227.
154 Ibid.

influential establishment was seminal, as was his role in advancing the cause of a new *vaidic* orthodoxy in the region.

As Paul Hacker has shown on the basis of literary works, it is impossible to trace the succession of teachers of the Śṛṅgēri maṭha to a date before the mid decades of the fourteenth century.[155] Epigraphic sources confirm this picture. "The inscriptional evidence", observes Hermann Kulke, "leaves no doubt that Śṛṅgēri became an important place only under Harihara I and Bukka I".[156] Inasmuch as the earliest known pontiffs, Vidyā Tīrtha and Bhāratī Tīrtha, were recipients of Saṅgama munificence, we may venture a guess that it was under them that the maṭha was established, and that the Saṅgama brothers played a role in it that was by no means small. If this is true, the story of Śṛṅgēri's help in founding the Vijayanagara state must be dropped in favour of the story of the latter causing the maṭha to be built!

Although popular as Vidyāraṇya, the pontiff was also known as Mādhavācārya.[157] This seems to have been the name given him after initiation as a saint. 'Vidyāraṇya', *forest of knowledge*, was perhaps his title. It was an apt title indeed, as his two widely influential works, the *Sarvadarśanasaṅgraha* and the *Parāśaramādhavīya*, amply demonstrate. Vidyāraṇya also wrote the *Jīvanmuktivivēka*.[158] In this outstanding work, he argued that knowledge of Brahman was not sufficient to cause liberation. Rather, the destruction of latent desires (*vāsanākṣaya*), and of the mind itself (*manōnāśa*), through the regular practice of yōga, and leading the strictly disciplined life of a renouncer, "renouncing even the fact that he is a knower of Brahman", was essential for liberation.[159]

Vidyāraṇya is also believed to be the author of the *Śaṅkaradigvijaya*, which popularized the story of Śaṅkara travelling across India and establishing maṭhas in the four corners of the subcontinent. Scholars, however, are divided about Vidyāraṇya's authorship of this work.

Vidyāraṇya's younger brother, Sāyaṇācārya, was a greater forest of learning. Bukka I (r. 1357-1377) and Harihara II (r. 1377-1404) commissioned him to carry out the ambitious project of writing commentaries on the Vēdas. The oeuvre that Sāyaṇa has left behind is at once prolific and profound. More than a hundred works are attributed to him.[160] A resume of his works will place his significance in relief.

As he belonged to the Taittirīya school of the *Kṛṣṇa Yajurvēda*, Sāyaṇa chose to commence his project by producing glosses on the *Taittirīya Saṃhita*, the *Taittirīya*

155 Cited in Kulke 1993: 235-236.
156 Ibid., 237.
157 Not to be confused with Madhvācārya (ca. 1197-98 - 1275-76), who propounded the *dvaita* system of *vēdānta*. We shall refer to Madhvācārya by his alternate name Ānanda Tīrtha throughout this work, in order to avoid confusion.
158 On this work, see Fort 1998: 97-113, and Goodding 2011.
159 Goodding 2011: 96.
160 On Sāyaṇa, see Galewicz 2009.

Brāhmaṇa, and the *Taittirīya Āraṇyaka*. This accomplished, he took up the *Ṛgvēda* and its *Brāhmaṇa* and *Āraṇyaka*, viz., the *Aitarēya Brāhmaṇa* and the *Aitarēya Āraṇyaka*, for commentary, which was followed by the *Sāmavēda* and eight of its *Brāhmaṇa*s, viz., the *Tāṇḍya*, the *Ṣaḍviṃśa*, the *Samavidhāna*, the *Ārṣēya*, the *Dēvatādhyana*, the *Chāndōgya*, the *Saṃhitōpaniṣad*, and the *Vaṃśa*. The other commentaries he wrote included the ones on the *Śatapatha Brāhmaṇa*, the Śaunakīya recension of the *Atharvavēda*, and twenty *adhyāya*s of the *Kaṇva Saṃhita*. Sāyaṇa also produced anthologies like the *Subhāṣita Sudhānidhi* and the *Puruṣārttha Sudhānidhi*, and works on a number of topics, like Dharmaśāstras (the *Prāyaścitta Sudhānidhi*), etymology (the *Mādhavīya Dhātuvṛtti*), medicine (the *Āyurvēda Sudhānidhi*), poetics (the *Alaṃkāra Sudhānidhi*), and *vaidic* rituals (the *Yajñatantra Sudhānidhi*).[161] That this project was dear to the Saṅgama rulers is borne out by the fact that they made scholarly assistance available to Sāyaṇa. Harihara II granted an *agrahāra* to Nārāyaṇa Vājapēyayāji, Narahari Sōmayāji, Paṇḍhāri Dīkṣita, Pañcāgni Mādhava, Nāgābharaṇa, and Nāgabhaṭṭa for their assistance in producing the commentaries.[162] Sāyaṇa himself received a grant. In 1377, Harihara II donated an *agrahāra* to a number of brāhmaṇas. Sāyaṇa was one of the recipients.[163] We learn from an inscription of the time of Kṛṣṇarāya (1513) that there was a village called Sāyaṇapura close to the capital, Vijayanagara.[164] The village was perhaps founded, or renamed, in honour of Sāyaṇa. So close was Sāyaṇa's relationship with the state that Cezary Galewicz recently chose to begin his monograph on the commentator by declaring that "[t]he legend of the man known to Indian history by the name of Sāyaṇa will probably remain forever tied to another legend, that of the empire of Vijayanagara."[165]

The Śṛṅgēri maṭha adhered to the *advaita* (non-dualist) school of Śaṅkara (ca. 788-820 CE). Or so it claimed, in spite of the tāntric influences it was subjected to. It is very likely, then, that the maṭha was not favourably disposed towards rival schools of thought and their establishments. One such establishment existed in the coastal town of Uḍupi down the *ghāt*s, viz., the famous Kṛṣṇa temple with its eight affiliate maṭhas. The Kṛṣṇa temple was the wellspring of the *dvaita* (dualist) school,

---

161 Modak 1995: 17-18.

162 Galewicz 2009: 96-97.

163 Annual Report of the Mysore Archaeological Department 1915, p. 42. Modak 1995: 31-32 speaks of another agrahara, Bukkarāyapura, granted in 1377 by Harihara II to sixty brāhmaṇas, including Sāyaṇa. He locates this grant in the Kṛṣṇarājapēṭe tālūk (of Maṇḍya district, although Modak refers to it as Hāsana district). I have not been able to trace this inscription. A similar inscription occurs in the Kṛṣṇarājanagara tālūk (of the neighbouring Maisūru district), though, in which Harihara II granted Bukkarāyapura to several brāhmaṇas. However, Sāyaṇa's name does not figure in the list of donees. If it is this grant that Modak is referring to, then it is likely that he has misread the word Hoysaṇa (i.e. Hoysaḷa) occurring in it as Sāyaṇa. See Kn 77, *Epigraphia Carnatica*, Vol. 5 (revised edition).

164 No. 277, *South Indian Inscriptions*, Vol. 4.

165 Galewicz 2009: 31.

which looked upon *advaita* as its biggest opponent. Understandably enough, Śṛṅgēri shared a very difficult relationship with Uḍupi.

The *dvaita* doctrine was systematically formulated in the thirteenth century by the Vaiṣṇava saint, Ānanda Tīrtha (ca. 1197-98-1275-76).[166] He lived in Uḍupi for the better part of his life. He was a master of the *vaidic* works such as the Saṃhitas, the Brāhmaṇas, the Āraṇyakas, and the Upaniṣads. He is known to have studied *advaita* independently, as well as under a teacher of considerable renown, before registering his disagreements and setting out to build his own system. With his great erudition, argumentative prowess, and charisma, Ānanda Tīrtha went on to exercise great influence over the praxis of sainthood in southern India. We must examine his life at some length.

Although there is no unanimity concerning the dates of Ānanda Tīrtha, a manuscript of his *Mahābhārata Tātparya Nirṇaya* used by Bhandarkar mentions Kali Era 4300 (CE 1199) as the date of his birth.[167] While this date does not occur in the printed version of text,[168] the succession list preserved in various monasteries mention 1197-98 as the year when Ānanda Tīrtha was born. That Ānanda Tīrtha lived for seventy-eight years enables us to place his death in the year 1275-76.

Ānanda Tīrtha is credited in hagiographic literature with the construction of the Kṛṣṇa temple at Uḍupi and its eight affiliate maṭhas.[169] There are no means to ascertain the veracity of this claim. The earliest legends concerning Ānanda Tīrtha are recorded in the *Maṇimañjarī*, written by Nārāyaṇa Bhaṭṭa, the son of one of his disciples Trivikrama. This fanciful work in eight chapters has, in fact, nothing much to tell us about Ānanda Tīrtha's life. Only in the eighth chapter is a terse and telescoped account given. There is no reference to the construction of the temple or the maṭhas in this account. An inscription from 1366 records a grant made by a certain Malliyadaṇṇāyaka to the god of Uḍupi.[170] The grant was made following the demise of a certain Sōvaladēvi, who had earlier made a grant. This suggests that the temple existed in the early half of the fourteenth century. However, the inscription is found in the Anantēśvara temple, not in the Kṛṣṇa temple. The Kṛṣṇa temple itself is known to have existed in the late fourteenth century. A grant was made to it in the time of Harihara II in 1395.[171] Another grant came its way in 1396.[172] We might on the basis of these evidences conclude that the temple existed in the later half of the fourteenth century. Given that Ānanda Tīrtha's death and the first known grant to the temple

---

166 On his dates, see Dasgupta 1991: 51-52.
167 Ibid., 51.
168 Ibid.
169 The eight maṭhas are Phalimāru, Adamāru, Pējāvara, Puttige, Sōde, Kṛṣṇapura, Śirūru, and Kaṇiyūru. The maṭhas were apparently named after villages originally held by them.
170 No. 306, *South Indian Inscriptions*, Vol. 7.
171 No. 299, Ibid.
172 No. 183, Ibid.

are separated only by a little over a century, it is not unreasonable to accept that the temple was built during Ānanda Tīrtha's lifetime or within a few years or decades of his death.

Epigraphic reference to the maṭhas is not found before the seventeenth century. A record from 1615, when Vēdavēdya Tīrtha, the adoptee (*karakamalasañjāta*) of Vādirāja Tīrtha, held the pontificate, speaks of eight villages (*aṣṭagrāma*) after which the maṭhas are named.[173] However, the existence of the maṭha during Vādirāja's time is alluded to in legends concerning his life.

If the account given in the *Maṇimañjarī* is to be believed, Ānanda Tīrtha was born as the incarnation of Vāyu (the wind god) to destroy the doctrines of Śaṅkara, who taught Buddhism under the veil of *vēdānta*. The account itself is fanciful. It identifies Śaṅkara as the son born out of wedlock to a widow. His real name is recorded as Maṇiman. He was an evil genius, who seduced a brāhmaṇa woman, converted people to his faith with the help of magic, and preached violence and immorality. His followers destroyed monasteries of their opponents, and indulged in sinful acts like killing cattle, women, and children. The teacher Satya Prajña was killed, and Prajñā Tīrtha converted to their faith by force. However, this line of teachers continued to practice their doctrine secretly. In this line was born Acyutaprēkṣa. Ānanda Tīrtha was his disciple.[174]

The life of Ānanda Tīrtha is elaborately described on the lines of the prevailing hagiographic conventions in Nārāyaṇa Paṇḍita's *Sumadhvavijaya*. Like the *Maṇimañjarī*, this work regards Ānanda Tīrtha as an incarnation of Vāyu. Here is the story:

A brāhmaṇa called Madhyagēha Bhaṭṭa lived at Pājaka in Paraśurāmakṣētra (the region between Gōkarṇa and Kanyākumāri) with his wife. He had a daughter, but there was no one to take his line forward as his two sons had died young. Madhyagēha Bhaṭṭa and his wife prayed to Lord Anantēśvara for twelve years, and as a result, were blessed with a son. He was named Vāsudēva.

As a child, Vāsudēva was intelligent, inquisitive, and adventurous, and showed signs of wanderlust. The hagiographer attributes a number of miracles to the young boy, including the slaying of a demon, and curing his teacher's son of a chronic headache by blowing wind into his ear. After initial schooling in a *gurukula*, Vāsudēva decided to renounce worldly life and become a disciple of Acyutaprēkṣa, much against the wishes of his father. But before leaving, he prophesied that Madhyagēha Bhaṭṭa would be blessed with another son. The prophecy came true. Acyutaprēkṣa initiated Vāsudēva into sainthood, and conferred the name Pūrṇabōdha upon him.[175] The boy was only ten years old at this time.

173 No. 302, Ibid.

174 *Maṇimañjari*, 6-8. For a summary of this account, see Dasgupta 1991: 52.

175 Elsewhere, and more popularly, he is known as Pūrṇaprajña.

One day Pūrṇabōdha expressed his wish to travel to Kāśi, and take a holy dip in the Gaṅgā. Acyutaprēkṣa was so deeply attached to his disciple that he was pained by the thought of his departure. Gaṅgā appeased the *guru* and the *śiṣya* by appearing in the lake Anantasarōvara nearby. The days that followed were, however, marked by frictions between Acyutaprēkṣa and Pūrṇabōdha. It began when Pūrṇabōdha defeated a *vaiśēṣika* scholar called Vāsudēva in a debate, and impressed by it, Acyutaprēkṣa decided to teach him a text of higher learning called *Iṣṭasiddhi*. This was an *advaita* text. Pūrṇabōdha pointed to several mistakes in it, which Acyutaprēkṣa had to concede. Pūrṇabōdha commenced a career in teaching, and began with *māyāvāda* (i.e., the *advaita* of Śaṅkara). Acyutaprēkṣa now turned to a recitation of the *Bhāgavatapurāṇa*. The manuscript he had was different from the one that a disciple listening to it had in his possession. The disciple pointed to the differences in some verses, whereupon Pūrṇabōdha, who was also present there, declared which one of the two versions was textually authentic. When challenged by Acyutaprēkṣa, he recited the subsequent section of the text to the surprise of those assembled there. Acyutaprēkṣa asked him when he had memorized these difficult sections, as he had never seen him do so. Pūrṇabōdha revealed that he had learnt them in his previous birth. Impressed by his scholarship, Acyutaprēkṣa subsequently nominated him as his successor, and gave him the name Ānanda Tīrtha.

In the following days, Ānanda Tīrtha frustrated many scholars, including Jyēṣṭhayati, a friend of Acyutaprēkṣa, and two Buddhist teachers, Buddhisāgara and Vādisiṃha, in various debates. He then began his discourses on the *vēdānta* by commenting on the *Brahmasūtras*, and challenging the existing commentaries of the rival schools, especially *advaita*. Upon the request of many eminent teachers of the day, including Acyutaprēkṣa's, he recited a new commentary on the *Brahmasūtras*.

Ānanda Tīrtha then set out on a tour of southern India in the company of Acyutaprēkṣa. It brought him to places like Viṣṇumaṅgalaṃ near Kāsaṟagōḍŭ, the Payasvini river valley, Tiruvanantapuraṃ, Kanyākumāri, Dhanuṣkōṭi, Rāmēśvaraṃ, Śrīraṅgaṃ, and other nearby places. At all these places, he had a sacred dip in the waters, and offered prayers. He also refuted rival teachers in debates at many places and won a number of admirers and followers. His next stopover was Śrīmuṣṇa. Here, he caused a water-tank called Daṇḍatīrtha to be excavated. From there he returned to the Payasvini valley, where at different places, he engaged in discourses and debates, defeating adversaries. He then wrote a commentary on the *Bhagavadgīta* and presented it to Acyutaprēkṣa and Jyēṣṭhayati.

Ānanda Tīrtha now turned to the north and travelled to Badarikāśrama (Badrīnāth in Uttarakhand) with the intention of obtaining permission to write a commentary on the *Brahmasūtras* from its celebrated author, Vēda Vyāsa. In the course of the journey, he held discourses at various places, and routed advocates of rival schools in debate after debate. He also collected a number of books during the journey. Upon reaching Badarikāśrama, he presented the commentary on the *Gīta* to Lord Nārāyaṇa (Viṣṇu) at the Anantamaṭha, and obtained his approval. In the following days, he performed penances. Meanwhile, Vyāsa invited Ānanda Tīrtha to his *āśrama* in Uttara Badari. Ānanda Tīrtha travelled across the snowcapped mountains and reached Vyāsa's *āśrama*. The two giants met in a divine union. There, Lord Nārāyaṇa manifested in front of Ānanda Tīrtha in another form and asked him to write a commentary on the *Brahmasūtra*s. Work on the commentary began at Badarikāśrama. Ānanda Tīrtha then travelled southwards and reached the river Gōdāvari, where a teacher called Śōbhanabhaṭṭa became his disciple. Ānanda Tīrtha returned to Uḍupi, where he presented his commentary on the *Brahmasūtra*s to Acyutaprēkṣa.

During his stay in Uḍupi, a storm caused a shipwreck in the sea. The ship was coming from Dvārakā. Ānanda Tīrtha saved the ship from destruction. The merchant who was sailing in the ship presented him with an image of Kṛṣṇa in gratitude. Ānanda Tīrtha built a temple for Kṛṣṇa at Uḍupi, and installed the image there. He then chastised a proud expert of *yajña*s, and had his teacher's son Vāsudēva perform a proper *yajña*. Then, he wrote the *Tantrasāra*, which laid out the rituals to be observed in the Kṛṣṇa temple.

After this, Ānanda Tīrtha set out on a second voyage to Badarikāśrama in the company of many disciples. He performed several miracles in the course of this journey, including making a king excavate a lake, walking on the river Gaṅgā along with his disciples, humbling highwaymen, and rescuing his disciple Satya Tīrtha by killing the tiger that had attacked him. At Uttara Badari, Vyāsa presented him with eight stone sculptures made sacred by the presence of Lord Lakṣmīnārāyaṇa. Vyāsa also instructed him to compose the *Mahābhārata Tātparya Nirṇaya*. On his return journey, Ānanda Tīrtha walked over the river Gaṅgā once again. During his four-month monsoon retreat (*cāturmāsa*) at Hastināpura, the Gaṅgā flowed down and bowed to him. At Kāśi, his disciples turned arrogant, and challenged him to a wrestling match. Ānanda Tīrtha defeated them effortlessly. Then he reduced the *advaita* teacher Indrapuri in a debate. Upon reaching Kurukṣētra, he dug the earth and revealed the mace used by him in his previous birth as Bhīma, the second of the five Pāṇḍava brothers.[176] At Hṛṣīkēśa (Ṛṣīkēśa), Lord Rudra invited him to accept *bhikṣā* (alms) and made his devotee offer him *bhikṣā*. Ānanda Tīrtha then came to Iṣupāta where he prayed to Paraśurāma. At Gōviṣaya (Goa), a king invited him and offered thousands of plantains and milk. Ānanda Tīrtha consumed them with ease. On another occasion at Gōviṣaya, he consumed four thousand plantains and thirty pots of milk offered by a brāhmaṇa called Śaṅkara.[177]

From Gōviṣaya, Ānanda Tīrtha returned to Uḍupi, and resumed his discourses on his *dvaita* system. Śōbhanabhaṭṭa, whom we met earlier on the banks of the Gōdāvari, arrived at Uḍupi, and was initiated as Padmanābha Tīrtha. Another learned teacher

---

176 Bhīma is believed to be the son of Vāyu, and Ānanda Tīrtha, an incarnation of Vāyu.

177 Our hero seems to have been quite a foodie. The motif of consuming large quantities of food occurs again and again in the *Sumadhvavijaya*. It compares with the gluttony of Bhīma in the *Mahābharata*.

came from the Kaḷiṅga country, became his disciple, and returned home to attain fame as Narahari Tīrtha. Throughout this period, Ānanda Tīrtha's discourses continued in Uḍupi.

One evening, Lord Śēṣa appeared in the sky with his entourage, which included the Sanaka brothers,[178] to listen to the discourses. It created a great sparkle of light in the sky. Ānanda Tīrtha's audience was surprised by the light. The great teacher explained to them how the light was caused, and offered them a glimpse of Śēṣa and his entourage. Then Śēṣa revealed himself and gave a colourful description of Vaikuṇṭha, the abode of Viṣṇu.

As the fame of Ānanda Tīrtha and his *dvaita* school began to spread far and wide, a number of adversaries arrived on the scene to challenge him. They approached Padma Tīrtha and Puṇḍarīkapuri of the Cōḷa country for help. Puṇḍarīkapuri challenged Ānanda Tīrtha to a contest, and predictably enough, he was defeated. Ānanda Tīrtha had entrusted the books in his possession to a certain Śaṅkarācārya. The māyāvādi opponents believed that our hero's knowledge was based on his books. So they employed a certain Padmanābha Tīrtha[179] to steal the books. Learning of this, Ānanda Tīrtha came to Ēkavāṭa with Jyēṣṭhayati, and humbled Padmanābha Tīrtha in a debate without the aid of books. The books were entrusted to the village headman with instructions to have them returned to Ānanda Tīrtha through the king.

The rest of the *Sumadhvavijaya* is rather dry (not that the events narrated above are otherwise). At Prāgyavāṭa, Ānanda Tīrtha spent one of his monsoon retreats. Here he spent his days in writing. It was here that the villagers brought the books stolen by Padmanābha Tīrtha to him. Ānanda Tīrtha refused to accept them, and advised them to have it returned through the king, Jayasiṃha. The king met him, and was moved by his spiritual charisma. He began to patronize the master, and became a trusted follower. Ānanda Tīrtha's adversaries were, nonetheless, unrelenting. They approached a certain Trivikrama Paṇḍita and urged him to defeat Ānanda Tīrtha in a debate. But Trivikrama Paṇḍita and his younger brother Śaṅkara were already great fans of the *dvaita* school. A debate followed, which was more in the nature of a humble Trivikrama Paṇḍita requesting Ānanda Tīrtha to clarify doubts on a number of points. It ended cordially. The rest of Ānanda Tīrtha's days were spent, predictably, in discourses and debates, routing rivals in both physical combats and intellectual exchanges, public works like building a check dam with a boulder to prevent flood in the river Bhadra, and filling the dried up lake of Daṇḍatīrtha in Saridantara by causing rain through a miracle. One of his last acts was to rescue his younger brother, who lived a woeful life after the death of his parents, from destitution. Ānanda Tīrtha initiated him as his disciple, who in course of time attained fame as Viṣṇu Tīrtha.

---

178 According to the Purāṇas, Sanaka, Sanandana, Sanātana, and Sanatkumāra were four leading sages and the sons of Brahma.

179 Not to be confused with Śōbhanabhaṭṭa, who was given this name after initiation.

After living a long life of play (*līlā*), Ānanda Tīrtha, who was by now popular as Madhvācārya, dissolved in the unmanifest, as they say in hagiographic parlance. He is believed to have suddenly vanished while discoursing on the *Aitarēya* commentary to his students at the Anantēśvara temple in Uḍupi.

The image of Ānanda Tīrtha that was constructed over the centuries, and recorded in the *Sumadhvavijaya*, has been crucial for the development of the *dvaita* system and its sainthood. There is in this image a combination of a number of attributes. Six of them are crucial for our purposes. One, Ānanda Tīrtha is endowed with divinity, emphasized by the fact that he is an incarnation of Vāyu, and meets with Vēda Vyāsa and Viṣṇu. Two, he is known for his physical strength, represented by acts like slaying a tiger and defeating men in wrestling encounters. Three, he performs miracles like walking on a river. Note that unlike the miracles of future saints from other traditions (discussed in chapters 5 and 6), these acts are not meant for the benefit or welfare of others. Four, he travels far and wide, and wins over people to his school, mostly through debates. Five, he is a rebel who rejects, and fights against, orthodox learning. Six, he is the fountainhead of a new school of knowledge. Of these attributes, valour and the performance of miracles are certainly downplayed, and travel and divinity occupy an intermediate position as if they are inevitable components of sainthood. The greatest emphasis in the narrative is on the fact that the saint calls orthodox knowledge into question, and develops and nurtures his own school. This embedded hierarchy of attributes[180] governed the image of sainthood in the *dvaita* school in the succeeding centuries. In the lives of the saints of Ānanda Tīrtha's tradition, valour and miracles was always peripheral in importance in articulating the personality of the saint, while travel and divinity were consistently recorded. The defining feature of the saint, however, was the challenge he posed to rival schools, and the force and conviction with which he argued his case. Although the *dvaita* school soon became one of the most deeply entrenched orthodoxies in the region, the noise it created by way of constant opposition to Śaṅkara's *advaita* enabled it to be represented as doctrinally radical. Here was the orthodox, masquerading as revolutionary.

The Madhva tradition has carefully preserved records of its genealogy beginning with Acyutaprēkṣa. Each maṭha had its own genealogy, too. Unlike the list of early teachers produced by the Śṛṅgēri maṭha, these were not fully invented genealogies, although many names are likely to have been smuggled into them at different times. Corroborative evidences in a number of cases establish the relative historical authenticity of the line of seers, although it is not to be taken as completely foolproof. Fantastic lists of succession were not, however, unknown, an instance of which is provided by Baladēva's commentary on the *Brahmasūtras*.[181]

---

180 We call it embedded because it is implicitly woven into the narrative rather than being stated explicitly.
181 Dasgupta 1991: 56.

Thus, the Madhvas of Uḍupi were the first in the region to produce a list of succession with a relatively high degree of historical credibility that has been carefully preserved and continued well into our times. In this, they were in all likelihood inspired by the list of succession preserved by the *viśiṣṭādvaita* schools of Tamilnadu.[182] Here is one such list of *dvaita* teachers of Uḍupi to the end of the nineteenth century:[183]

Ānanda Tīrtha (or Madhvācārya)
↓
Padmanābha Tīrtha
↓
Narahari Tīrtha
↓
Mādhava Tīrtha
↓
Akṣōbhya Tīrtha
↓
Jaya Tīrtha
↓
Vidyādhirāja Tīrtha
↓
Kavīndra Tīrtha
↓
Vāgīśa Tīrtha
↓
Rāmacandra Tīrtha
↓
Vidyānidhi Tīrtha
↓
Raghunātha Tīrtha
↓
Raghuvarya Tīrtha
↓

182 The *viśiṣṭādvaita* line of succession commenced with Nāthamuni, who compiled the works of the twelve Vaiṣṇava saints, the Āḻvārs, as the *Nālāyira Divyaprabandhaṃ* in the tenth century. He was succeeded by Puṇḍarīkākṣa, Rāmamiśra, Nāthamuni's grandson Yāmunācārya, and Rāmānuja in that order. See Farquhar 1967: 240-242. See also Dutta 2014 for an account of early hagiographic representations of Rāmānuja.

183 Dasgupta 1991: 56. The historical significance of tracing such genealogies of succession will be discussed in chapter 4.

Raghūttama Tīrtha
↓
Vēdavyāsa Tīrtha
↓
Vidyādhīśa Tīrtha
↓
Vēdanidhi Tīrtha
↓
Satyavrata Tīrtha
↓
Satyanidhi Tīrtha
↓
Satyanātha Tīrtha
↓
Satyābhinava Tīrtha
↓
Satyapūrṇa Tīrtha
↓
Satyavijaya Tīrtha
↓
Satyapriya Tīrtha
↓
Satyabōdha Tīrtha
↓
Satyasannidhāna Tīrtha
↓
Satyavara Tīrtha
↓
Satyadhāma Tīrtha
↓
Satyasāra Tīrtha
↓
Satyaparāyaṇa Tīrtha I
↓
Satyakāma Tīrtha
↓
Satyēṣṭi Tīrtha
↓
Satyaparāyaṇa Tīrtha II
↓
Satyavit Tīrtha

In his works, Ānanda Tīrtha is believed to have refuted the works of twenty-one commentators who came before him. The commentators are enumerated by Śēṣa, who was a disciple of Chalāri Nṛsiṃhācārya, the author of a commentary on Nārāyaṇa Paṇḍita's *Sumadhvavijaya*. The list includes the redoubtable Śaṅkara and Rāmānuja.[184] Ānanda Tīrtha's works followed the widely established tradition of expounding the doctrine in the form of hermeneutically oriented commentaries on the *prasthānatraya*,[185] and other *vaidic* and brāhmaṇical works. Thirty-seven works are attributed to him. These included a commentary on the *Bhāgavatapurāṇa*, the *Bhagavadgīta*, the *Brahmasūtra*s, Upaniṣads like the *Aitarēya Upaniṣad*, the *Taittirīya Upaniṣad*, the *Chāndōgya Upaniṣad*, the *Bṛhadāraṇyaka Upaniṣad*, the *Īśāvāsya Upaniṣad*, the *Kaṭhōpaniṣad*, the *Kēnōpaniṣad*, the *Praśnōpaniṣad*, the *Muṇḍakōpaniṣad*, and the *Māṇḍūkyōpaniṣad*. Besides, he wrote commentaries on parts of the *Ṛgvēda*, the *Aitarēya Brāhmaṇa*, and the *Aitarēya Āraṇyaka*. His masterpiece was the *Mahābhārata Tātparya Nirṇaya*, allegedly an exposition of the real meaning and spirit of the *Mahābhārata*. In this work, he described the world as real and characterized by five distinctions (*pañcabhēdā*), viz., the distinction between the self (*jīva*) and god (*īśvara*), the distinction between one self and the other, the distinction between matter (*jaḍa*) and god, the distinction between matter and matter, and the distinction between matter and the self.[186] This theory was the cornerstone of his *dvaita* school.

Ānanda Tīrtha was the pioneer of the new *vaidic* orthodoxy in the region. The *dvaita* doctrine he promulgated was certainly a serious challenge to the *advaitic* orthodoxy, as it affirmed the reality of the world. The world, according to this doctrine, was not *māyā*, but a substantial reality. But the first step towards upholding the reality of the world was already taken a century before Ānanda Tīrtha, when Rāmānuja systematized the tenets of the *viśiṣṭādvaita* school. We must, therefore, dwell at some length on Rāmānuja's intellectual contributions in order to understand how he recast the debate on the ontological status of the world.

Rāmānuja (ca. 1017-1137) was a profoundly influential teacher. He was a disciple of Yāmunācārya (ca. 966-1038), who in turn was the grandson of Nāthamuni (ca. 900-950), who had compiled the works of the twelve Vaiṣṇava saints of Tamilnadu, called Āḻvārs, in the *Nālāyira Divyaprabandhaṃ*. Rāmānuja thus had a rich intellectual legacy to inherit. It was a combination of four elements: i) classical *vēdānta* articulated in the form of commentaries on the *prasthānatraya* texts, ii) the ideal of devotion or *bhakti* with its emphasis on intense personal relationship between the devotee and the deity,

184 Ibid., 53.

185 The *prasthānatraya* or 'the three movements' are the *Brahmasūtra* of Bādarāyaṇa (i.e. Vēda Vyāsa), the *Bhagavadgīta*, and the Upaniṣads. The *vaidāntic* traditions of India, which include the *advaita*, the *dvaita*, the *viśiṣṭādvaita*, the *dvaitādvaita*, the *śuddhādvaita*, and many other schools, regard the *prasthānatraya* as the source of their authority. Most *vaidāntic* doctrines are in the form of commentaries on the *prasthānatraya*.

186 *Mahābhārata Tātparya Nirṇaya*, 1.69-71.

iii) the temple-centred *āgamic* rituals of the tāntric Pañcarātra tradition, and iv) the *paurāṇic* ontology narrativized in the *Bhāgavatapurāṇa*, and more importantly, in the *Viṣṇupurāṇa*.[187]

Rāmānuja made a significant departure from Śaṅkara's scheme of things when he identified the world as real and substantial.[188] Matter was, therefore, a major ontological factor in the articulation of his doctrine. The Buddhists had reflected upon the nature of matter for a long time. But unlike the Buddhist systems in which a specific god was absent, the doctrine of Rāmānuja had the quality of a theology. God (in his form as Viṣṇu) was central to this system. Recognizing the world as real and substantial, then, generated the need for describing the difference between god and the world, and how they were connected to each other. In his *Śrībhāṣya*, a commentary on the *Brahmasūtras*, Rāmānuja elaborated upon this idea of difference in a matter of fact way by emphasizing that the perception of difference and their recapitulation during memory were possible only because each object had an essential attribute of its own, which made it different from the other. In the absence of such essential attributes, it would be impossible to distinguish between, say, a horse, and an elephant.[189] Rāmānuja argued that experience, in its forms as knowledge, comprehension, and consciousness, is simply an attribute of the experiencing self.[190] The individual self, therefore, possesses an attribute, viz., the faculty of knowing. It is not merely a reflection of the supreme self devoid of attributes, as Śaṅkara had claimed.

This foregrounding of difference had its logical corollary in the fact that the difference between the self and the body had also to be clearly understood. Thus, reflections on the body came to occupy an important position in this system of theology. Rāmānuja addressed this question by regarding Brahman as *śarīri*, i.e., embodied, or the one endowed with a body. Interpreting verses from the *Viṣṇupurāṇa*, he argued that Brahman possessed a body, variously called *śarīra*, *rūpa*, *tanu*, *aṃśa*, *śakti*, and *vibhūti* by the *Purāṇa*. In this theory of embodied Brahman, the *śarīri* was the substance, the *śarīra* or body, its attribute. This was a radical move away from the manner in which the *Bhagavadgītā*, an important *prasthānatraya* text, framed the relationship between the body (*dēha* or *śarīra*) and the embodied one (*dēhi* or *śarīri*). Although the *Gītā* dwelt at length on the (phenomenological) presence of the body, its avowed position was that the body was, in the ultimate analysis, corporal, and subject to decay, unlike the *ātman*, which was extra-corporal, and eternal, indestructible, and immeasurable.[191] The body, was, therefore undesirable. Making

---

187 The influence of the *Bhāgavatapurāṇa*'s order of things is only implicit and embedded in Rāmānuja's works, his explicit and long-standing engagement being with the *Viṣṇupurāṇa*.

188 See Bartley 2002: 27-68 (i.e. chapter 2) for a discussion.

189 *Śrībhāṣya*, 1.1.1.

190 Ibid. However, Rāmānuja hastens to clarify that experience itself has no attributes, as it is not an object to be known.

191 *Bhagavadgītā*, 2.18.

this "undesirable" object substantial, and more crucially, an attribute of Brahman, changed the way in which South Asian traditions of renunciation in particular and intellectual traditions in general looked at the world.

Isn't there a distinction between the *śarīri* and the *śarīra* in Rāmānuja's scheme of things? Yes, there is, and this is one of its points of emphasis as well. But the crucial point is that the *śarīra* is substantial (*dravya*) inasmuch as the world is substantial, and at the same time, an attribute (*guṇa*) of the *śarīri*. Everything that exists is identical with Brahman only by virtue of the relationship of body and soul between them. Whatever is different from Brahman exists as an entity only by being his body.[192] It is thus that difference (*bhēda*) and likeness (*abhēda*) are both affirmed simultaneously. How can a substance be a substance, and at the same time the attribute of another substance? The answer is provided through the simile of a lamp and the light emanating from it. The light is real, and substantial in its own right. At the same time, it is an attribute of the lamp that is also real and substantial.[193] This relational ontology, called *dharmabhūtajñāna*,[194] endowed an attribute with substance. Knowledge, i.e., *brahmajñāna*, involved a proper understanding of this relational ontology and its causes. The intention to know could arise without the intervention of god. As Elisha Freschi observes, "Intentions need the support of God to be turned into actions but one can conceive independently the desire to take refuge in God and this is the root of one's future attitudes and deeds."[195]

How was *brahmajñāna* to be known? Rāmānuja's answer to this question was simple and disappointingly prescriptive: *brahmajñāna* was to be learnt from a *guru*. It is the *guru* who teaches the aspirant to say: "In me all is born, by me all things are sustained and in me all things are dissolved. I am the secondless Brahman" and that "I am that Brahman that illuminates all things, which is truth, knowledge and bliss absolute". The knowledge thus acquired is a knowledge from the mediate (*parōkṣa*), which over time becomes immediate (*aparōkṣa*).[196] An intensely personal bond between the *guru* and the disciple is called for, as P.N. Srinivasachari writes in his monograph on the *viśiṣṭādvaita*:

> the *ātman*, who belongs to Brahman, somehow superimposes on himself the idea that he belongs to *prakṛti*, sleeps in and as matter in the *pra|aya* state, identifies himself with the body of a god or an animal or a man in creation and subjects himself to the wheel of *samsāra* with all its hazards and hardships till he is made to realise his folly by a loving *guru*.[197]

192 *Śrībhāṣya*, 1.1.1.
193 Srinivasacari 1943: 300.
194 Ibid., 33.
195 Freschi 2015: 292.
196 Srinivasachari 1943: 89.
197 Ibid., 136-137.

The loving *guru* is therefore central to the acquisition of knowledge and the practice of sainthood. Thus, an aspirant "cannot rely on the inner light of reason without the grace of God and the *guru*".[198]

This emphasis on a personal and emotional bond with the *guru* cannot be seen as an inherent trait of renunciation in South Asia. Some of the oldest works on renunciation from the subcontinent present no signs of such intimacy. In the *Praśnōpaniṣad*, for instance, the relationship the teacher Pippalāda shares with his six students is remarkably formal. One may even call it mercenary. Having learnt the knowledge of Brahman, the students pay tributes to Pippalāda—in words and in kind—and leave him without cherishing any emotional bonds. No residues of intimacy are left behind. We never come across any attempt to establish an enduring bond between the *guru* and the *śiṣya*.[199] This seems to have been the case at least till the early second millennium CE. In the absence of any attempt to address this question historically, it is difficult to say when, why, and how the practice of configuring the *guru-śiṣya* relationships in intimate terms gained currency. All that can be said is that it was well known by the end of the twelfth century when the forebears of the later day Vīraśaivas began to represent themselves as being protected by the eight-fold armours (*aṣṭāvaraṇa*), beginning with the *guru*.[200] As far as I can trace, the earliest expression of the new chemistry between the teacher and the student goes back to the Mantrayāna school of Buddhism in Tibet. The story of Nārōpa's (ca. 1016-1100) impassioned engagement with his guru Tilōpa (ca. 988-1069) seems to embody the first known instance of its kind. Nārōpa's patience and conviction about the infallibility of Tilōpa makes him endure a number of recurring ordeals that the latter expects him to overcome. Nārōpa, nevertheless, remains unshakable in his resolve and reverence for his *guru*.[201] As intense as this is the relationship the celebrated Milarēpa shared with his teacher Marpa, who was the greatest of Nārōpa's students.[202] This new ideal seems to have soon found its way into Nepal from where it was carried to the north Indian plains, perhaps by the Nātha (Kānphaṭā or Bārāpanthī) *yōgis*. Gōrakṣa (Gōrakhanātha), to whom the founding of the Nātha tradition of renunciation is attributed, is said to have shared a close relationship with his *guru*, Matsyēndra.[203]

The position the *guru* enjoyed in South Asian systems of renunciation after the twelfth century was ethically far-reaching, if not decisive. What it involved was a displacement of agency *(kartṛtva)* and action (*kriya*). The self freed itself from

198 Ibid., 174.

199 We are discussing the relationship involved between the teacher and the aspirant disciple in the practices of renunciation, not the formal *gurukula* education during *brahmacarya*.

200 The eight armours are *guru*, *liṅga*, *jaṅgama*, *pādōdaka*, *prasāda*, *vibhūti*, *rudrākṣa*, and *mantra*. For a discussion, see Nandimath 2001: 326-32.

201 On Nārōpa, see Guenther 1995.

202 On Milarēpa, see Evans-Wentz 1950.

203 Briggs 2007: 229-34.

the burden of agency and action by investing them in the *guru*, who, though real, functioned as an abstract figurehead as far as the dynamics of this displacement was concerned. Thus, *guru* could be invoked as a concept—as the Vīraśaivas did by including him in the *aṣṭāvaraṇa*—without there being an explicit need to invoke a specific individual as *guru* to whom obeisance is paid. This abstraction enabled the sixteenth-century poet Mēlpattūr Nārāyaṇa Bhaṭṭadiri from the neighbouring Kerala to transform everything in the world into a *guru* from which he has something to learn. If the god-compassionate makes up his mind, anything can turn into a source of learning.[204] The earth teaches patience, the wind detachment, and the sky-teacher (*gaganaguru*) immanence.[205] Water teaches purity, fire omnipresence, and the sun and the moon, changelessness behind the shifting hues and shades.[206] The hunter, the python, the ocean, the fly, the beetle,[207] the elephant, the bee, the deer, the fish, Piṅgalā the courtesan, the pelican,[208] the child, the virgin, the artisan, the snake,[209] the spider, the hornet, and the body which teaches renouncement by reminding us of its ultimate fate of ending up as filth or ash,[210] are all transformed into teachers. With agency and action displaced from the self, what remained was the act—without the intentional component—and its result. Both were designated as *karma*. The question of agency was of course not completely dismissed, as the self was always said to be susceptible to the burdens of accumulated *karma*. But the *karma* question became less and less troubling over the centuries, particularly after the fifteenth century, when many new techniques—like listening to the *Rāmāyaṇa*, the *Mahābhārata*, the *Bhāgavatapurāṇa*, or stories from the *paurāṇic* tradition, or chanting the god's name, or visiting centres of pilgrimage—were invented to secure liberation and freedom from the backlashes of *karma*. Even heinous crimes such as *brahmahatyā* (killing a brāhmaṇa) could be absolved with ease. The figure of the *guru* and its avowed relationship with the self enabled the transformation of agency and action—which were functionally real though conceptualized as displaced—into a ritualistic, recursive, and therefore non-existent form, making the self's powers of volition ethically redundant. The displacement of agency and action—which was more of a deferral than displacement—had a historically significant outcome. It released the self from the question of responsibility. The new self engaged in duty (also called *karma*), but without being responsible or answerable to anyone. It produced knowledge and beauty, wielded authority, created wealth, and longed for the realization of Brahman, all for their own sake and not because the self nurtured a sense of responsibility.

204 "*tvat kāruṇyē pravṛttē ka iva nahi gurur lōkavṛttē'pi bhūnan*", *Nārāyaṇīyaṃ*, 93.3.
205 Ibid.
206 Ibid., 93.4.
207 Ibid., 93.5.
208 Ibid., 93.6.
209 Ibid., 93.7.
210 Ibid., 93.8.

It should therefore not be surprising that no Indian language had an equivalent for the word 'responsibility' in its vocabulary, until words like *hoṇegārike*, *javābdāri*, *uttaravādittvaṃ*, *cumatala*, *zimmēdārī*, and so on were coined or appropriated in the nineteenth and the twentieth centuries to signify it.[211]

Invoking the *guru* was one way of transcending responsibility.[212] There were perhaps many other ways of doing it. One of them is of particular interest to us. This was *līlā*, or the concept of a cosmic play as constituting the universe.

Līlā was a worldview, or more appropriately, an ontology of the world. It described the world as a play of the supreme self or Brahman, variously identified as Rāma, Kṛṣṇa, Śiva, Viṣṇu, etc. Whether this supreme self was endowed with essential attributes (*guṇa*) was of course a theological question often debated.[213] But its ability to orchestrate the cosmic play, either consciously or through the mediation of *śakti* or *māyā*, was widely accepted after the twelfth century, and more pronouncedly after the fifteenth century. The visible and the invisible worlds, which constitute the universe, were the unfurling of this play. The world did not exist as anything other than the play. Thus, the supreme self was the cause of the world. According to some traditions, Brahman created the world. According to others, the world was always present without being subjected to creation or destruction, and merely reflected in the form of the manifest world, like the city reflecting in the mirror, due to *māyā*.[214]

Rāmānuja is among the earliest teachers to argue that the manifest world is a *līlā* of god. The *Śrībhāṣya* begins by invoking god as the one who creates, maintains, and destroys the whole world with his sport.[215] Rāmānuja accepts the position of the *Brahmasūtras* that the world is but a mere play (of Brahman)[216] and that there was no motive behind creation.[217] He further refutes charges of partisanship and cruelty on Brahman for having created an unequal world by endorsing the *Brahmasutras*' idea of dependence (*sāpēkṣa*) in creation. Brahman, says Rāmānuja, depends upon the

---

211 Here, we make a conceptual distinction between duty and responsibility. Duty is enforced by an external agency like state, community, family, convention, law etc., whereas responsibility emerges from within, and is governed by one's conscience.

212 Literature concerning the image of the *guru* in south Asia after the twelfth century is neither extensive nor compelling. See Devadevan 2010c: 263-308 for a preliminary discussion. The importance of *guru* in the emerging religious systems of this period has not gone unnoticed, though. "It is peculiar", writes Galewicz, "for many religious traditions of medieval India, and most characteristic of the group of works we are dealing with here, that the persons of *gurus* and the institution of the *guru* as such are paid the highest possible respect." Galewicz 2009: 54.

213 This refers to the *saguṇa-nirguṇa* debate.

214 The simile is from the popular *Dakṣiṇāmūrti Stōtraṃ* 1 ("*viśvaṃ darpaṇa dṛśyamāna nagarī tulyaṃ*").

215 "*akhila bhuvana janma sthēma bhaṅgādi līlē*", *Śrībhāṣya*, invocation.

216 "*lōkavat tu līlā kaivalyaṃ*", *Brahmasutras*, 2.1.33.

217 "*na prayōjanavattvāt*", *Brahmasutras*, 2.1.32.

karma of the souls for creation. Hence a world full of suffering and inequality.[218] This unconvincing argument is based on the authority of the *Bṛhadāraṇyaka Upaniṣad*, that virtue and vice lead to virtue and vice, respectively.[219] How, then, did Brahman create the first soul and the first *karma*? Rāmānuja states, on the authority of the *Kaṭhōpaniṣad*, the *Bṛhadāraṇyaka Upaniṣad*, and the *Bhagavadgītā*, that the soul, *karma*, and matter have no beginning.[220] At the same time, *līlā* is independent of the *karma* or past actions of Brahman, and also not directed towards a goal in the future. "The Lord's action", as John Braisted Carman summarizes it, "is not determined by karma, nor does he have to achieve some unrealized goal, for all the Lord's desires are already fulfilled. When the Lord periodically creates, maintains, and destroys the universe, he acts in sovereign freedom for the sheer joy of self-expression".[221] So, it is the sheer joy of self-expression that makes god engage in the great cosmic sport of creating matter (*jaḍa*) and the body (*śarīra*) (that are anyway already in existence, as they have no beginning!), imbuing them with reality and substance, and making them attributes of his own substance.

Rāmānuja was certainly borrowing the idea of *līlā* from the *Bhāgavatapurāṇa* and Nammāḻvār's *Tiruvāymoḻi*.[222] In the *Tiruvāymoḻi*, god is said to be playing in the poet's heart without showing him the body.[223] He is a miracle-worker[224] and a marvel of contradictions,[225] who created the great drama of the Mahābhārata war.[226] These images might have gained wide popularity after Nāthamuni incorporated them into the *Nālāyira Divyaprabandhaṃ*, conferring them with canonical status. Rāmānuja had access to these images; for wasn't he the disciple of Nāthamuni's grandson Yāmunācārya?[227]

The *viśiṣṭādvaita* was a revolutionary doctrine. It brought the world in general and the body in particular to the centre-stage of reflection. Earlier systems mostly deployed the body and the world for purposes of similes or to establish their unreal and/or destructible status in relation to Brahman. Medical treatises, like the *Suśruta*

---

218 *Śrībhāṣya*, 2.1.34.

219 *Bṛhadāraṇyaka Upaniṣad*, 3.2.13.

220 *Śrībhāṣya*, 2.1.35. This is a major inconsistency in Rāmānuja's system, but Rāmānuja seems to be in no mood to resolve it.

221 Carman 1994: 83-84.

222 Note, however, that the *Bhāgavatapurāṇa* was not of much importance for Rāmānuja, and even Vēdānta Dīkṣita. Rāmānuja, instead, held the *Viṣṇupurāṇa* in high regard.

223 *Tiruvāymoḻi*, 6.9.5, as translated in Ramanujan 1993: 21. The *Tiruvāymoḻi* is a Tamil text, and the poet does not use the expression *līlā* in it, although the idea is embedded in his imagery.

224 Ibid., 7.8.1.

225 Ibid., 7.8.3.

226 Ibid., 7.4.5.

227 The question of *līlā* awaits systematic historical research. Devadevan 2010c: 263-308 makes a set of preliminary assessments. The essays compiled in Sax 1995 offer a good starting point for further research. Also see Hawley 1981.

Saṃhitā, were of course professionally obliged to discuss the body. But it was rare to find discourses on the body in texts expounding religious systems. The Jaina theorists were among the earliest to acknowledge the body as real. The Yōga school and the *Bhagavadgītā* also laid emphasis on the body as real, and prescribed methods for its nurture and/or control. However, not until the twelfth century did the body figure as an essential object of reflection in South Asian systems of thought. The *viśiṣṭādvaita* endowed the body and the world with an ontological status that was at once real and substantial.

An understanding of the self or the supreme would henceforth be incomplete without an understanding of the body. This was the first step in the evolution of the consciousness that the body and the world were available for reflections, and their ontologies open to causal explanations. Neither the *Bhagavadgītā* nor systems like Yōga ever attempted to offer causal explanations for the existence or creation of the body. That this worldly shift in theology occurred at a time when the rank and file of landholders expanded exponentially and brought forth a deeply entrenched class of peasant proprietors who asserted their selfhood and worldly wealth in ways hitherto unknown explains why the *viśiṣṭādvaita* became the most influential system of theology in south India after the twelfth century, influencing even systems that were antagonistic to it, as we shall see. Thus, when Ānanda Tīrtha produced his doctrine of five distinctions, the idea that the world was real was already known to south Indian theological systems for over a century. It was in this context that Vidyāraṇya, the arch Advaiti of the fourteenth century, advocated not only the destruction of latent desires (*vāsanākṣaya*), but also the destruction of mind itself (*manōnāśa*). He certainly knew that the body was real, although his denial of its reality was remarkable for its refined reasoning.

Vidyāraṇya died in 1386. Sāyaṇa outlived him by only a few months. He passed away in 1387. Twelve years later, the famous Chisti saint of Dilli, Sayyīd Muhammad al-Hussaynī, better known as Hazrat Khvājā Bandānavāz Gēsūdarāz, reached Daulatābād. The Bahmani ruler Firūz Śāh accorded him a warm welcome, invited him to Kalaburagi, and offered him space to build his *khānkāh* (hospice). Bandēnavāz, as the saint came to be known in the region, was already seventy-nine years old at that time. He lived in Kalaburagi until his death at the age on 101 on 1 November 1422.[228]

Bandēnavāz was the son of Sayyīd Yūsuf al-Hussaynī of Khūrāsan, who had become a disciple of Hazrat Nizāṃ-ud-dīn Auliyā in Dilli. His family claimed descent from Muhammad, the Prophet. Yūsuf was popularly known as Rājū Kattāl. Bandēnavāz was born in Dilli. At the age of seven, in 1328, the family moved to Daulatābād when Muhammad bin Tughlak ordered migration of the residents of Dilli to his new capital. Rājū Kattāl died in 1330 and was interred in Daulatābād. Three years later, in 1333,

228 The following account of Bandēnavāz's life is based on Eaton 2005: 33-58 (i.e., chapter 2). Also see Papan-Matin 2010: 175-178 and Jestice 2004: 311 for a brief biography.

the family returned to Dilli. In 1336, Bandēnavāz and his brother Sayyīd Candān al-Hussaynī became disciples of the Chisti saint, Nāsir-ud-dīn Mahmūd, popularly known as Cirāg-e-Dilli (the light of Dilli). Nāsir was the preeminent disciple of Nizāṃ-ud-dīn Auliyā, who had died in 1325. Under his tutelage, Bandēnavāz turned into a recluse and spent long periods in isolation, lost in books and meditation. Candān al-Hussaynī continued with his worldly pursuits. Bandēnavāz was seriously affected by the cholera (or a spillover of the great plague that caused the Black Death in Europe, Central Asia, and China?) that struck Dilli in 1356. Nāsir-ud-dīn nursed him back to life, and recognized him as his spiritual successor through the symbolic act of giving him his prayer carpet, before dying in September that year. For the next forty-two years, Bandēnavāz lived in Dilli and attracted a wide following. He left Dilli on 17 December 1398 after learning of Tīmūr's destructive march towards Dilli. He travelled through Bahādurpūr, Gvāliyar, Jhānsi, Candēri, Vaḍōdarā and Khaṃbaṭ, and reached Daulatābād late in 1399, from where he reached Kalaburagi at the instance of Firūz.

The relationship between Firūz and Bandēnavāz remained cordial until 1403. In that year charges of heresy came to be made against Bandēnavāz on the grounds that the works he taught in his hospice included the heretical *Fusus al-Hikhaṃ* of Ibn al-'Arabi (1165-1240). Firūz's brother Ahmad Śāh Bahmani, who was a claimant to the throne, threw in his lot with Bandēnavāz. The Shaikh seems to have supported Ahmad's claim to the throne. His relationship with Firūz soared. In 1409, Bandēnavāz moved to a new location away from the fort. The Sultān also grew contemptuous of the Shaikh as the latter, who excelled in ecclesiastical learning, was poor in secular sciences like rhetoric and geometry, which the Sultān had mastered.[229] In 1422, when Firūz was on his sickbed trying to promote his son as the next Sultān, Ahmad paid a visit to Bandēnavāz, and on 21 September, usurped the throne after a brief confrontation with Firūz's forces. Firūz died on 2 October. A month later, on 1 November, Bandēnavāz also breathed his last. Before his death, Bandēnavāz nominated his son Sayyīd Asghar al-Hussaynī as his successor to the *khānkāh*. Thus was introduced the principle of hereditary succession among the Sūfis in the Deccan.[230] Ahmad also granted land to the *khānkāh*, although he soon stopped patronizing the Chisti order and turned to the Kādiris of Iran as part of a change in royal policy. The control over land, hereditary succession, the brief support extended by the Bahmani state, and the image of a ripe-old man rebelling against the Sūltan, these factors led to the popularity of Bandēnavāz in the region. Shortly after his death, his mausoleum in Kalaburagi became a leading centre of pilgrimage. It has continued to be so well into our times.

Bandēnavāz was a proponent of *sama'*, the practice of listening to the singing of mystical poetry to the accompaniment of percussion instruments. The *band sama'* (closed band), involving a limited audience and the use of a tambourine, was his

229 Eaton 2005: 52.
230 Ibid., 55.

innovation. Singing turned out to be a powerful means of propagating Sūfism in the Deccan.

Bandēnavāz was the Sāyaṇa of the Islamic world. He wrote prolifically in Arabic, Persian, Urdu, and Dakhni, producing nearly two hundred books on a variety of ecclesiastical themes. These included commentaries on the *Korān* and the *Hadīth*s.

The projects of Rāmānuja, Ānanda Tīrtha, Vidyāraṇya, Sāyaṇa, and Bandēnavāz were harbingers of a greater project undertaken in the fifteenth century at Haṃpi, whose impact was pervasive and whose consequences, far-reaching. The impetus for this project seems to have come from Mahaliṅgadēva, a resident of Puligeṟe (where Ādayya destroyed a Jaina *basadi* three centuries earlier). It was carried out under the able supervision of Jakkaṇārya and Lakkaṇṇa Daṇḍēśa, two military commanders under the Vijayanagara king Dēvarāya II (r. 1424-1446), who were also entrusted with civil assignments as functionaries of the state. This project was instrumental in the consolidation of beliefs, practices, and narratives that would eventually come to congeal as Vīraśaivism.

Mahaliṅgadēva bore titles such as *Puligerepuravarādhīśvara* and *Vārāṇasīndra.* He wrote the *Ēkōttaraśatasthala* and a commentary on Allama Prabhu's *vacana*s under the name, *Prabhudēvara Ṣaṭsthalajñānacāritravacanada Ṭīke.* With this commenced the historical enterprise of compiling the *vacana*s of the twelfth-centuries *śaraṇa*s, producing glosses on them, and composing hagiographies of the *śaraṇa*s and narratives of encounters between them. An early attempt in this direction was made in 1369, when the poet Bhīma wrote the influential *Basavapurāṇa*,[231] a hagiographic account of the life of Basava, inspired by Pālkurike Sōmanātha's *Basavapurāṇamu* in the Telugu (ca. 1200). But the new enterprise was more orthodox than Bhīma's, and doctrinally rigorous and elaborate. Mahaliṅgadēva's disciple was Kumāra Baṅkanātha, who wrote the *Ṣaṭsthalōpadēśa* and the *Prabhudēvara Ṭīkina Vacana.* Jakkaṇārya was Baṅkanātha's adopted son (*karajāta*), and his entry into Vijayanagara service gave a great fillip to the project. Jakkaṇa was himself the author of the *Ēkōttaraśatasthala*, inspired by Mahaliṅgadēva's work of the same name. Mahaliṅgadēva had another disciple, known by the title Girīndra. He wrote a commentary on Jakkaṇa's *Ēkōttaraśatasthala.*

Among the other illustrious participants in the project, Lakkaṇṇa Daṇḍēśa has already been named. He wrote the encyclopedic *Śivatatvacintāmaṇi.* Maggeya Māyidēva was another contributor, who lived in Dēvarāya II's time. He came from Aipura (also called Magge?) on the river Malaprabha.[232] He was the author of the

231 This epoch-making work has yielded the largest number of manuscripts for a Kannada literary text, after Kumāravyāsa's version of the *Mahābhārata* in the language, the *Karṇāṭa Bhārata Kathāmañjari.*

232 It is not unlikely that he was a weaver with the name, Maggada Māyidēva, i.e., Māyidēva of the Magga ('the loom').

Śatakatraya, the *Anubhavasūtra*, the *Ēkōttaraśatasthalaṣaṭpadi*, the *Ṣaṭsthalagadya*, the *Prabhugīta*, and a few *vacanas*. The works of Gurubasava, a lesser-known writer, were innovative in form, framed as they were as dialogues between a *guru* and his disciple. He wrote seven works, the *Śivayōgāṅgabhūṣaṇa*, the *Sadgururahasya*, the *Kalyāṇēśvara*, the *Svarūpāmṛta*, the *Vṛṣabhagīta*, the *Avadhūtagīta*, and the *Manōvijaya*. These are collectively known as *Saptakāvya*. At the instance of Gururāya, a *mahāpradhāna* under Dēvarāya II, Candra alias Candraśēkhara wrote the *Virūpākṣāsthāna* and the *Gurumūrti Śaṅkaraśataka*. Candra was a polyglot, and claimed proficiency in eight languages.

The Vijayanagara court hosted a number of renouncers, who lived in different parts of Karnataka at the time. Tradition identifies 101 of them, and calls them the *nūrondu viraktaru* or the 101 Viraktas. Some of them were also poets. Among them was Cāmarasa, the author of the outstanding hagiographic account of the life of Allama Prabhu, the *Prabhuliṅgalīle*. This work was recited to great appreciation in Dēvarāya II's court. Kallumaṭhada Prabhudēva was another Virakta known for his literary works. He composed the *Liṅgalīlāvilāsacāritra*, and a commentary on the *Mantragōpya* attributed to Allama. The recalcitrant Karasthala Nāgaliṅga, a goldsmith from southern Karnataka, was a third Virakta credited with literary compositions. He wrote a number of *vacanas* and a short work called the *Karasthala Nāgidēva Trividhi*.

Closely related to the Vijayanagara project was the work of Śivagaṇaprasādi Mahādēvayya, who wrote the *Śūnyasaṃpādane*, a narrativized anthology of twelfth-century *vacanas* centering on the life of Allama. It turned out to be a successful work, inspiring three more *Śūnyasaṃpādanes* in the fifteenth and the sixteenth centuries, one each by Halageyārya, Gummaḷāpurada Siddhaliṅga Yati, and Gūḷūru Siddhavīraṇṇoḍeya.

It is not easy to characterize the nature of this great project, because although they were addressed to a limited audience, they engaged with multiple concerns and served multiple purposes. It tried to consolidate and integrate the several Śaiva traditions that had sprung into life after the organized groups of the earlier period, such as the Kāḷāmukhas and the Kāpālikas, had begun to show signs of disintegration. Many disorganized groups, like the Viraktas, the Ārādhyas, the Jaṅgamas, the Ārūḍhas, etc., were brought together as part of this integration. Their orders of succession, practices of renunciation, and systems of knowledge were elaborated, widely commented upon, and defined as constituting Vīraśaivism. Saints from various other traditions were also appropriated. For instance, Cāmarasa's *Prabhuliṅgalīle* speaks of Allama Prabhu confronting Gōrakṣa (Gōrakhanātha, the founder of the Nātha or the Kānphaṭā tradition), at the end of which the latter becomes his disciple.[233] This legend is repeated in the *Śūnyasaṃpādane*. Muktāyakka is another saint who figures

233 *Prabhuliṅgalīle*, 19.

prominently in the works of this project. She might be none other than Muktābāi, the sister of Jñānēśvara and a major figure in the Vārkharī tradition of Maharashtra.

These works were informed by a new image of selfhood that had been evolving since the twelfth century. This self was the reified expression of men and women who had in the course of the preceding centuries gained greater access to wealth in the form of land and money, and begun to assert their political authority at the locality and the regional levels. In other words, this self was the creation of a class that was affluent, or at least confident about its potentials of upward mobility. Like the individual merchant who began to dissociate himself from the merchant syndicates, and like the peasant proprietors who had begun to transact business independently of the *nāḍu* assembly, this new self was beginning to assert its autonomy in different ways. It was most ingeniously done with the help of discourses, reflections, and commentaries on the human body.

In most traditions, the body was represented as foul, polluted, and undesirable. A clear distinction was made between the body (*dēha* or *tanu*) and the self (*tānu*) or the soul (*ātman*) that resides in it. The idea was to argue that the self continued to be immaculate and incorruptible in spite of residing in the despicable body. We must dwell upon this idea at some length.

In a popular *vacana* attributed to Basava, a distinction is made between the body and the temple. We are told that things standing (*sthāvara*) will fall apart, while the moving ones (*jaṅgama*) will not.[234] It might appear that the *vacana* is expressly making a case for the body. This, however, is not the case. While it is not hard to find more such *vacana*s from a corpus exceeding 20,000, they add up in the narrativized anthologies to produce a cumulative picture of the body as undesirable. There are numerous instances where this is explicitly stated. Cripple me, blind me, deafen me, and place me at the feet of your *śaraṇa*s, says another *vacana* attributed to Basava.[235] Elsewhere in the corpus, we are told to worship the lord before age, grey, and death takes us.[236] More ruthless is the treatment of the body in the *vacana*s attributed to Akka Mahādēvi. The body is dirt, we are told,[237] and after it has known the Lord, who cares if the body feeds a dog or soaks up water?[238] All that perhaps matters is a prayer: O Cennamallikārjunā, don't say those you love have a body.[239]

Cāmarasa tries to offer a reasonable-sounding critique of the body. In the conversation between Gōrakṣa and Allama, the latter says, "If *kāya* (the body) is strengthened, then *māyā* (illusion) is strengthened; if *māyā* is strengthens, then *chhāyā*

---

234 See Ramanujan 1973: 70 (No. 820) for the most popular translation of this *vacana*. Also see the discussion of this *vacana* (pp. 1-4), which is however marked by formalist over-reading.
235 Ibid., no. 59, p. 52.
236 Ibid., no. 161, p. 60.
237 Ibid., no. 12, p. 98.
238 Ibid., no. 117, p. 109.
239 Ibid., no. 157, p. 113.

(shadow, i.e. the unreal) is strengthened; there is no accomplishment (*siddhatana*) if *kāya*, *māyā*, and *chhāyā* are strengthened."[240] Gōrakṣa was the progenitor of a system that believed in *kāyasiddhi*. The primacy this system gave the body, drew from the idea that the body and the self were identical, and that the only way to overcome suffering was to strengthen the body and make it hard like a diamond (*vajrakāya*). The Nāthas developed yogic practices with this goal in mind. It is this worldview that Allama challenges in the *Prabhuliṅgalīle*. His response to Gōrakṣa's declaration that "I am the body"[241] is in the form of a time-tested trope: "can the fool, who considers the dirty loathsome body that is a sewer of bone, skin, shit, piss, and blood, know the self?"[242] The conversation between the two giants does not resolve the matter. There is a final round of physical confrontation. Gōrakṣa insists Allama to strike him with a dagger. Allama accepts it reluctantly, and strikes Gōrakṣa hard. The dagger hits Gōrakṣa with a '*khaṇil*' sound. The earth shakes, the mountains tremble to cast boulders, but not a hair of Gōrakṣa's is cut off. Amazing indeed is Gōrakṣa's diamond body (*vajrapiṇḍaśarīra*). But Allama is not impressed. "Will the accomplished one's body make a '*khaṇil*' sound?", he asks. Gōraḳsa is taken aback by Allama's response. If attaining a diamond body is not accomplishment, what is? Strike me, and learn for yourself, replies Allama. Gōrakṣa strikes him. The dagger passes through Allama's body as if passing through empty space. Allama remains unhurt. Gōrakṣa realizes that real accomplishment lies in transforming the body into a void (*bayalu* or *śūnya*), not in making it hard like a diamond.[243]

Nijaguṇa Śivayōgi (ca. 1500), while endorsing the wretchedness of the body, makes another interesting argument in the *Paramānubhavabōdhe*. According to him, sometimes I say that "I am the body", and at other times that "the body is mine". The latter implies possession, and we can possess only things external to us; on the other hand, the former does not suggest possession, but unity instead. Surely then, there is some confusion here about the status of the body, which, Nijaguṇa argues, is reason enough to reject the body.[244]

Discussions concerning the body are elaborate in the *Śūnyasaṃpādane* tradition. Halageyārya's version of the text may be examined as an example. Here, Siddharāma is represented as a believer in *prāṇaliṅga*. According to this position, the body was the *pīṭha* (platform) hosting the *prāṇa* (breath), which was the *liṅga*. What then was the need for an external object or symbol (*kuṟuhu*)? Allama on the other hand swore by *iṣṭaliṅga*, i.e., an external object of one's choice, representing the *liṅga*. The *iṣṭaliṅga*

240 *Prabhuliṅgalīle*, 19.37.
241 Ibid., 19.21.
242 Ibid., 19.22.
243 Ibid., 19.25-35.
244 *Paramānubhavabōdhe* 3.3.2. See 3.1-8 for an extensive argument. Also see Devadevan 2009b for a critique of this argument.

was to be placed on one's palm (*karasthala*) and worshipped constantly. The emphasis was on the togetherness (*saṅga*) of the body (*aṅga*) and the *liṅga*, and not their unity. Allama held that the inner (*antaraṅga*) and the outer (*bahiraṅga*) complemented one another. And so did the tangible (*iṣṭaliṅga*) and the intangible (*prāṇaliṅga*), and the real and its symbol. One had to transcend the symbolic, but this was to be done by holding on to the symbolic.[245] It is for this reason, perhaps, that Halageyārya's Allama speaks not of the dissolution of the body (*dēha*), but the dissolution of body-consciousness (*dēhabhāva*).[246] Like most of his contemporaries, Halageyārya framed his thought in terms of binaries, but it sprang from deep reflections, and was marked by a profound measure of ideational integrity. It is thus that he is unable to imagine the unmanifest without imagining the manifest, just as light is impossible without darkness, and truth unthinkable without untruth.

In his *Anubhavāmṛta* (ca. 1675), Mahaliṅgaraṅga made his rejection of the body more explicit. Bones, nerves, and marrow are born of father's filth, mother's blood turns into blood, flesh and skin, the distinction between man and woman is merely of form, the body is not the self, but only a moving pot of shit.[247] Father's filth ripens in the mother's womb that discharges filthy blood month after month to produce a filthy body that is not the self.[248] Raṅga also dismisses the view that the breath (*prāṇa*) is the self.[249] What the *Anubhavāmṛta* introduces to us is a sublime self that is incorruptible in spite of its earthly associations. The eighteenth century saint Cidānanda Avadhūta goes to the extent of saying that the long association which the self has had with the body has made it as woe-begotten as the latter, but it remains omnipotent enough to retain its resilience and inhibit the body's waywardness.[250] The self may inhabit the body and deliberate through the filth and refuse of the material world, but it retains an indestructible core whose essence is too pristine to suffer wounds and scars on account of its engagements with the profane world.

The emphasis of the above discussion was on the rejection of the body that was widely advocated during and after the fifteenth century in the Deccan region. We must not, however, regard this as springing from a deep desire to see the body dissolve into the unmanifest. Such elaborate reflections on the body point to the centrality the body had in the emerging systems of thought, a fascination that brought the body to this central position, and a reification of this fascination in the

245 *Śūnyasaṃpādane* of Halageyārya, 252-260.
246 Ibid., 190. In Gūḷūru Siddhavīraṇṇoḍeya's version, Allama says, without the manifestation of *aṟivu* (knowledge), *kuṟuhu* will not be eliminated (*Śūnyasaṃpādane* of Gūḷūru Siddhavīraṇṇoḍeya, 3.106). In Halageyārya's version it is *maṟahu* (forgetfulness) that is said to remain as long as *aṟivu* in not manifest.
247 *Anubhavāmṛta*, 3.37.
248 Ibid., 3.38.
249 Ibid., 3. 40-43.
250 *Jñānasindhu* 27.23-45.

form of intellectual reflections. That it was the warmth of the body that was desired, and not its disavowal, is underlined by the parapraxis contained in these works. For wasn't Akkamahādēvi on the look out for a *guru* who could teach her how to unite with Śiva without the dissolution of the body?[251] The body is the ultimate form of possession. Owning a body differs fundamentally from owing a house, possessing a piece of land or acquiring an object of desire. For, unlike these, the body is not merely a source but also the destination of desire. Libidinal experience can have its source in an object external to the body, but the experience itself is sensory, and therefore, primarily a bodily experience. And so is accomplishment. It has to be sensed. Maurice Merleau-Ponty was perhaps right when he identified the body as "the mirror of our being".[252] Small wonder then that Allama Prabhu, in another instance of parapraxis, asks Gōrakṣa who it is that attains *siddhi* after the body is destroyed.[253]

It is tempting to prolong this discussion concerning the body. The sources on hand offer rich material for this discussion. But our present purpose has already been served. The rejection of the body was not a rejection. It was the ruse of a new self that longed for a body.

The tradition of reflecting upon the body, inaugurated by the *viśiṣṭādvaita* school, found fertile expression among the Śaivas of Karnataka. So did the other two categories: *guru* and *līlā*. We have noticed earlier that the *guru* was the first of the eight armours identified by the Vīraśaivas. The revered *guru* was the only valid source of knowledge for an aspirant. He or she imparted knowledge, and dispelled the darkness of ignorance. This, however, was not in the form of instructions given in a monastery to a mute and submissive student. For, the recipient of knowledge was a future teacher, and had to be recognized for all practical reasons as an incipient *guru*. The emphasis, therefore, was on imparting knowledge in a dialogic context. And exemplifying this process of knowledge transmission was Basava's *anubhava maṇṭapa*, where Allama arrived and engaged in long debates with other *śaraṇa*s who accepted him as their teacher. The four extent *Śūnyasaṃpādane*s embody this mode of representing the *guru*.

The idea of *līlā* also had a tremendous appeal to the Śaivas. But they did not restrict its scope to representing the world as a play of the supreme, but expanded it to incorporate the acts of the *śaraṇa*s, which were also regarded as *līlā*. Kallumaṭhada Prabhudēva's work was befittingly called the *Liṅgalīlāvilāsacāritra*. Here, he described creation as follows:

> thus, the undivided, sphere-shaped, great embodiment of luminance, the Mahāliṅga, was divided into the *liṅga* and the *aṅga*, as it worshipped itself and performed *pūja* in the sport of

---

251 "What great teacher have I today, from whom the way of uniting with Śiva without the dissolution of the body can be gained?" *Prabhuliṅgalīle*, 10.30. (Translation mine).

252 Merleau-Ponty 1962: 171.

253 *Prabhuliṅgalīle*, 19.26.

līlā. Thus was it divided into two: the Mahāliṅga gained five faces and became the Liṅgamūrti known as the five-faced. When a part of the effective power of luminance of the dynamism of the consciousness that illuminates the Liṅgamūrti was separated, it became the *aṅga* called *ātma*. The Liṅgamūrti's place was told in both the *liṅga* and the *aṅga* thus formed.

līlayā sahitaḥ sākṣādumāpatiritīritā
līlayā rahitaḥ paścāt svayaṃbhuriti kathyatē

When the Mahāghanaliṅga is *līlā*, he is called Umāpati. When *līlā* ceases, he becomes Svayaṃbhu (self-born). This is the meaning of this text.[254]

Creation, for Kallumaṭhada Prabhudēva, was a divine sport, as it was for the proponents of *viśiṣṭādvaita*. But as opposed to the *viśiṣṭādvaitis*, the acts of the saints also were represented as *līlā* in the Vīraśaiva works. Every act of Allama was regarded a *līlā* played by him, and his hagiography by Cāmarasa aptly called *Prabhuliṅgalīle*. Accounts on the life of the saints could therefore incorporate supernatural acts like miracles and magic. The representation of the acts of the *śaraṇa* as *līlā* was governed by the idea that the *śaraṇas* were members of Śiva's entourage (*śivagaṇa*) who had incarnated on earth to carry out a predestined mission, or play. The poet Bhīma considered even killing Jaina saints, breaking up their heads, and the destruction of Jaina shrines by the Vīraśaivas as acts of *līlā*.[255]

By the sixteenth century, mundane acts of devotees were also being referred to as *līlā*. Thus, in Śāntaliṅgadēśikan's *Bhairavēśvara Kāvyada Kathāmaṇisūtra Ratnākara*, Annadānēśvara is said to have obtained the throne of Nīlagunda through *līlā*.[256] Devotees of Śiva live in *līlā*, says Gubbiya Mallaṇārya in his *Vīraśaivāmṛtapurāṇa*, and those who insult such devotees will fall into the great abyss of hell, upside down.[257]

We must now turn to one final aspect of the great Vijayanagara project. This was by any reckoning the most influential outcome of the initiatives of Mahaliṅgadēva and his peers. Strange as it may seem, the tradition it invented has not yet been fully acknowledged as an invented tradition by modern day historiography. Historians of our times have for some reason not extended their gift of skepticism to bear upon this invented tradition. The result is that the myth of Kalyāṇa, Basava, the *anubhava maṇṭapa*, and a great twelfth-century revolution has lingered on in the academic repertoire as well as in the popular imagination.

The city of Kalyāṇa rose to prominence in the early eleventh century. It seems to have had humble beginnings in the late tenth century as an important stopover on a trade route. It was an unpleasant city in terms of its geography. There were no rivers nearby, the Bhīma and the Kārañja being many miles away from the city. The

254 *Liṅgalīlāvilāsacāritra*, 3.7. (Translation mine).
255 *Basavapurāṇa*, 50.72-73.
256 *Bhairavēśvara Kāvyada Kathāmaṇisūtra Ratnākara*, 1.9.
257 *Vīraśaivāmṛtapurāṇa*, 3.10.51.

land was dry, but capable of throwing up a substantial surplus if properly irrigated, but the region was not topologically conducive for building lake networks like those in southern Karnataka or the Kāvēri delta. Agriculture tended to be rain-fed. In the neighbourhood of Kalyāṇa was the village of Mayūrakhiṇḍi (Mōrkhaṇḍi), which resembled Kalyāṇa in its topography. The Rāṣṭrakūṭas had ruled from here for a while in the eighth century but moved to Mānyakhēṭa (Māḷakhēḍa) in the ninth century. For some reason, the Cāḷukyas, who overthrew the Rāṣṭrakūṭas in ca. 973 and established themselves at Mānyakhēṭa, moved to the old base of the Rāṣṭrakūṭas over half a century later. Kalyāṇa became their new headquarters. They ruled from here for a century and a half in the eleventh and the twelfth centuries.

The Cāḷukyas transformed Kalyāṇa into a great city and built a fort at a strategic location. The Tripurāntaka temple (which has not survived) was a major landmark of the city. Kalyāṇa hosted Vijñānēśvara, the great lawgiver of the *Mitākṣara* fame. And here in the court of Vikramāditya VI lived Bilhaṇa from Kashmir, who wrote in honour of his patron one of the most celebrated work in Sanskrit: the *Vikramāṅkadēvacarita*.[258] To him is also attributed the *Caura Pañcāśika*. Kalyāṇa is also likely to have been the place where the Cāḷukya king Sōmēśvara III wrote the *Mānasōllāsa*.

By the late twelfth century, the high noon of the city's prosperity had come to pass. Its importance declined after the Kaḷacūri chief Bijjaḷa II usurped the throne in 1162. Bijjaḷa II and his son ruled from their headquarters Maṅgaḷavāḍa, and had Kalyāṇa as one of their outposts (*nelevīḍu*). The rebel Kaḷacūri claimant Kannara (Karṇa) tried to establish himself at Kalyāṇa. Bijjaḷa II had appointed Basava, the nephew of one of his functionaries Baladēva, as his treasurer, and had given his (adopted?) sister Nīlāṃbike in marriage to him. Basava was a devout Śaiva who was born in a brāhmaṇa family at Bāgēvāḍi (now Basavana Bāgēvāḍi). As a young boy, he had rebelled against orthodox brāhmaṇa practices and torn away his sacred thread. He stayed for a while at Kūḍalasaṅgama where the Kṛṣṇa meets the Malaprabha, and studied under a Śaiva teacher. During his stay at Maṅgaḷavāḍa as Bijjaḷa II's treasurer, he organized feeding (*dāsōha*) for wandering Śaiva saints, the Jaṅgamas. A number of Jaṅgamas reached Maṅgaḷavāḍa to obtain his patronage. Among them was Allama Prabhu, a drummer-turned-saint from the city of Baḷḷigāve. The feeding was organized with abject disregard for prevailing caste norms. Basava seems to have spent a large amount of money on feeding. Charges were levelled against him of misappropriating funds from the royal treasury. He was also accused of violating norms of commensality, as he had partaken food from the house of a low caste devotee of Śiva called Saṃbhōḷi Nāgayya. His relationship with Bijjaḷa II deteriorated. Bijjaḷa II was killed in 1167 by a certain Jagadēva who appears to have been a henchman of Sōmēśvara IV, the surviving scion of the erstwhile Cāḷukyas. In the confusion that led to the killing of Bijjaḷa II, Basava left Maṅgaḷavāḍa, and met his end at Kūḍalasaṅgama under mysterious

---

258 On the *Vikramāṅkadēvacarita*, see Bronner 2010.

circumstances. Kaḷacūri rule ended in 1184, and Sōmēśvara IV returned to power. His rule ended in ca. 1199. With this, the history of the Cāḷukyas came to an end. Kalyāṇa also ceased to be the nerve centre of the region's political and economic life.

Harihara's *Basavarājadēvara Ragaḷe* (ca. 1175) is the first hagiographic account on the life of Basava. In this work, Basava is found to be active in Maṅgaḷavāḍa. This is hardly surprising. Among the twelfth-century *śaraṇa*s, only some, such as Maḍivāḷa Mācayya, Bāhūru Bommayya, and Telugu Jommayya are known to have lived in Kalyāṇa. What is of interest, though, is the fact that apart from Basava's nephew Cannabasava, Allama Prabhu is the only major contemporary *śaraṇa* from among the composers of *vacana*s, whom Basava is said to have ever met. In Harihara's accounts, there are no allusions to his meeting with Akkamahādēvi, Siddharāma, Maḍivāḷa Mācayya, and the other important *śaraṇa*s. Harihara is also silent on the existence of the *anubhava maṇṭapa*, the hall of experience, where the *śaraṇa*s are believed to have met in order to discuss a wide range of issues from the sublimity of the spiritual world to the waywardness of everyday life.

An important change occurred in the hagiographic accounts, when in Pālkurike Sōmanātha's *Basavapurāṇamu*, some of the *śaraṇa*s met with Basava. More importantly, the scene of action shifted to Kalyāṇa. Sōmanātha was evidently relying on stories that circulated among the believers in centres of pilgrimage like Śrīśailaṃ. Inasmuch as Bijjaḷa II had killed the Cāḷukya king of Kalyāṇa and seized his throne, it was not difficult to imagine the activities of his treasurer Basava in that city. Given the symbolic significance of the city, Bijjaḷa II might have wished to bring Kalyāṇa under his control. In fact, Harihara's *Kēśirāja Daṇṇāyakara Ragaḷe* identifies Permāḍi (Bijjaḷa II's father) as the ruler of Kalyāṇa,[259] although we know from history that Permāḍi ruled from Maṅgaḷavāḍa as subordinate to Sōmēśvara III and Jagadēkamalla II, and contracted matrimonial alliance with the family of his masters. The discrepancy, which unwittingly crept into Sōmanātha's account, reached the Kannada world through Bhīma's *Basavapurāṇa*. Bhīma's work, and the circulation of Sōmanātha's poem in various forms, profoundly informed the project of Mahaliṅgadēva, Śivagaṇaprasādi Mahādēvayya, Jakkaṇa, Lakkaṇṇa Daṇḍēśa, and others. These works also formed the basis for most accounts produced in the late fifteenth, the sixteenth, and the seventeenth centuries on the lives of the *śaraṇas*.

There were many variants of this story. But there was consensus on its broad outlines. Basava, the treasurer of Bijjaḷa II, was an ardent devotee of Śiva, and the brother-in-law of his patron. He organized feeding (*dāsōha*) for the *śaraṇa*s, which attracted *śaraṇa*s from as far away as Saurāṣṭra and Kashmir. To further the cause of the *śaraṇa*s, Basava set up the *anubhava maṇṭapa* in which *śaraṇa*s sat down to discuss and debate the nature of the self, the essence of the supreme, and the right practices required for realizing the supreme, and to criticize superstitions, rival

259 *Kēśirāja Daṇṇāyakara Ragaḷe*, 1.31-32.

belief systems, and inequalities based on caste and gender. A throne called *śūnya siṃhāsana* was created. Allama occupied this throne. The *śaraṇa*s composed *vacana*s in large numbers to expound their views and ideals.

The experiment turned out to be fatal, as the non-Śaiva orthodoxy forced Bijjaḷa II to punish Basava for violating caste norms. At Bijjaḷa II's bidding, two *śaraṇa*s, Haraḷayya and Madhuvayya, were blinded. This was done to create terror among the *śaraṇa*s. A great mayhem followed. A devout *śaraṇa* called Jagadēva was instructed by his peers to take revenge on the king. Accordingly, Jagadēva killed Bijjaḷa II. Basava left Kalyāṇa, and became one with the *liṅga* (*liṅgaikya*) by drowning in the waters at the confluence of the Kṛṣṇa and the Malaprabha in Kūḍalasaṅgama.

This was the story promoted through the works of Pālkurike Sōmanātha and Bhīma. That the scene of action in these works was Kalyāṇa formed the basis for most works produced as part of the Vijayanagara project under Jakkaṇa and Lakkaṇṇa Daṇḍēśa, in which Kalyāṇa became a metonymy of sorts. In the course of time, the story underwent further changes. A reason was invented for the blinding of Haraḷayya and Madhuvayya. The former was a Mādiga (tanner) and the latter a Brāhmaṇa, the new story contended. Under Basava's influence, the Brāhmaṇa had given his daughter in marriage to the Mādiga's son, a *pratilōma* marriage that shocked the orthodoxy, and forced Bijjaḷa II to mete out the punishment on Haraḷayya and Madhuvayya.

Unfortunately, it is this version that is passed off as history in most modern accounts.[260] Expressions like Kalyāṇa-krānti (the revolution of Kalyāṇa), Basava-krānti (the Basava revolution), Śaraṇa-caḷuvaḷi (the *śaraṇa* movement), and Vacana-caḷuvaḷi (the *vacana* movement) evokes passionate responses from the Kannada vernacular academia, bordering on the fanatic.[261] Not only has this story of revolution enamoured hundreds of Grade C researchers, it has passed muster with such thoughtful scholars as D.R. Nagaraj, M.M. Kalburgi, and A.K. Ramanujan. The academic, literary, and popular works produced on Basava, his revolution, and its spillovers (including anthologies of *vacana*s, and critical and popular editions of Vīraśaiva literature) run into over a million printed pages. What is missed in the process is a fascinating history of the making of the myth of Kalyāṇa, and how the myth became a driving force behind several systems of renunciation in the region after the fifteenth century.[262]

---

260 Instances are too many to be listed out. But see Desai 1968 and Chidanandamurthy 2007 for a general history. Also see Ramanujan 1973; Schouten 1995; Ramaswamy 1996; and related essays in Kalburgi 2010.

261 See Devadevan 2009: 90-96, for a critique of this position.

262 Devadevan 2007.

4 Heredity, Genealogies, and the Advent of the New Monastery

Bandēnavāz Gēsūdarāz initiated the practice of hereditary succession in his hospice, which was a new development in the Deccan region. That the hospice received a perpetual land grant from Ahmad Śāh Bahmani (r. 1422-1436) was historically decisive in this context. Succession to the control of land reinforced the principle of heredity, and consolidated the position of the hospice as a political force in the region, placing the hospice on a firm footing. It led to the creation of strong images of tradition and continuity that came to be explored through representational strategies deployed in the legends and hagiographies. A compelling model, based on heredity and succession to landed wealth, was created for other monastic traditions to emulate. Among the fallouts of this far-reaching development was the evolution of lineages of succession within the monastery, both real and imagined.

The principle of hereditary succession to landed wealth was pregnant with potentials to bring forth radical transformations, not just in the realm of monastic establishments, but also in other institutional domains. In an insightful study of the emergence of the *aṃbalavāsi* (temple-dwelling) castes in Kerala, Kesavan Veluthat has shown that groups like the *poduvāḷ*s, the *vāriyar*s, etc., did not enjoy the status of distinct castes during the ninth, the tenth and the eleventh centuries, when the Cēras of Mahōdayapuraṃ (ca. 844-1122) held sway over large parts of Kerala. These groups were recognized as so many brāhmaṇas, carrying out secular functions related to the temple. In the course of time, they gained hereditary access to land by way of service tenures granted in lieu of periodic remuneration. Hereditary control over land consolidated their position within the temple and also as a closely-knit endogamous group, leading to their evolution as castes.[263] This is the most ingenious explanation to date for the emergence of castes in India before the institution underwent the great transformation of the nineteenth and twentieth centuries as a result of the decennial census and the introduction of electoral politics.[264] There seems to have been no caste in premodern India that did not enjoy hereditary access to land in some capacity or the other. This does not mean that all castes owned land. Our emphasis is on *hereditary access* and not on *ownership*. It involved a wide range of access in a variety of capacities like owners, rentiers, tenants, occupants, holders of cultivation rights, and agrestic labour, both bonded and free. There were a large number of groups that exercised no hereditary control over land. Modern ethnography identifies them as

---

263 Veluthat 2013: 132-144 (i.e., chapter 9).

264 Cf. Talbot 2001: 48-86 (i.e., chapter 2) for a discussion in the context of Andhra, where it is argued that caste was amorphous and less frequently invoked. Stress is instead laid on 'a typology of statuses' (Ibid., 55-61). It may, however, be noted that many of these 'status' titles are now caste titles. Also see Sharma 2007: 5-7 for an argument against the status theory.

tribes. Thus, the nature of access to land is crucial for any discussion on caste in premodern India.

The practice of granting land for religious purposes is as old as the later *vaidic* period in India (ca. 800-600 BCE),[265] and making land grants with the generation of agrarian resources and revenue in mind, as old as the first century BCE.[266] In the Deccan region, land grants were widely prevalent after the fourth century. Among the recipients of these grants were individual brāhmaṇas, the corporate group of brāhmaṇas, temples, and Buddhist and Jaina establishments. The grant made to the brāhmaṇas was called *brahmadēya*. The temple grant was originally called *dēvabhōga*, and later, *dēvadāna*. Historians identify these as eleemosynary grants. In Tamilnadu, there were a few other forms of eleemosynary grants like *paḷḷiccandaṃ*, *śālābhōgaṃ*, *kaṇimuttūṟṟŭ* and *veṭṭāppēṟŭ*. The *paḷḷiccandaṃ* was a Jaina grant, and the *śālābhōgaṃ*, an endowment made to a school (*śālā*) that had apart from imparting religious and secular knowledge, a leading military function to perform.[267] The nature of *kaṇimuttūṟṟŭ* and *veṭṭāppēṟŭ* are not clear from the records. In Karnataka, inscriptions speak of grants like *kīḻguṇṭe* (to the family of a soldier who died fighting), *bittuvaṭṭa* (for the maintenance of a tank), *bāḻgaḻccu* (a form of subsistence grant, or pension), *aṇugajīvita* (given to a relative or a member of the royal family or an elite), and *parōkṣavinaya* (in honour of someone else).[268]

At least since the ninth century, the potential of money and gold as interest-bearing capital made the emergent elites gradually withdraw from the practice of granting land. Land grants were made extensively, but endowments of money or gold in lieu of land were made in greater numbers, registering a new development in the praxis of charity. In many cases, a fixed share of revenue or produce from a piece of land was also set aside as grant instead of transferring ownership or cultivating rights. Inscriptions provide us with numerous instances of land being given away for religious purposes. But after the tenth century, it had turned into a less preferred practice vis-à-vis the practice of granting revenue or gifting money and gold.

---

265 Examples occur in texts like the *Aitarēya Brāhmaṇa* (Sharma 2007: 97) and the *Śatapatha Brāhmaṇa* (Ibid., pp. 90-91). That the practice was known is confirmed by the reservations against it in some of the text, although Sharma notes that "actual instances of land gifts are lacking" (Ibid., p. 91). Land grants continued in the 600-300 BCE period, as suggested by stray references like the Buddhist 'Lohicca Sutta', *Dīghanikāya* 12.

266 The earliest known instance of this kind comes from the later half of the first century BCE. An inscription of the Sātavāhana queen Nāganika records the grant of two villages as part of a series of *vaidic* sacrifices organized under her aegis. At least 64,503 *kārṣāpaṇa*s were spent on these sacrifices, in addition to 44,340 cows, and a number of horses, chariots, elephants, pots, silver containers and clothes. See No. 3 in Mirashi 1981.

267 On the military roles of the schools, see Veluthat 2013: 152-164 (i.e., Appendix II).

268 Devadevan 2009a: 60.

The rank and file of landholders had already swollen by the twelfth century, making individual landholders a force to reckon with.[269] Holding land on a hereditary basis also made the family a deeply entrenched institution. Inscriptions begin to enumerate family lines with much greater frequency. Genealogy had until this time remained the preserve of kings and saints. In the case of the later, it was the succession of saints or the *guruparaṃparā* that was emphasized, not the order of succession in a given monastery. In instances not related to kings and saints, records only named the Ego, and in many cases, his or her father. Cases of enumerating more than two generations were altogether rare. The Bedirūr grant of the Gaṅga king Bhūvikrama, dated 634, provides one such example, in which five generations are named, beginning with Bāṇa Vidyādhara Prabhumēru Gavuṇḍa, and ending with the recipient of the grant, Vikramāditya Gāvuṇḍa.[270] An interesting instance from a village near Dāvaṇagere gives the genealogy of a family of courtesans. It reads: "Maidamarasa's concubine Kāḍacci, Kāḍacci's daughter Kāḷabbe, Kāḷabbe's daughter Āycabbe, Āycabbe's daughter Kaḷiṅgabbe, Kaḷiṅgabbe's lord Pallaharaki Paraki's daughter Kaḷiṅgabbe, Kaḷiṅgabbe's son Parakayya". This genealogy was doubtless a result of the control over land the family enjoyed. The inscription is found in a village called Kāḍajji, a clear indication that the village was founded by or in honour of Maidamarasa's concubine.[271]

After the twelfth century, inscriptions carrying genealogies of the families concerned increased in number by leaps and bounds. An inscription from Gōvindanahaḷḷi, dated 1236, mentions Kētaṇa and Bōgayya I as the father and grandfather, respectively, of the recipients of the grant, Bōgayya II and his brother Murāri Mallayya.[272] Note that Ego carries his grandfather's name, a common practice in southern India until recently. An inscription from Beḷḷūru in the Nāgamaṅgala district is a veritable feast for the historian hunting for genealogies. It commences with the name of Sindeyanāyaka, who excelled in cattle-raids. He has three sons, matchless in valour: Māceyanāyaka I, Ādityadēva, and Valleyanāyaka. Māceyanāyaka I's sons are Rāceyanāyaka, Māceyanāyaka II, Manaha, Malleyanāyaka, Cikkēnāyaka, Sindeya, Śrīraṅga, Āditya, and Ballāḷa. Such was the Beḷḷūru family, which in all likelihood established the village. In that village lived Bhaviseṭṭi. His wife was Sūcikabbe. Their son, Kētiseṭṭi married Mañcave. Paṭṭaṇasvāmi and Maṇḍalasvāmi were their sons. Maṇḍalasvāmi was the donor of the grant. He was married to Mallave. His sons were Kētamalla and Kāḷeya. Mañcaseṭṭi and Māḷeya were his sons-in-law.[273]

269 Karashima 1984 discusses the evidence in the context of Tamilnadu. See also Karashima 2009: 9-10 for an interesting summary. No comparable study exists for Karnataka.

270 No. 29, Ramesh 1984.

271 Dg. 17, *Epigraphia Carnatica*, Vol. 11.

272 Kr. 39, *Epigraphia Carnatica*, (revised edition), Vol. 6.

273 Ng. 80. *Epigraphia Carnatica*, (revised edition), Vol. 7.

This description of the family, bordering on madness, was unthinkable in the ninth or the tenth century. Hereditary access to land had begun to find a number of reified expressions, among them religious genealogies, castes, and entrenched familial legacies. Understandably enough, the past, upon which stories of succession are based, was also gaining in importance. It was in this context that the invention of traditions, discussed in the preceding chapter, took place.

Complementing this development was the increasing monetization of economic transactions. This process had commenced in the late ninth and the early tenth century. By the late eleventh century, the value conversion of coins had become possible. A glaring example of this is found in an inscription dated 1098, where the conversion of *lokki-ponnu* (the coin minted at Lokkiguṇḍi, now Lakkuṇḍi) into *navilu-ponnu* (the coin minted at Navilūru?) is mentioned.[274] Transactions were now being made increasingly in cash. By the close of the fourteenth century, inscriptions came to be suffused with details of payment in cash. Under the Vijayanagara rulers, remittance of revenue to the treasury was invariably in cash, although collection continued to be in kind. As early as 1348, an inscription from coastal Karnataka spoke of "*bārakūra parivarttanakke saluva bārakūra gadyāṇa*", i.e., the Bārakūru Gadyāṇa payable at the Bārakūru exchange.[275] An inscription from 1458 mentioned "*bārakūra parivarttanakke saluva kāṭi gadyāṇa*", i.e., the Kāṭi Gadyāṇa payable at the Bārakūru exchange.[276] Prescribed in an inscription of 1386 was "*maṅgalūru kāṭi gadyaṇa*", which brings to light the Kāṭi Gadyāṇa of Maṅgalūru.[277] The Kāṭi Gadyāṇa, circulating in coastal Karnataka, had therefore different values at Bārakūru and Maṅgalūru, and the difference was reckoned through the expression *parivarttana*, exchange or circuit. The liquidity and exchange rate of coined money had attained remarkable complexity by the fourteenth century.

Trading initiatives also became increasingly specialized. A thirteenth-century inscription from Haḷēbīḍu refers to Akkiya Cavuḍiseṭṭi (Cavuḍiseṭṭi, the rice merchant), Āneya Hariyaṇṇa (Hariyaṇṇa, the elephant trader), Hattiya Kāmiseṭṭi (Kāmiseṭṭi, the cotton merchant), Nūlara Nakharaṅgaḷu (the yarn dealers collective), Meṇsina Pārisadēva (Pārisadēva, the pepper merchant) and Nūlara Nāgiseṭṭi (Nāgiseṭṭi, the yarn merchant).[278] Rural markets to the south of the Tuṅgabhadra were effectively under the control of local traders. Merchants were also beginning to make their supralocal presence felt. In the thirteenth century, some of them like Ēcayya and

274 Bellary 20, *Kannada University Epigraphical Series*, Vol. 1.

275 No. 231, *South Indian Inscriptions*, Vol. 7. The inscription does not give us the exact date, but only states that it was issued in the Sarvadhāri year, when the Vijayanagara king Harihara held the throne. Sarvadhari occurred in 1348 and 1408. Harihara II ruled from 1377 to 1404, but Harihara I was the king between 1347 and 1356, which enables us to identify the date as 1348.

276 No. 336, Ibid.

277 No. 189, Ibid.

278 Bl. 322, *Epigraphia Carnatica*, (revised edition), Vol. 9.

Baladēvaseṭṭi from Kopaṇa (Koppaḷa on the northern banks of the Tuṅgabhadra) and Kētiseṭṭi of the shop in Koṭṭuru (in the Tuṅgabhadra valley) were active in Haḷēbīḍu.[279] Merchants from northern Karnataka, Kerala, and Tamilnadu traded frequently in the south. However, such supralocal mobility was not seen on the part of merchants from southern Karnataka, which reinforces our suggestion (made in chapter 3) that the southern merchants came from the peasant proprietor class, whose interest in the local agrarian networks made them less prone to take up itinerant pursuits.

In this context of monetization, alienating money by way of making endowments to religious establishment was perhaps losing its preference. The practice continued, but on a substantially lesser scale. By the late fourteenth century, the older practice of making landed endowments returned to the centre-stage. Brāhmaṇas, temples, and other religious establishment began to receive land once again. In most cases, the grants were perpetual, providing hereditary control to the recipients. The grants made to the monastery of Śṛṅgēri by Harihara I and Bukka, and the endowment made to the Uḍupi temple during the reign of Harihara II,[280] are noteworthy examples of land grants regaining their lost importance. These instances contrast sharply with the grants made by the Cōḻa king Rājarāja I to the Bṛhadīśvara temple of Tañjāvūr[281] or the celebrated Tiruvālaṅṅāḍu copperplate grant of his son Rājēndra I,[282] where only a part of the revenue from the villages earmarked for the purpose was made over. They also stand out vis-à-vis the 1117 grant of the Hoysaḷa king Viṣṇuvardhana to the Cannakēśava temple he built at Belūru, where only the transit toll (*suṅka*), including the revenue payable in cash (*ponnāya*) from the villages listed, were given away.[283]

By the late fifteenth century, the effects of hereditary control over land, acquired through various means such as gift, purchase, and inheritance, were also seen on the monasteries. A number of new monasteries emerged, each with its own land, genealogy of seers, and stories about the past to tell.

While these developments were common to large parts of the Deccan, the region to the north of the Tuṅgabhadra experienced two other developments that had a telling effect on its political economy. The expansion of the *jāgīrdāri* system under the Bahmani rulers rooted the already-strong landed interests even more deeply. Given the large land holdings and the militia that the landlords commanded, the possibilities of insubordination or unrest among the subject peasantry were remote. At the same time, the Bahmani state embarked upon a new enterprise. Under the merchant from Iran, Mahmūd Gavān (1411-1481), who entered Bahmani service in 1453 and became chief minister in 1458, the state became a preeminent trader, exercising considerable

279 Ibid.

280 No. 299, *South Indian Inscriptions*, Vol. 7.

281 Inscriptions published in *South Indian Inscriptions*, Vol. 2, Part I and II.

282 No. 205, *South Indian Inscriptions*, Vol. 3, Part III.

283 Bl. 16, *Epigraphia Carnatica*, (revised edition), Vol. 9.

control over long-distance trade, including naval trade. This initiative was different from the earlier ones in South India during the Cōḻa and the Cēra rule, where the state only facilitated trade and enlisted traders into its service as revenue farmers. Under Gavān, the state became a *de facto* trader, filling the vacuum left behind by the decline of great trading syndicates such as the Ayyāvoḷe Ainūrvar, the Maṇigrāmaṃ, etc. Gavān was in fact honoured with the title *Malik al-Tujjar*, Prince of Merchants, by the Bahmani ruler Humāyūn (r. 1458-1461 CE).[284]

This was a pioneering development. Soon, the prospects of trade came to be exploited by more and more states and chiefdoms, and many of them became active traders in the course of the sixteenth and the seventeenth centuries.[285] The arrival of the Portuguese, the Dutch, and the British facilitated the expansion of this process.

In contrast to the Vijayanagara state, which promoted rural monetization and minted coins of lower denominations that circulated in the networks of local trade, the Bahmani state was more drawn towards supralocal transactions. The use of coined money by the Bahmanis in rural transactions was less impressive. Coins uttered by the Bahmani mints were of higher denominations, and used in large-scale trading and revenue transactions. Their presence in routine local-level market transaction networks was feeble. In a richly documented study, Phillip B. Wagoner has shown that it was the Vijayanagara *honnu* that circulated in the local market networks of the Bahmani territory.[286] A large segment of the peasantry remained unorganized and outside of the purview of active interventions from the state and the great landed interests of the day. This peasantry inhabited the harsh terrains of northern Karnataka, where the presence of the state had remained poor for centuries. Recalcitrance was rife here. At the same time, expansion of agriculture was also possible in these areas, although poor rainfall and the absence of effective irrigational installations affected the volume of surplus generated. Yet, there existed the strong likelihood of merchants—who turned increasingly to the local markets after the state moved out of them to turn into a major supralocal trader—to be attracted towards this virgin field. To what extent this possibility was explored by the merchants is not clear. Like many other aspects of the fifteenth and the sixteenth century political economy, it continues to await study. There is, however, at least one major instance of mercantile involvement with the peasantry that culminated in a significant transformation of monasteries in the region.

Sometime in the last quarter of the fifteenth century, a saint called Ārūḍha Saṅgamanātha arrived in Vijayanagara. He was also known as Diggi Saṅgamanātha after the village Diggi in the Yādagiri district, where he lived for some time. We know next to nothing about his life. Legends concerning his acts float in abandon

284 Eaton 2005: 65.
285 Subrahmanyam 1990.
286 Wagoner 2014.

in the Yādagiri, Kalaburagi, Vijayapura,[287] Bāgalakōṭe, and Rāyacūru districts. As his name indicates, he belonged to the Ārūḍha tradition, although legends told by the *khānkāh* of Candā Sāhēb of Gūgi (Shaikh Candā Hussaynī) consider him to be a Virakta.[288] Saṅgamanātha and Candā Sāhēb were close friends, and influenced each other deeply. The name Hussaynī suggests that Candā Sāhēb belonged to the family of Bandēnavāz. Saṅgamanātha's influence on him was so deep that he accepted a saffron headgear, worn to this day by descendants of his *khānkāh*.[289] Candā Sāhēb's influence on the Ārūḍha was as profound. Saṅgamanātha adopted the green robe, cap, and other paraphernalia of a Sūfi.[290]

At Vijayanagara (Haṃpi), Saṅgamanātha met a merchant called Basava. It is likely that Saṅgamanātha gave him the name Basava. The twelfth century Basava was a devotee of lord Saṅgamanātha of Kūḍalasaṅgama, whom he also regarded as his *guru*. Was this old relationship being reenacted in the late fifteenth century between the Ārūḍha and the merchant? Yes, as we shall presently see.

Basava was the son of Malliśeṭṭi and Liṅgamma of Vijayanagara. He is known to the vernacular academia as Koḍēkallu Basava after the place on the river Kṛṣṇa where he eventually came to rest. We, too, shall call him Koḍēkallu Basava to distinguish him from the Basava of the twelfth century. The account of his life is known to us from the *Nandiyāgamalīle*, composed by his descendent Vīrasaṅgayya. According to Basavalinga Soppimath, who has carried out a mediocre study of Koḍēkallu Basava (under the guidance of the illustrious M.M. Kalburgi!), Vīrasaṅgayya completed the work in 1589. This conclusion is based, according to him, on the reference to the Rudra Besiki 'year' mentioned by Vīrasaṅgayya. As an expression, Rudra Besiki is not easily decipherable. But the stanza in question identifies Virōdhi as the year.[291] Virōdhi fell in 1589-90, but the other details do not correspond with this year. The work was completed on a Monday on the fourteenth lunar day in the month of Kārtīka.[292] No Monday fell on a fourteenth lunar day in Kārtīka in 1589. Virōdhi occurred again in 1649-50 and 1709-10. There is one date in 1649, where all details mentioned by Vīrasaṅgayya fall in place: 18 October 1649. It was a Monday, the fourteenth lunar

287 Bijāpura (Bijapur), as renamed by the Government of Karnataka in 2014.
288 Tarikere 1998: 79.
289 Ibid.
290 Such exchanges are taken to be instances of religious synchronism by the vernacular academia. In an important, but poorly articulated critique of this position, Tarikere 1998 argues that the synchronism thesis regards different traditions as autonomous and watertight entities, which however was hardly the case in practice. Religious traditions were porous and, at the popular level, they tended to enmesh into one another in complex ways that involved conflict, negotiations, exchanges, conciliation, acceptance, and assimilation to an extent that made a distinction between one tradition and the other impossible.
291 Virōdhi is the twenty-third in a cycle of sixty years, used in traditional calendar systems in India.
292 *Nandiyāgamalīle*, 15.50.

day in Kārtīka. This must be identified as the date when the poet completed the *Nandiyāgamalīle*. Soppimath argues that the poet was the great grandson of Koḍēkallu Basava, although the person named here is neither the poet nor the great grandson of Koḍēkallu Basava. The description in the *Nandiyāgamalīle* is as follows: Koḍēkallu Basava's son was Saṅgayya I, his adopted son Appājayya, his son Saṅgayya II, his son through his wife Liṅgājamma, Vīrasaṅgayya,[293] the son (not named) borne him by his wife Nīlājamma, his son Basavarājayya, his married son (not named), and his son Vīrasaṅgayya, the poet.[294] The poet is, therefore, eighth in line after Koḍēkallu Basava, meaning that at least two centuries had elapsed between the time of our hero and his hagiographer. A date of ca. 1450 for the birth of Koḍēkallu Basava, therefore, does not seem to be unreasonable.

According to the poet, Liṅgamma and Malliśeṭṭi found Koḍēkallu Basava in a forest, after the children they brought forth and the ones they adopted had all died young.[295] Malliśeṭṭi was a successful trader. Koḍēkallu Basava was also trained to become one. At a young age, he is said to have come into contact with the saint, Emme Basava.[296] The poet does not supply us with sufficient information on the nature of this contact. It is known that Emme Basava was the proponent of *kālajñāna*, i.e., prophecy, as a form of knowledge. Many of his *kālajñāna* compositions have come down to us. He also received a grant from the Vijayanagara ruler Tirumalarāya, which seems to have been confiscated by another maṭha under circumstances that are not known to us.[297] Later in his life, Koḍēkallu Basava emerged as a major advocate of *kālajñāna*, which does not of course make it likely that he learnt it from Emme Basava. For, Tirumalarāya's inscription recording the land grant to Emme Basava is dated 1543, when Koḍēkallu Basava, had he been alive, would be an old man in his eighties or nineties. We must therefore concede, against the testimony of the hagiographer, that it was the hero of the *Nandiyāgamalīle* who influenced Emme Basava, and not the other way round.

Koḍēkallu Basava was married to Kāśamma, the daughter of the merchant couple, Saṅgājamma and Paṭṭaṇaśeṭṭi Liṅgaṇṇa. Liṅgaṇṇa was perhaps a moneylender, and known for the compound interest he charged, if the expression *cadura baḍḍi* is any

293 For some reason, Soppimath declines to read the next stanza, and identifies this Vīrasaṅgayya, Koḍēkallu Basava's grandson's grandson, as his great grandson and the poet. Soppimath 1995: 46.
294 *Nandiyāgamalīle*, 15.48-49.
295 Ibid., 8.7. Such tropes are not unknown in hagiographic literature from the region.
296 Ibid., 10.19.
297 Nj. 115, *Epigraphia Carnatica*, Vol. 3.

indication.[298] Kāśamma was still a child at the time of marriage.[299] In the course of time, Koḍēkallu Basava became a leading trader. It was at this juncture in his life that Ārūḍha Saṅgamanātha reached Vijayanagara.[300] Koḍēkallu Basava was immediately drawn towards the Ārūḍha's magnetic persona. Saṅgamanātha trained him in his system of renunciatory practices, provided him with four 'invisible' servants, gave him the eleven variants of his new script, and made him wear the robe of skin (*carmāṃbara*).[301] Before doing so, the saint made Koḍēkallu Basava realize who he was in his fourteen previous births. In his first birth, Koḍēkallu Basava was the embodiment of the letter Ōṃ (*ōṃkārarūpa*). In the second birth, he was the thousand-headed one (*sahasraśīrṣa*). And then, he was born as Pūrvācārya, Vṛṣabhēndra, Nandi, Atuḷabhadra, Bhōgēśa, Tirujnāni Sammandhi, Hanuma, Rōmakōṭi, Allama Prabhu, Basava, Muhammad, and Guptagaṇēśvara in that order.[302] Note that four of them are historical figures. Tirujnāni Sammandhi was one of the sixty-three Śaiva Nāyanārs of Tamilnadu, Tirujñānasaṃbandhar. Allama Prabhu and Basava were contemporaries in the mid-twelfth century. And Muhammad was the great prophet who founded Islam.

Koḍēkallu Basava's relationship with Saṅgamanātha does not seem to have augured well with others in the city. A certain Gāṇigara Niṅgaṇṇa (Niṅgaṇṇa, the oil presser) asked Koḍēkallu Basava to stay away from the saint, and in consequence, lost his life.[303] The merchant's wife Kāśavva levelled charges against Saṅgamanātha, and, like the oil presser, had to pay with her life. Koḍēkallu Basava is said to have sent her to Śiva's abode.[304]

After killing his wife, Koḍēkallu Basava left Vijayanagara on horseback, and reached Baḷḷigāve (where Allama had lived over two centuries ago). Here, he met Nīlamma and expressed his desire to marry her. Nīlamma seems to have been reluctant. When she asked why he sought her hand, Koḍēkallu Basava replied that she was his wife, Nīlamma, in his previous birth as Basava, and had angrily left him for not bestowing children upon her; he had returned to redress her grievance.[305] What transpired thereafter is not clear. There was resistance to the alliance, either from Nīlamma, or from her parents, the *pañcavaṇṇige* couple Cannājamma and

298 Ibid., 10.32. The word *cadura* is used elsewhere in the text the mean 'clever' (cf. 10.52 and 10.53). So, it is not unlikely that the Paṭṭaṇaśeṭṭi who collected interest (*baḍḍi*) is referred to as the clever one. Soppimath however reads *baḍḍi* (or *vaḍḍina*, as it apparently occurs in the version he consulted) as the name of a town to which Saṅgājamma and Liṅgaṇṇa belonged! See Soppimath 1995: 50.
299 *Nandiyāgamalīle*, 10.49; 10.66.
300 Ibid., 11.26.
301 Ibid., 11.34-35.
302 Ibid., 11.32-33.
303 Ibid., 11.30.
304 Ibid., 11.44.
305 Ibid., 11.65.

Siddhayya, or from both daughter and parents. Koḍēkallu Basava carried the girl away, forcefully. They were pursued. In the encounter that followed, Koḍēkallu Basava's men succeeded in repulsing those who came looking for them. Some of the pursuers (one hundred, according to the *Nandiyāgamalīle*) died fighting.[306] Cannājamma and Siddhayya gave in. Koḍēkallu Basava and Nīlamma returned to Baḷḷigāve, where their marriage was solemnized with great pomp and show.[307]

After their marriage, Koḍēkallu Basava and Nīlamma set out on a long voyage along with their followers. They came to Rācōṭi (perhaps Rāyacōṭi in the Kaḍapa district of Andhra),[308] where Nīlamma gave birth to a son.[309] The boy was called Rācaṇṇa or Rācappa, possibly named after the place of his birth. Their next station was Soṇḍūru (Saṇḍūru in the Baḷḷāri district, famous for its Kumārasvāmi temple).[310] The second son, Guhēśvara, was born here.[311] Kappaḍi (Kūḍalasaṅgama in the Bāgalakōṭe district) was their next stopover.[312] Here, Nīlamma gave birth to the third son, Saṅgayya I,[313] also known as Cannasaṅgayya and Karasaṅgayya.[314]

The journey continued. It brought Koḍēkallu Basava to a coastal town in the Koṅkaṇa country, which attracted rich trade and enterprise. Here, he met a certain Kañcagāra Kaḷiṅga, who was obsessed with the desire of having a vision of Lord Śiva. He had tried many paths, including Jaina and Muslim, but without success. Koḍēkallu Basava showed him the right path, and Kaḷiṅga had a glimpse of Śiva.[315] Further on, Koḍēkallu Basava reached Vaḍabāḷa, found the saint Nāganātha hidden in a forest in the form of a serpent, fed him milk, and transformed him into a man.[316] According to Soppimath, the legend suggests that Koḍēkallu Basava initiated Nāganātha into the Nātha tradition and sent him to Vaḍabāḷa.[317] While this is an interesting suggestion, there is no evidence either in the *Nandiyāgamalīle* or in any other sources that Nāganātha of Vaḍabāḷa belonged to the Nātha tradition.[318] The encounter itself is

306 Ibid., 11.71.
307 Ibid., 12.16-38.
308 Ibid., 12.44.
309 Ibid., 12.52.
310 Ibid., 12.57.
311 Ibid., 12.63.
312 Ibid., 12.65. It is here that Basava had died in 1168.
313 Ibid., 12.70.
314 Ibid., 12.69. The expression Karasaṅgayya suggests that the boy was a *karajāta*, i.e., an adopted son. An alternate and less persuasive version refers to him as Karisaṅgayya, i.e., Saṅgayya, black (*kari*) in complexion.
315 Ibid., 13.3-23.
316 Ibid., 13.24.
317 Soppimath 1995: 53.
318 Soppimath in fact believes that Koḍēkallu Basava also belonged to the Nātha tradition. This only points to his poor understanding of both the Koḍēkallu and the Nātha traditions.

unlikely although Soppimath affirms its likelihood,[319] as studies place Nāganātha and his disciples in the period between 1354 and 1458.[320] It must be noted here that according to oral legends, Nāsir-ud-dīn Cirāg-e-Dillī (d. 1356) moved to the Deccan and settled down here, where he came to be worshipped as Nāganātha.[321] It is believed that in the fair of Nāganātha, the palanquin cannot be lifted unless the following *dīn* is called: "*nāsiruddīn cirāg ki dōstāra dīn haraharā*".[322] Similar calls of Nāsir's *dīn* are made in the traditions of Māṇikaprabhu and Bakaprabhu in the Bīdara district.[323]

From Vaḍabāḷa, Koḍēkallu Basava went to Ujjayini, where two traders welcomed him, and offered him hospitality. We do not know if Ujjayini is the famous town known by that name in Mālava, or Ujini in Baḷḷāri district, which is known as Ujjayini in the Vīraśaiva literature. The former is not unlikely in view of the fact that the next leg of his tour took Koḍēkallu Basava to northern India. From Ujjayini, he is said to have gone to Ausikandara. It is not possible to identify this place, although it seems to be hinting at a name such as Sikandarābād, Sikandarpur or Sikandrā. It is tempting to identify Ausikandara with Sikandrā, the new town built by Koḍēkallu Basava's contemporary and the Lodi Sultān, Sikandar Lōdi (r. 1489-1517). This is supported by the fact that the next town in the journey was Pulabhāra where Koḍēkalla Basava succeeded in winning over the Vaiṣṇavas through a miracle.[324] Pulabhāra is certainly Bhilvāḍā in Rajasthan, known for its Vaiṣṇava connections. However, the poet says that Koḍēkallu Basava helped a family of peasants, Bommagoṇḍa, his brother Basavagoṇḍa, elder sister Maiḷaladēvi, and a younger sister, in augmenting their agrarian income, and received a gift from them.[325] This makes the identification of Ausikandara with Sikandrā tenuous. We must, however, bear in mind that the *Nandiyāgamalīle* was composed nearly two centuries after the events recorded there had taken place. The legends, under oral circulation, are likely to have undergone a number of changes in the course of transmission. The route described by the poet is also irregular, and shows no signs of coherence. Koḍēkallu Basava left Pulabhāra and reached Mahā Cinna,[326] which in all likelihood is Mahā Cīna, the name by which China was known in India. That Koḍēkallu Basava visited China cannot be accepted as a fact of history. It had, however, a function to serve in the hagiography's order of things, viz., the visit of a saint to places strange and unknown, and finding acceptance there. After Mahā Cinna, Koḍēkallu Basava turned to the south, reached Kurukṣētra[327] where by

319 Ibid., 54.
320 Ibid., 53, n. 40.
321 Tarikere 1998: 4; 42. The historical Nāsir is not known to have travelled to the Deccan region.
322 Ibid., 42.
323 Ibid.
324 Ibid., 13.40-42.
325 Ibid., 13.34-40.
326 Ibid., 13.43.
327 Ibid., 13.63.

the touch of his feet, those who had died in the battle of Kurukṣētra—the Pāṇḍavas, the Kauravas, and their allies—came back to life.[328] He then continued the southward journey to reach Kalyāṇa.[329]

At Kalyāṇa, he sat down to copy the scripts found engraved on a stone. Soppimath posits that Muslim invaders were destroying the *vacana*s of the twelfth century *śaraṇa*s, and that Koḍēkallu Basava's visit to Kalyāṇa was meant to salvage as much of this literature as possible by copying them into the obscure script, *amaragannaḍa*.[330] There is no evidence to substantiate this argument. When Koḍēkallu Basava was at Kalyāṇa, the lord of the world (*lōkapati*) sent words for him. The name of the *lōkapati* is recorded as Isupāśca. This, certainly, was Yūsuf Bādśāh or Yūsuf Khān, who founded the Ādil Śāhi state of Vijayapura in 1489. Koḍēkallu Basava was not keen on meeting the king. He was, however, forcibly taken to the Sultān's palace (perhaps in Vijayapura). Koḍēkallu Basava reached the royal harem, where Isupāśca struck him with a dagger. Predictably enough, the dagger did not hurt the saint. It passed through his body as if moving through water, in a manner that brings Allama's encounter with Gōrakṣa to mind.[331] The king became his devotee, and asked for a gift of five bundles of *vacana*s, and some hair.

Inasmuch as Koḍēkallu Basava was hailed as an incarnation of Muhammad the Prophet, the hair he gave Isupāśca came to be preserved in Vijayapura as a relic of the Prophet's. We know that the hair now preserved in the Hazratbal mosque of Kashmir as Muhammad's relic was brought from Vijayapura. In all likelihood, this is the hair of Koḍēkallu Basava.

Koḍēkallu Basava was now on the final leg of his journey. He had travelled widely, and performed many miracles. Nowhere did he convert people to his faith. Even at Pulabhāra, where the Vaiṣṇavas became his devotee, it is a glimpse of Viṣṇu that he showed the Vaiṣṇavas. In other words, he made them gain a better understanding of their own faith. Did he really travel to far off places like Bhilvāḍā and Kurukṣētra? Or was it only a fiction introduced by the poet, or a figment of the imagination that crept into the legend in the course of the two centuries when it transmitted orally? These questions may be of interest to the positivist historian. What is more interesting for our purpose is that in this long journey, his meeting with only four classes of people are reported: merchants and artisans, peasants and their family, saints and the saintly ones, and rulers and their men. If the poet did not have a historically credible picture of the events concerning Koḍēkallu Basava's life, he certainly knew the classes that the merchant-turned-saint engaged with, which might well have been those same

328 Ibid., 13.65.
329 Ibid., 13.66.
330 Soppimath 1995: 57.
331 *Nandiyāgamalīle*, 14.5.

classes that patronized the maṭha in the poet's own lifetime. Herein lies the real significance of the *Nandiyāgamalīle*, as far as our analysis is concerned.

Having seen the world extensively, Koḍēkallu Basava decided to settle down. He reached Sagara, near Diggi, where there was a settlement of soothsayers. Very little is said about the soothsayers. Koḍēkallu Basava criticized them for trading off great secrets (*parama rahasyagaḷu*) for a few grains of millet.[332] He told them that they could not achieve *amaratva* (immortality) just by calling themselves (members of) Amara Kalyāṇa.[333] We thus learn that the soothsayers had constituted an assembly called Amara Kalyāṇa. Koḍēkallu Basava prevailed upon the soothsayers, and succeeded in transforming them into peasants.[334] The soothsayer-turned-peasant families came to be known as *ettinavaru*, 'those with the ox'. This was the beginning of Koḍēkallu Basava's efforts to build a group of followers and found an establishment of his own. The *ettinavaru* have remained devotees of Koḍēkallu Basava to this day.

From Sagara, he moved northeastwards to Nāgāvi, where he won over a certain Guṇḍa Basava and his son, Īrappayya, to his fold.[335] This family is known as *kattiyavaru*, 'those with the donkey'.[336] The family has retained its ties with the monastery at Koḍēkallu to this day. The present pontiff of the Koḍēkallu maṭha belongs to this "family of donkeys". We know from other sources that Guṇḍa Basava was a revered saint in and around Nāgāvi. He was also a poet, who composed many *ḍaṅgura* songs.[337] In these songs, he referred to Nāgāvi as Dharma Kalyāṇa. His tomb is worshipped in Nāgāvi by descendants of his family. Īrappayya is also held in high regard by the Nāgāvi tradition.

It is of great interest that the first two groups of followers, whom Koḍēkallu Basava enlisted into the service of his project, claimed affiliation with Kalyāṇa. In the case of the soothsayers of Sagara, the word might not have meant anything more than a congregation. Guṇḍa Basava's allusion to Dharma Kalyāṇa, on the other hand, seems to be making the claim that Nāgāvi was as great, or as sacred, as Kalyāṇa itself.

After leaving Nāgāvi, Koḍēkallu Basava passed through Kulakundi, and arrived at Koraḷibeṭṭa, where he cured a merchant called Maliśeṭṭi or Mallaṇṇa of leprosy.[338] He then reached Ikkaḷi, and brought the family of a certain Mādappa into his fold. Mādappa's father Rāghappa was initially reluctant to join the Order, but became a devotee following a miracle in which Koḍēkallu Basava appeared before him in the form of Śiva.[339] Seven families from Ikkuḷige are believed to have moved with him to

332 Ibid., 14.13.
333 Ibid., 14.14.
334 Ibid., 14.22.
335 Ibid., 14.26-37.
336 Ibid., 14.37.
337 Songs sung to the accompaniment of a percussion instrument called *ḍaṅgura*.
338 Ibid., 14.38-39.
339 Ibid., 14.40-49.

Koḍēkallu as devotees. Their descendants now live in Koḍēkallu, and the number of families has increased to fifty.[340]

The great journey ended at Koḍēkallu. This was a pastoral settlement, controlled by a hunter called Hanuma Nāyaka.[341] Koḍēkallu Basava bought land from the hunter, and also conferred recognition upon him as a king.[342] With Hanuma Nāyaka's help, he transformed Koḍēkallu into a flourishing village of trade and enterprise.[343] Then he sat down at the *haddugunḍu* rock on the outskirts of the village to compose his poems (*vacanavākya*).[344] But he was back in action soon, perhaps for want of resources. He raised a band of troops, raided villages, and sent the troops to fight the Bādśāh.[345] The Bādśāh was defeated, and forced to grant a few score (*kelavu viṃśati*) villages to Koḍēkallu Basava.[346]

What followed next was crucial. Although this is not explicitly stated in the *Nandiyāgamalīle* (composed by a man poor in intellect), there is circumstantial evidence in support of this development. Koḍēkallu Basava believed in the legend, narrativized in Bhīma's *Basavapurāṇa* and the works of the great Vijayanagara project sponsored by Jakkaṇa and Lakkaṇṇa Danḍēśa, that Basava hosted a large number of *śaraṇa*s in Kalyāṇa in his day, and organized the *anubhava maṇṭapa* in which the great pioneers of Vīraśaivism discussed and debated on spiritual and worldly matters that were of concern to them. Lakkaṇṇa Danḍēśa had perhaps believed that the Vijayanagara project of compiling the *vacana*s, and consolidating the floating legends on the *śaraṇa*s into standardized hagiographies, were an attempt to relive the great experiment of Kalyāṇa which, according to him, was a historical fact, but as a matter of fact, was imagined into existence in the late fourteenth and the early fifteenth century. Lakkaṇṇa Danḍēśa considered Vijayanagara to be the new Kalyāṇa. He called it Vijaya Kalyāṇa.[347] We cannot be certain on whether or not he had developed a systematic view on the idea of Vijaya Kalyāṇa. This seems unlikely indeed. By the time of Koḍēkallu Basava, Kalyāṇa had turned into a powerful metaphor, and was deployed to signify such villages, congregations, etc., as were sought to be represented as sacred. Amara Kalyāṇa and Dharma Kalyāṇa are instances in this regard that are known to us. The image of Kalyāṇa as sacred was not restricted to narratives and traditions centering on Basava and Allama Prabhu. The *Saundaryalahari*, a major text

---

340 Soppimath 1995: 62.

341 *Nandiyāgamalīle*, 15.15.

342 From this humble beginning, Hanuma Nāyaka and his successors grew in strength, and eventually established the chiefdom of Surapura. On the Surapura chiefdom, see Aruni 2004.

343 *Nandiyāgamalīle*, 15.18.

344 Ibid., 15.19.

345 Ibid., 15.20-21.

346 Ibid., 15.24-25. Later on in the narrative, it is stated that the number of villages granted was eighteen (*daśa-aṣṭa*), a conventional number. Ibid., 15.28.

347 See the articles in Bhusanuramatha 1988.

of the Śrīvidyā tradition, composed sometime in the fifteenth century (and attributed to Śaṅkara by Vallabha and many others who came after him) enumerates it in a list of eight holy cities.[348] Koḍēkallu Basava aspired to build upon this image. The idea that occurred to him was ingenious. He decided to reenact the (imagined) *anubhava maṇṭapa* of Basava. This would be the last Kalyāṇa, and the most perfect. He called it Kaḍeya Kalyāṇa (the Last Kalyāṇa). It was also known as Amara Kalyāṇa, which is perhaps due to the role played in the project by the soothsayers of Sagara, who had once identified themselves as Amara Kalyāṇa.

As part of this initiative, Koḍēkallu Basava set up an *anubhava maṇṭapa*. He put himself in the shoes of Basava. His wife Nīlamma might have played the role of Nīlamma and Akkamahādēvi. An *anubhava maṇṭapa* was not complete without an Allama or a Cannabasava.[349] Who were to occupy these positions? This question led to a dispute, which only points to the significance of the experiment in the eyes of the participants. Koḍēkallu Basava chose Paramānanda Guru of Hebbāḷa, a saint who hailed from Tamilnadu and was teacher to his *guru* Ārūḍha Saṅgamanātha, to occupy the position of Allama. A recalcitrant saint from Tamilnadu, Maṇṭēsvāmi or Maṇṭēliṅga,[350] appears to have claimed this position for himself. In hagiographic accounts of Maṇṭēsvāmi, he is represented as Allama. We may venture the guess that one of Koḍēkallu Basava's sons, Guhēśvara, also aspired to the position of Allama. The name Guhēśvara, which in all likelihood was a title, seems to be pointing in this direction.[351]

The position of Cannabasava was also in demand. Who occupied it is not known. Koḍēkallu Basava's son Saṅgayya I was known as Cannabasava. And so was a saint from Sālōṭagi, known for his *ḍaṅgura* songs. Cannabasava of Sālōṭagi was familiar with Koḍēkallu Basava and his project, although there is no indication that he was a claimant to the office of Cannabasava. A third Cannabasava lived in the village of Galaga. He was a member of the Maṇṭēsvāmi faction. This is confirmed by the presence of the shrine of Maṇṭēsvāmi's disciple Gurubhāra Liṅgayya within the shrine housing his tomb. He is likely to have been a candidate put up by Maṇṭēsvāmi for the position of Cannabasava.

Following his failure to be crowned Allama, Maṇṭēsvāmi moved to the south to establish a tradition of his own. He might have wished to call it the First Kalyāṇa (Ādi Kalyāṇa) in striking contrast to Koḍēkallu Basava's Last Kalyāṇa. In the oral epic sung by the nīlagāras, he is said to have visited the chaotic Ādi Kalyāṇa, and restored order.

---

348 *Saundaryalahari*, 49. The other seven cities are Vaiśāli, Ayōdhyā, Dhāra, Mathurā, Bhōgavati, Avanti and Vijayanagara. It is the reference to Vijayanagara and Kalyāna (Kalyāṇi in the text), which enables us to place the text in the fifteenth century.

349 Cannabasava was Basava's nephew through his sister Nāgavva.

350 It has also been argued that Maṇṭēsvāmi was of Telugu origin. See Jayaprakash 2005: 7-32 (i.e., chapter 2).

351 Guhēśvara is a corruption of Goggēśvara, the signature used by Allama in his *vacanas*.

Maṇṭēsvāmi succeeded in winning the support of Rācappa, the son of Koḍēkallu Basava. Rācappāji rebelled against his father, left for the south with Maṇṭēsvāmi, and became a revered saint among the small group of nīlagāras devotees who hold him and his master Maṇṭēsvāmi in great esteem.[352] It is not expressly stated anywhere that Rācappāji rebelled against his father; however, to this day, the Koḍēkallu and Maṇṭēsvāmi traditions share relationships that are far from cordial, pointing to the unpleasant circumstances of the departure of Maṇṭēsvāmi and Rācappāji from Koḍēkallu. Rācappāji and Siddappāji, another of Maṇṭēsvāmi's disciples, established close relationships with an emerging family of chiefs in the Maisūru region. Ties of matrimony were also forged. It is this family that eventually rose into prominence under Rāja Oḍeya (r. 1578-1617) and his successors, and built the Woḍeyar (*sic*) state of Maisūru.[353]

What became of Koḍēkallu Basava is not known. According to the *Nandiyāgamalīle*, after obtaining villages as grant from the Bādśāh, Koḍēkallu Basava met a certain Maḷeya Prabhu, who was eager to see Śiva and fell at his feet to help him. Koḍēkallu Basava sent him to the abode of Śiva.[354] The reference, here, is to Maḷeya Mallēśa, a ubiquitous rainmaker whom it is difficult to locate in history. His encounter with, and his death at the hands of, Koḍēkallu Basava may point to a hostile encounter our hero had with devotees from the Maḷeya Mallēśa tradition. Next, Koḍēkallu Basava began to attract devotees from far and wide. Maṇṭēsvāmi of the Drāviḍa country (Tamilnadu) was afflicted with leprosy, and was on the verge of death. He asked his disciple Gurubhāra Liṅgayya to offer him a vision of the *guru*. Gurubhāra Liṅgayya remembered Koḍēkallu Basava, and Koḍēkallu Basava appeared in his mind to tell him where he lived. Accordingly, Maṇṭēsvāmi left for Koḍēkallu, where he was received with kindness by Koḍēkallu Basava and Nīlamma. The couple nursed him back to health, and adopted him as a son. And then Koḍēkallu Basava left the world, asking Maṇṭēsvāmi to raise an army and take care of it until his return in the next birth.[355] Before passing away, he sealed his writings in three boxes, had them dumped into the river Kṛṣṇa, and asked king Bali of the Nāga world to preserve and worship them until his return.[356]

Koḍēkallu Basava, "the incarnation of Muhammad the Prophet", had lived a fabulous life indeed. He was endowed with a fertile imagination and a sharp intellect. He composed poems that were splendid pieces of craftsmanship, innovative in form, rigorous in semantic pursuit, and at times more modern than most 'modernist' poetry of the twentieth century. But Maṇṭēsvāmi's rebellion and Rācappa's departure might

352 On Maṇṭēsvāmi, see Indvadi 1999 and 2004.

353 On Rāja Oḍeya and the consolidation of Oḍeya political influence, see Simmons 2014.

354 Ibid., 15.29.

355 Ibid. 15.30-41.

356 Ibid., 15.43-46.

have left him dejected. Kaḍeya Kalyāṇa collapsed. His third son Saṅgayya I also left Koḍēkallu along with the Vaiṣṇava saint-poet Kanakadāsa for reasons that are not clear. It will not be wrong to guess that Koḍēkallu Basava died a rich man, powerful, influential, learned, and saintly, but profoundly sad.

What did Koḍēkallu Basava accomplish in the course of his seemingly disoriented life that bordered on the tempestuous? In trying to address this question, we must at the outset place the fact in bold relief that he came from a family of merchants. The two women he married were also from merchant families. Vijayanagara and Baḷḷigāve, the locations of his early years, were flourishing centres of commerce. Among the places he visited was a coastal town, bristling with trade and enterprise. When he finally settled down at Koḍēkallu, he transformed the village into a trading centre. It was the interests of the mercantile and artisan groups that Koḍēkallu Basava's enterprise represented.

In the course of his journey, he met an artisan, Kañcagāra Kaḷiṅga, who's spiritual needs he fulfilled. Towards the end, he met a trader, Malisețți, whom he cured of leprosy. Neither of them made any presents to Koḍēkallu Basava. They were not brought into the fold of the Koḍēkallu maṭha in any capacity either. The *Nandiyāgamalīle* and other surviving traditions (both written and oral) do not recognize any merchant or artisan group as early followers of the Koḍēkallu tradition. We must then say that this was a monastery *of* the mercantile groups, not a monastery *for* them.

This contrasts with Koḍēkallu Basava's engagement with the peasantry. At Ausikandara, he helped a peasant family to expand their agrarian income, and secured their allegiance, although they were not made followers of the monastery. The peasants showered rich gifts on him. At Sagara, he made the soothsayers take to agriculture, and brought them into his fold. The *Nandiyāgamalīle* captures in a nutshell the historical process through which mercantile groups in northern Karnataka tried to establish coercive relationships of dependence with the peasantry. It also demonstrates how monasteries in the region were powerful enough to facilitate the expansion of agriculture in the drier belts, regulate production relations of the day, coerce the complacent peasantry to build ties of dependence with the enterprising mercantile and artisan groups, and act as powerful centres of surplus appropriation and redistribution.

Koḍēkallu Basava was also the representative of a major centrifugal tendency. We have seen that a number of saintly genealogies and practices had appeared in the region in the preceding centuries. Under Jakkaṇa and Lakkaṇṇa Daṇḍēśa, earnest attempts were made to integrate many of these into a single system called Vīraśaivism through new narratives, which were polyphonic, had multiple nodes and internodes, but at the same time, centered on the figure of Allama Prabhu or Basava. Disputes raged, concerns varied, and the points of emphases differed from author to author. Nevertheless, the narratives shared strong intertextual linkages, which enabled the development of a semiotic pool from which participants in this great project drew their vocabulary with gay abandon. In the process, the cryptic and the inaccessible were being rendered familiar, if not always intelligible. Koḍēkallu Basava's project struck at the very heart of this centripetalism. He drew from the same narrative structures, borrowed his vocabulary from the same semiotic pool, but deployed them to charge traditions of renunciation at various places such as Nāgāvi, Vaḍabāḷa, Galaga, Sālōṭagi, and Sagara—which had never developed fully or had lost their original fortune—with a new energy. He invested these traditions with a sense of autonomy in their own right, and made them locally entrenched and capable of regulating production relations, surplus appropriation, and redistribution. The production of narratives was also scrupulously abjured, which explains why few among these new saints had hagiographies composed in their honour, and none before the seventeenth century.

That the Koḍēkallu tradition represented mercantile interests in the expansion of agriculture in the drier reaches of northern Karnataka did not exhaust its entrepreneurial spirit. Equally significant was the fact that it represented mercantile interest in the emerging military labour market. Mercenary recruits from the peasantry were a common feature of the armies of the subcontinent until the end of the eighteenth century when, beginning with Lord Wellesley's Subsidiary Alliance, these armies began to be systematically disbanded. It was common for renouncers to appear in the army as warriors. They were also instrumental in recruiting mercenaries from the peasantry. It is not surprising, then, that Koḍēkallu Basava is credited in the *Nandiyāgamalīle* with raising an army. He helps Hanuma Nāyaka in building a station of troops (*pāḷya*) that functioned as the headquarters of a chiefdom.[357] Besides, he gathered people to form a militia for himself, with which he raided villages in the area.[358] Koḍēkallu Basava is also said to have sent his troops to fight the Bādśāh, i.e. Yūsuf Khān.[359] We do not know if Koḍēkallu Basava was alive in 1565, when decisive battles were fought in the backyard of Koḍēkallu at places variously identified as Tāḷikōṭe, Rakkasagi, Taṅgaḍagi, and Banahaṭṭi between a confederacy of the Deccani Sultāns, and the Vijayanagara forces led by Rāmarāya, which culminated in a fatal blow to Vijayanagara and the death of Rāmarāya. It would not surprise us to learn that the Koḍēkallu militia had participated in this battle, although this is not borne out by evidence.[360]

Warrior-saints were found across many parts of south Asia between the fifteenth and the nineteenth century.[361] "After the creation of the Delhi Sultanate around the fifteenth century," writes Carl Olson, "warrior ascetics became significant participants in the political realm, and they were identified by carrying an iron lance."[362] As early as the late thirteenth century, warrior-Sūfis like Shaikh Sarmast accompanied the

357 *Nandiyāgamalīle*, 15.20.
358 Ibid., 15.21.
359 Ibid.
360 Kodekallu lies at a distance of less than an hour's journey on horseback from all these places.
361 Lorenzen 2006: 37-63, (i.e., chapter 2).
362 Olson 2015: 93.

invading Sultāns of Dilli.[363] The cult of the warrior-saint was certainly entrenched in various parts of the subcontinent by this time. By the fifteenth century, it had evolved into a form of military labour entrepreneurship. This entrepreneurship was dependent upon the peasantry, which provided mercenary labour. Thus, the peasant was the backbone of the warrior-saint cult.[364]

It is in this context of military labour entrepreneurship that another of Koḍēkallu Basava's initiatives assumes its importance. Northern Karnataka has a rich tradition of fortunetellers, or people endowed with the knowledge of time (*kālajñāna*). They were itinerant men and women who played a significant role in the exchange of information and spread of rumours. The men, known as *sāruvayya*s (i.e., 'those who spread the word'), trace their origin to Koḍēkallu Basava. The women, called *koravi*s, begin their prophecy by invoking the goddess Mahālakṣmī of Kolhāpura and Koḍēkallu Basava.[365] The *sāruvayya*s and *koravi*s were not Koḍēkallu Basava's innovations; the latter are, for that matter, found even in other parts of south India. The tradition of soothsaying seems to have existed in Karnataka before the time of Koḍēkallu Basava. Its origins remain obscure. In all likelihood, their role in the circulation of information and rumour was of no mean consequence. The genius of Koḍēkallu Basava rests in the facts that he was able to give the practice a new shape in the form of *kālajñāna*, and succeeded in organizing a network of *sāruvayya*s and *koravi*s, who brought their charismatic presence as 'knowers of time' to bear upon the assignment given to them of gathering information and spreading rumour. For, as an entrepreneur in the military labour market, Koḍēkallu Basava is sure to have known the importance of information and rumour in the art of warfare. The invoking of his name by *sāruvayya*s and *koravi*s to this day is evidence for the foundational role he played in orchestrating this network.

We must now ask an important question: What did Koḍēkallu Basava represent? He was a successful merchant. He travelled widely, and succeeded in convincing people of his greatness. He was devoted to his teacher, and killed people who came in his way. He dressed weirdly, caused bloodshed, performed miracles, cured people of diseases like leprosy, built a settlement of flourishing trade and enterprise, conferred 'kingship' on a hunter, confronted the king and brought him into submission, obtained land grants from the king, bestowed riches upon the believers, caused people to change their vocation, initiated the process of agrarian expansion in one of the driest areas of the region, built a militia, raided villages, reinforced local production relations and surplus appropriation, established a monastery, created new forms of knowledge, divined the future, wrote poetry, and made Śiva appear in front of his

363 Eaton 1978: 23-27.
364 In the context of north India, William Pinch has documented and commented upon the relationship, which the warrior-saint shared with the peasantry. See Pinch 1996. Also see Pinch 2006.
365 Viraktamath 2005: 63.

devotees. There should be no harm in suggesting, sarcastically, that our hero might as well have found proof for Fermat's Last Theorem, had he been presented with it. Koḍēkallu Basava represented the acme of a new selfhood that had begun to register its presence in the literary traditions of the early fifteenth century and snowballed, from the late fifteenth century onwards, into an ethic that would underwrite the dimensions of the individual and his or her self-awareness.

Our protagonist's case is by no means an exceptional one. William Pinch makes the following observation in the context of renouncers in the Gaṅgā valley:

> Monks...had strong opinions that informed and were informed by the goings-on in Gangetic society. They were willing and able (indeed expected) to leave behind the secure confines of the monastery, the contemplation of sacred texts and images, and the cycles of ritual and worship, to engage themselves in society's all-too-temporal concerns. Prior to 1800, such engagements included soldering, trade, banking, protecting pilgrimage sites and religious endowments, and enlisting as mercenaries in the armies of regional states.[366]

In the course of the fifteenth and the sixteenth centuries, the political economy in the region underwent further changes. With a substantial segment of long distance trade coming under the state's control, wherein the state either traded directly or functioned as regulator with an eye on the revenue, the exercise of control over rural markets began to develop a measure of autonomy in its own right. This was especially true of transactions in grain and sundry supplies, including oil and coarse cloth. Local trading networks were now centred on agrarian products, which brought them under the control of the landed elites. The increased demand for cash crop products reinforced the local trader's dependence on landlords. Among these cash crops were cotton, oilseed, and betel leaves. New crops introduced by the Portuguese, like red chili and cashew nut, might also have been under circulation, although it is unlikely that these were in great demand before the nineteenth century. In a hagiography of the seventeenth-century saint Sāvaḷagi Śivaliṅga, we find mention of the peasant landlords bringing a group of traders under their control. These were itinerant traders. They were many in number,[367] and dealt in nutmeg, masālā leaves, clove, areca nut, coconut, *koraku*, sugar, *manaki*, etc.[368] The peasantry had come under increased control of military entrepreneurs and landlords through processes that we will take up for discussion in chapter 5. In the new dispensation, where local mercantile groups in northern Karnataka became increasingly dependent on agrarian products, landlords found themself placed in an advantageous position that was historically decisive.

From the sixteenth century, a large number of monasteries began to appear in northern Karnataka. These represented the interests of the landed classes, as they

366 Pinch 1996: 6.

367 The expression is *nūrāru*, literally 106, but used colloquially to indicate 'hundreds'.

368 *Sāvaḷagi Śrīśivaliṅgēśvarapurāṇa*, 4.43.

supplied agrarian products on the one hand, and controlled the peasantry that supplied military labour on the other. Like the monastery founded by Koḍēkallu Basava, these establishments functioned in a centrifugal manner.[369] There was another respect in which the new monasteries were fundamentally different from the ones that existed in earlier centuries. The older monasteries drew their authority from their scriptures or textual traditions, or from the vision (*darśana*) they sought to accomplish, or the practices of renunciation they had developed. The new monasteries also had scriptures and books that were regarded as sacred. They developed their own unique visions of the Supreme, as well as practices of renunciation that led to the realization of these visions, but the scriptures, visions, and practices were no longer sources of authority. They were only among the essential functional components of the monastery, not the defining feature of what the monastery represented. The new source of authority was the figure of the individual in the form of a *guru*. The founder of the monastery was often the most revered of the *guru*s. His word, both written and oral, and his ideals, represented through legends, were worthy of adoration by the followers—notably worthy of adoration, not emulation. The works of Koḍēkallu Basava and his son Rācappa were preserved in the monastery in the form of manuscripts. The manuscripts were worshipped during festival and other special occasions, and read out like the chanting of *mantra*s. Their study was open only to the pontiffs and aspirants to the pontificate, and not to the followers.

The emphasis on the individual as the source of authority had two important consequences: (1) having lost their authority, texts, visions, and practices were now only secondary in importance, with bars removed from subjecting them to revision, discarding them at convenience, and drawing authority from sources of any other tradition; and (2) archetypal *guru* figures could be brought into the imagined genealogies of these traditions, irrespective of which tradition they actually belonged to. Thus, in the Mahānubhāva tradition, we have the following genealogy of teachers:[370]

Nāsir-ud-dīn Cirāg-e-Dillī alias Ādinātha alias Nāganātha

↓

Macchēndranātha

↓

Gōrakhanātha

↓

Gahinīnātha

↓

369 This tendency was by no means restricted to saints and their establishments. It also governed the political developments of the day. See Wink 1986.

370 Tarikere 1998: 56.

Nivṛttinātha
↓
Jñānēśvara
↓
Sōpāṇa
↓
Muktābāyi
↓
Visōbā Khēcara
↓
Cāṅgadēva
↓
Nāmdēv Siṃpi

The genealogy commences with a fourteenth century Sūfi saint of the Chisti order from Dilli, who is regarded as the teacher of Macchēndranātha or Matsyēndra, the mythical *guru* of the (eleventh-century?) founder of the Nātha tradition, Gōrakhanātha. Saints of the Vārkarī tradition of Maharashtra, such as Nivṛttinātha, Jñānēśvara, and Muktābāyi, also figure in this line of teachers.

The Chisti Order metamorphosed into the Caitanya tradition in parts of the Deccan.[371] Here, as in the case of the Mahānubhāva line, Nāsir-ud-dīn Cirāg-e-Dillī alias Nāganātha was identified as the founder. His disciples were Ala-ud-dīn Lāḍlē Maśāik or Rāghava Caitanya of Āḷande, Bandēnavāz or Kēśava Caitanya of Kalaburagi, and Śahāb-ud-dīn Bābā or Bābājī Caitanya of Mayināḷa. Rāghava Caitanya's line of disciples included Siddaliṅga of Āḷande and Majuṃdār of Junnār, Bandēnavāz was teacher to Navakōṭi Nārāyaṇa of Kalaburagi,[372] and Śahāb-ud-dīn, the teacher to Tukārāṃ.[373] In addition to the Caitanya tradition, Nāsir-ud-dīn Cirāg-e-Dillī appears as the teacher of a number of other traditions founded by the following *gurus*:[374]

1. Datta Caitanya of Vaḍabāḷa
2. Rāmabhaṭṭa of Māṅgāvi
3. Raghunātha of Khilāri
4. Timmaṇṇa Dhanagāra of Indūru
5. Kṛsṇābāyi of Hirve

---

371 Of course, this was not a fully developed tradition in its own right and, in addition, it should not be confused with the Gauḍīya Caitanya tradition.
372 Interestingly, Navakōṭi Nārāyaṇa is a title given to a chief called Śrīnivāsa Nāyaka, who later became a popular saint, Purandaradāsa.
373 Tarikere 1998: 56.
374 Ibid.

6. Ēkaliṅga Tēli of Maṇūru
7. Hegrāsasvāmi of Mahōḷa, and his three *khalīfās*, viz., Ajñānasiddha of Narēndra, Narēndrasiddha of Vaḍabāḷa, and Siddhaliṅga of Mahōḷa
8. Varadamma of Maṇūru
9. Baḍavva of Mārḍi
10. Narasiṃha of Apēgāv
11. Bahirāṃbhaṭṭa of Paiṭhāṇ

In another legend, Allama Prabhu is represented as Alaṃ Kamāl-ud-dīn and as the progenitor of five traditions:[375]

1. Himavanta Svāmi of Muḷagunda
2. Siddharāma of Sonnalāpura

    ↓

    Basava of Kalyāṇa

    ↓

    Cannabasava of Uḷavi
3. the sixty-three *purātanas* (i.e, the Nāyanārs of Tamilnadu)
4. Amīn-ud-dīn of Vijayapura

    ↓

    Fakīrappa of Śirahaṭṭi

    ↓

    Māḷiprabhu of Muḷagunda
5. Rāmaliṅga Āḷe of Kōlhāpura

That Sūfis like Nāsir-ud-dīn Cirāg-e-Dillī, Alā-ud-dīn Lāḍlē Maśaik, Bandēnavāz, and Śahāb-ud-dīn Bābā were worshipped as Ādinātha or Nāganātha, Rāghava Caitanya, Kēśava Caitanya, and Bābājī Caitanya respectively, corresponds to the fact that many Siddha saints were worshipped as Sūfis with Islamic names. Prominent among them were Allama Prabhu, regarded as Alaṃ Kamāl-ud-dīn, and the seventeenth-century saint poet Mōnappa or Mōnēśvara of Tinthiṇi, worshipped as Mōn-ud-dīn or Maun-ud-dīn. The annual fair of Mōnappa at Tinthiṇi is also referred to as *urus*, a Sūfi expression. The *urus* commences with the following call of *dīn*:

> *ēk lākh aiśī hazār pāñcō pīr paigaṃbar*
> *jītā pīr maun-ud-dīn kāśīpati har har mahādēv*

This may be loosely translated as: there are 1,80,000 saints, five of them are prophets, Maun-ud-dīn is the living prophet, hail Mahādēv, the lord of Kāśī.

375 Ibid.

These historical developments cannot be attributed to the singular initiatives of Koḍēkallu Basava, as antecedent developments are known to have taken place. Ahmad Śāh Bahmani (d. 1436), who patronized Bandēnavāz, is buried in Aṣṭūru in the Bīdara district. On his tomb is inscribed the word 'Allamaprabhu' in Devanagari letters.[376] The centripetalist initiatives of Jakkaṇārya and Lakkaṇṇa Daṇḍēśa also involved the use of teachers from diverse traditions, among them Gōrakṣa (Gōrakhanātha) and Muktāyakka (Muktābāyi), and adherents of *iṣṭaliṅga*, like Allama, and followers of *prāṇaliṅga*, like Siddharāma. There is a tomb-replica in Māḍyāḷa, where Koḍēkallu Basava is worshipped as Allama.[377] It was in the hands of Koḍēkallu Basava, though, that these developments found systematic expression and reinforcement. His ability to thoroughly integrate them with the class interests of the day served as a model for organization of class relations, and made the new monasteries of northern Karnataka a historically decisive force and an entrenched phenomenon.

Even as Koḍēkallu Basava was refashioning the praxis of renunciation in the north, the southern and coastal parts of Karnataka saw the rise of a diametrically opposite tendency in the praxis of sainthood. This was the Vaiṣṇavite *dvaita* sainthood promoted by the Kṛṣṇa temple of Uḍupi. Vyāsarāya, Vādirāja, Śrīpādarāya, Purandaradāsa, and Kanakadāsa were the preeminent representatives of this tendency, although all of them were not adherents of *dvaita*.[378] The lives of these saints shed precious light on the concerns of this emergent tradition, and its spheres of engagement.

Vādirāja was the pontiff of the Sōde maṭha, one of the eight monasteries of Uḍupi. He was a disciple of the *guru*, Vāgīśa Tīrtha. The *guru* was a devotee of Viṣṇu in his form as Bhūvarāha (the boar). Once, when he was observing his four-month monsoon retreat at the Kuṃbhēśvara temple in Kuṃbhāśi, a couple from the village of Hūvinakere, Sarasvatī Dēvi and Rāmācārya, arrived to seek his blessings.[379] They had no children. Vāgīśa Tīrtha prophesied that Bhūvarāha would bless them with two sons. He urged them to offer the first son to the Sōde maṭha. In due course, Sarasvatī Dēvi gave birth to two sons. The elder son, born in ca. 1480, was named Bhūvarāha. The couple handed him over to the *guru*. Vāgīśa Tīrtha initiated the young boy into sainthood and renamed him Vādirāja, literally 'a king among debaters'.

Vādirāja studied under Vāgīśa Tīrtha and evolved into a master of orthodox learning (such as logic, rhetoric, poetics, grammar, literature, and *vēdānta*). His skills

---

376 Ibid., 67.

377 The worship of a tomb (*gaddige*) is popular in the region. This was introduced by the Sūfis. There are also tomb-replicas (*tōru-gaddige*), where the replica of a tomb is worshipped in commemoration of a revered saint. On tomb worship in Karnataka, see the discussion in Assayag 2004.

378 Kanakadāsa, for instance, was a follower of Rāmānuja's *viśiṣṭādvaita* (evidence for which is presented in Kalburgi 2010 Vol. 4: 378-379), although he is regarded a *dvaita* saint by most scholars (which is not supported by evidence).

379 They are also known by the name Gaurī Dēvi and Dēvabhaṭṭa.

in debating were exceptional, and regarded within the tradition as second only to Ānanda Tīrtha's. The Vijayanagara king is believed to have conferred upon him the title of Prasaṅgābharaṇa Tīrtha, a jewel of oratory.

It is believed that each of the eight monasteries of Uḍupi was given charge of the affairs of the Kṛṣṇa temple for a period of two months in a circular roster. Vādirāja extended the period to two years. This was apparently done to provide time for the pontiffs to travel far and wide to engage in debates, and win over followers to their creed. Or so the modern-day hagiographer of Vādirāja, Aralu Mallige Parthasarathy, would have us believe.[380] A pontiff, who was in charge of the temple for two years, would take charge again only after fourteen years. Vādirāja put this valuable time to use, travelled to Kerala in the south and Gujarat in the north, and toured extensively in the Koṅkaṇ region, including Goa. At all places, he allegedly excelled in debates, and defeated numerous rivals. As a result, the rank of his followers began to swell.

Vādirāja visited many centres of pilgrimage across the subcontinent, and wrote an account of these centres, entitled *Tīrtha Prabandha*. Divided into four parts, the west, the north, the east, and the south, this work is of considerable interest for understanding the significance of a centre of pilgrimage to the *dvaita* practitioners of Uḍupi in the sixteenth century. Table 10 provides a list of these centres.

The list in the *Tirtha Prabandha* includes not only place-names, but also a number of rivers: Nētrāvati, Payasvini, Suvarṇā, Varadā, Dharmagaṅgā, Śālmali, Tāpti, Narmadā, Bāṇagaṅgā, Gōmatī, Kṛṣṇā, Gōdāvari, Kālindī, Gaṅgā, Phalgu, Tuṅgabhadra, Kāvēri, Tāmraparṇi, and Ghṛtamālā. It also refers to the mountain range of Sahyācala, and a forest, Naimiṣāraṇya.

It is clear from Table 10 that Vādirāja's interest was mostly in coastal Karnataka, which should not be surprising. What is of interest, though, is the conspicuous absence of centres of pilgrimage in mainland Karnataka. Harihara, Baṅkāpura, and the little-known Bidirahaḷḷi (Vēṇugrāma) are the only places named. We shall return to this question in chapter 6. Even more conspicuous is the absence of leading centres of pilgrimage such as Kēdāra (Kedarnath), Ṛṣīkēśa, Haridvāra, Gaṅgōtri, and Yamunōtri in the north. Śrīśailaṃ occurs in the list, but Siṃhācalaṃ does not. Śrīraṅgaṃ finds mention, but not Kāḷahasti, although the river Suvarṇamukhi flowing nearby is noticed. Uḍupi's rival, Śṛṅgēri, is also missing.

380 Parthasarathy 2011: 34.

Table 10. List of Pilgrimage Centres described in Vādirāja's Tīrtha Prabandha[381]

Sl. No.	West	North	East	South
1.	Paraśurāmakṣētra	Kṛṣṇavēṇi	Gaṅgā Delta	Śrīraṅgaṃ
2.	Uḍupi	Paṇḍharāpura	Purī	Candra Puṣkariṇī
3.	Pājaka	Gōdāvari	Śrīśailaṃ	Kāvēri
4.	Vimānagiri	Kālindī	Ahōbala	Vṛṣabhācala
5.	Śivakṣētra	Prayāga	Tuṅgabhadra	Nūpuragaṅgā
6.	Nandikēśvara	Gaṅgā	Haṃpi	Darbhaśayana
7.	Madhyavāṭa	Kāśi	Ānēgondi	Rāmasētu
8.	Vētravati Narasiṃha	Gayā	Tirupati	Rāmēśvaraṃ
9.	Nētrāvati	Viṣṇupāda	Suvarṇamukhi	Dhanuṣkōṭi
10.	Kumāradhārā	Phalgu	Kāñcīpuraṃ	Tāmraparṇi
11.	Uppinaṅgaḍi	Mathurā	Tiruvaṇṇāmalai	Mahēndraśaila
12.	Subrahmaṇya	Vṛndāvana	Tirukōyilūr	Kanyākumāri
13.	Payasvini	Ayōdhyā	Vṛddhācalaṃ	Śucīndraṃ
14.	Suvarṇā	Naimiṣāraṇya	Śrīmuṣṇa	Anantaśayana
15.	Kuṃbhāśi	Hastināvatī	Kuṃbhakōṇaṃ	Ghṛtamālā
16.	Gautamakṣētra	Kurukṣētra		Tiruvanantapuraṃ
17.	Kōṭēśvara	Śaṃbala		
18.	Śaṅkaranārāyaṇa	The 6 Prayāgas		
19.	Kollūru	Badarī		
20.	Sahyagiri			
21.	Harihara			
22.	Vēṇugrāma			
23.	Baṅkāpura			
24.	Varadā			
25.	Dharmagaṅgā			
26.	Śālmali			
27.	Sōde			
28.	Mañjuguṇi			
29.	Ēṇabhairavakṣētra			
30.	Gōkarṇa			
31.	Kōlhāpura			
32.	Tāpti			
33.	Narmadā			
34.	Prabhāsa			
35.	Bāṇagaṅgā			
36.	Dvārakā			
37.	Gōmatī			
38.	Cakratīrtha			
39.	Śaṅkōddhāra			
40.	Gōpīcandana			
41.	Siddhapuri			
42.	Puṣkara			

381 Source: *Tīrtha Prabandha*.

During his sojourn at Pūnā, Vādirāja noticed that Māgha's Sanskrit work, the *Śiśupālavadha*, was being honoured by the learned men of the city. He challenged the greatness of this work, and spread the falsehood that a greater work exists at Uḍupi and would be produced before them within nineteen days. He then sat down to compose the *Rukmiṇīśavijaya*, completed it in nineteen days, presented it to the scholars of Pūnā, and won praise for it.[382] In the following years, he wrote a number of other works, like the *Yuktimallikā*, which was a summary of the essence of the *Brahmasūtra*s, the *Lakṣābharaṇa*, a commentary on the *Mahābhārata*, the *Gurvarthadīpikā*, a commentary on Jaya Tīrtha's *Nyāyasudhā* and *Tatvaprakāśikā*, and the *Pāṣaṇḍamatakhaṇḍana*, a critique of rival schools. More than seventy works in Sanskrit are attributed to him, many of them short *stōtra*s in praise of god. Vādirāja also wrote numerous songs in Kannada, and a handful of longer devotional works too, like the *Bhramaragīte*, the *Lakṣmīśōbhāne*, the *Vaikuṇṭhavarṇane*, the *Tatvasuvvāli*, the *Svapnapada*, the *Guṇḍakriye*, etc.

Vādirāja's oeuvre was remarkable for its vast and encyclopedic learning. His defence and exposition of the *dvaita* system were admirable for the deep understanding they presented. However, Vādirāja was only adhering to the system developed by Ānanda Tīrtha and Jaya Tīrtha, too faithfully so to speak, without making original contributions to develop the system further. He made no innovations in terms of arguments or descriptions of the cosmology to expand and refine the system. On rare occasions, he used proverbs with rustic wisdom as metaphors in his work. One such instance, meant to proclaim Kṛṣṇa's immanence, occurs in the *Bhramaragīte*: the wise ones say that the *aśvattha* (pipal tree), which confers the required boon upon the world, was born of crow's droppings.[383] In the *Lakṣmīśōbhāne*, he says: who has ever hidden an elephant in a measuring bowl? Can a mother's womb hold Śrīhari, who ruled many ten million unborn eggs and atoms from the pores of his body?[384] One may certainly wish that this use of rusticity could be consistently found in his works.

Some incidents in the life of Vādirāja are of interest to us. Once a *jāgīrdār* in a town was celebrating his son's wedding. Unfortunately, a snake bit the groom, and he fainted. Learning that Vādirāja was camping in the town, the *jāgīrdār* carried the groom to him. Vādirāja placed the groom on his lap, and prayed to Goddess Lakṣmī for a remedy. Lakṣmī instructed him to sing a song that described her marriage with Viṣṇu. Vādirāja sang the *Lakṣmīśōbhāne* he had composed earlier. The groom was miraculously freed of the venom.[385]

382 Māgha's *Śiśupālavadha* is generally regarded as the most difficult text in Sanskrit *kāvya* literature. To produce a work that excels the *Śiśupālavadha* was to outshine and dethrone the best. This is not an uncommon tendency in hagiographic convention.

383 *Bhramaragīte*, 46.

384 *Laksmīśōbhāne*, 5.44.

385 Parthasarathy 2011: 103.

On another occasion, a childless *jāgīrdār* approached Vādirāja with the request to confer a son upon him. Vādirāja sent him back saying that he was not destined to have a child in this life, and that he had to wait until his next birth to have his wish fulfilled. The disappointed *jāgīrdār* met a magician, who fulfilled his wish in exchange for an amount of five thousand gold coins. Two thousand coins were paid immediately with the agreement that the rest of the money would be paid after the child was born. When the child was born, the contented *jāgīrdār* gave eight thousand gold coins to the magician, far in excess of what he had originally promised. He showed off the child proudly to Vādirāja, when the latter visited the village again. Vādirāja told the *jāgīrdār* that it was not really a child but a demon implanted by the magician with instructions to return back to him after slaying the *jāgīrdār* and his wife at the age of six. He then sprinkled holy water from his jar on the child, and lo!, the child was transformed into the demon. Vādirāja conferred special powers on the demon and instructed him to kill the magician. The story urges us to concede that Vādirāja's timely intervention saved the *jāgīrdār* and his wife from disaster.[386]

Vādirāja was once hosted by the Jaina chief Tirumalarasa Cauṭa of Mūḍabidari. In the *pūjā* chamber of the chief's house was the beautiful image of a Jina, made of emerald. "What image is this?" Vādirāja asked the chief. "It is the Jina I worship," Tirumalarasa replied. "No", Vādirāja refuted, "this looks like the image of Viṭṭhala". He urged the chief to gift him the figure if upon closer examination it turned out to be an image of Viṭṭhala. The chief agreed. Vādirāja took the Jina image in his hands, where it transformed miraculously into an image of Viṭṭhala. Tirumalarasa had no choice but to forego the cherished emerald image.[387]

Vādirāja spent his last years in Sōde. The chief of Sōde, Arasappa Nāyaka, built the Trivikrama temple and installed the Lakṣmī Trivikrama image there in honour of Vādirāja. In these years, Vādirāja oversaw the construction of the Candramauḷīśvara, the Māruti, and the Śrīkṛṣṇa temples, and the Dhavaḷagaṅga lake at Sōde. He passed away at Sōde, sometime after 1571.[388] Conventional accounts have ascribed him a long life of 120 years, placing his death in the year 1600.

There are many points of convergence between the lives of Koḍēkallu Basava and Vādirāja. Both were great masters of their respective systems. Both composed poetry, travelled widely, defeated adversaries, built temples or monasteries. Yet, it is the differences that strike us most. Koḍēkallu Basava was hostile to the king, although he promoted a petty chief. He built an army and functioned as a leading warrior-saint. He performed miracles, and caused qualitative changes in the economic conditions of his followers. Vādirāja on the other hand maintained cordial relations

386 Ibid., 104-105.

387 Ibid., 105.

388 In 1571, Vādirāja received a grant from the Keḷadi chief Rāmarāja Nāyaka (No. 34, Jois 1991). So his death might have occurred after this date.

with the Vijayanagara rulers and the chiefs under them, such as the Nāyakas of Sōde and Keḷadi. Building an army was not his forte. Nor are anecdotes told of how he brought material prosperity into the lives of his followers. Vādirāja did not perform miracles, certainly not on a scale comparable to Koḍēkallu Basava's. He was able to miraculously cure the son of a *jāgīrdār* of snakebite, but only with the blessings of Lakṣmī, and by following a course mentioned by her. The story of rescuing a *jāgīrdār* from the demon-child and the incident where the Jina image metamorphosed into an image of Viṭṭhala have enough supernatural content in them to qualify as miracles. But, Vādirāja is not revered within the tradition as a miracle-worker. The respect he commands comes from the fact that he was an embodiment, and vigorous promoter, of orthodox knowledge and submissive devotion. To put the contrast between the two saints in a nutshell, Koḍēkallu Basava represented the ethic of enterprise, Vādirāja, the ethic of complacency.

Let us briefly examine the life of another major saint of the *dvaita* tradition. Śrīpādarāya was born sometime in the early fifteenth century (perhaps 1404) at Abbūru on the banks of River Kaṇvā in the Cannapaṭṭaṇa tālūk of Rāmanagaraṃ district, between Beṅgalūru and Maisūru. His parents Giriyamma and Śēṣagiriyappa gave him the name Lakṣmīnārāyaṇa. Giriyamma's elder sister was the mother of the saint Brahmaṇya Tīrtha, whose maṭha exists in Abbūru.[389]

Lakṣmīnārāyaṇa's childhood seems to have been spent in poverty. His parents owned a herd of cattle, which the boy took out for grazing. Once, the saint Svarṇavarṇa Tīrtha of Śrīraṅgaṃ happened to be visiting Abbūru to meet with Puruṣōttama Tīrtha, who had attained some renown in the region. On the way, he chanced upon Lakṣmīnārāyaṇa and was attracted by the boy's character. He expressed his desire to have the boy as a disciple. Puruṣōttama Tīrtha summoned Giriyamma and Śēṣagiriyappa, and urged them to hand over Lakṣmīnārāyaṇa to Svarṇavarṇa Tīrtha, as he would initiate the boy into brāhmaṇahood through the rite of *brahmōpadēśa*, and take care of his schooling. That the boy's cousin Brahmaṇya Tīrtha had to be given away to the monastery was already cause for bitterness in the family. Giriyamma was reluctant to give her son away. But the request had come from the revered Puruṣōttama Tīrtha. She had no choice but to yield.

Svarṇavarṇa performed the rite of *brahmōpadēśa*, and began training the boy. In some years' time, Lakṣmīnārāyaṇa was initiated into renunciation and recognized as Svarṇavarṇa's successor to the pontificate. He was sent to Vibhudēndra Tīrtha for higher learning. Under Vibhudēndra's tutelage, Lakṣmīnārāyaṇa became an expert in the *dvaita* system. A test of his knowledge was held under the supervision of Raghunātha Tīrtha. Lakṣmīnārāyaṇa excelled in the test by commenting upon a major text of the system. It was Raghunātha Tīrtha who conferred upon him the name

---

389 Varadarajarao 1987: i.

Śrīpādarāya. In the course of time, Śrīpādarāya succeeded Svarṇavarṇa to become the eighth pontiff of the monastery at Śrīraṅgaṃ.[390]

Some years later, Srīpādarāya set out on a long pilgrimage, which brought him to Paṇḍharpur in southern Maharashtra, which was the preeminent centre of the Vārkharī tradition. Here, he found two large chests on the banks of the river Bhīma. One of them contained an image of Raṅgaviṭṭhala. Śrīpādarāya became a devotee of this deity and began worshipping him. However, he failed to open the other chest.

In the course of his tour, Śrīpādarāya reached Muḷabāgilu in the Kōlāra district of Karnataka. The place was associated with another saint, Akṣōbhya Tīrtha, who is said to have drawn an image of Yōgānarasiṃha with cinders. Akṣōbhya is also said, in a fictitious story, to have engaged Vidyāraṇya in a debate at Muḷabāgilu, in which the redoubtable *viśiṣṭādvaita* master, Vēdānta Dēśikan, acting as referee, declared Akṣōbhya victorious. Śrīpādarāya decided to settle down here, and built a monastery on the outskirts of the town.

The reasons for Śrīpāda's migration from Śrīraṅgaṃ to Muḷabāgilu are not clear from the hagiographies. In the early decades of the fourteenth century, the Uttamanaṃbi family of Śrīvaiṣṇavas (of the Rāmānuja tradition) had become powerful at Śrīraṅgaṃ. They were also successful in attracting Vijayanagara support for their cause.[391] It is likely that the Uttamanaṃbis entered into conflicts with the *dvaita* school of Śrīpāda, forcing him to move out of Śrīraṅgaṃ. Alternately, Śrīpāda might have aspired for patronage from the Vijayanagara rulers. If he sought out royal support, we must conclude that he made little gains until the 1470s and 80s, when the Saṅgama control over southern India declined and the Sāḷuva aspiration to replace them became manifest. Many a saint seems to have succeeded in forging a strategic alliance with the Sāḷuvas. Kandāḍai Rāmānujadāsar was one such saint. "The available evidence", writes Arjun Appadurai, "makes it difficult to identify this person. But it seems fairly certain that he rose from obscurity to prominence by the appropriate manipulation of his "discipleship" to prominent sectarian leaders and his trading of this credential for political currency under the Sāḷuvas at Tirupati".[392] It is for this reason that the Uttamanaṃbis had to make concessions for Rāmānujadāsar, although they were still in control of Śrīraṅgaṃ.[393] Like Rāmānujadāsar, Śrīpādarāya was also successful in establishing a close relationship with the Sāḷuva state.

Sometime around the year 1475, Brahmaṇya Tīrtha passed away. His young disciple Vyāsarāya (b. ca. 1460), whom Brahmaṇya had nominated his successor, left for Kāñcīpuraṃ to continue his studies. From there, he reached Muḷabāgilu, where

---

390 This monastery is believed to have been founded by Ānanda Tīrtha's disciple Padmanābha Tīrtha.

391 Appadurai 1981: 88.

392 Ibid., 89.

393 Ibid.

he accepted Śrīpādarāya as his teacher. Śrīpāda turned out to be a foundational influence on Vyāsarāya.

The relationship the *guru* shared with his new disciple was divinely ordained, and is exemplified by a story. Once, Śrīpādarāya entrusted Vyāsarāya with the task of carrying out the daily worship at the monastery in Muḷabāgilu. In the course of his *pūjā*, Vyāsarāya chanced upon an unopened chest. This was one of the two chests Śrīpādarāya had found at Paṇḍharpur. No one had succeeded in opening the chest. Vyāsarāya picked up the chest, and opened it effortlessly. From the box emerged Lord Veṇugōpāla, playing his flute. In his ecstasy, Vyāsarāya picked up a *sāḷagrāma* stone placed nearby, and began beating it like a drum and dancing it to the tunes. The other disciples in the monastery were surprised by the miracle, and reported it to Śrīpādarāya. No sooner did Śrīpādarāya arrive on the scene than Vēṇugōpāla froze into an image. Śrīpādarāya realized that of the two images he had retrieved from Paṇḍharpur, the image of Raṅgaviṭṭhala was meant for him and that of Vēṇugōpāla for his disciple. Vyāsarāya was permitted to own the image and worship it.[394]

It was around the time when Vyāsarāya reached Muḷabāgilu that the Saṅgama state of Vijayanagara was disintegrating. Sāḷuva Narasiṃha, who had designs to establish a kingdom of his own, was very active during this period. He established contacts with Śrīpādarāya and became one of his leading benefactors. According to a legend, Sāḷuva Narasiṃha had put to death the Tirupati temple priest and his son on charges of corruption. Thus, he incurred the sin of killing a brāhmaṇa (*brahmahatyādōṣa*), which was one of the five great sins (*pañcamahāpātaka*). He found no help from anybody in securing release from this sin. At this time, news reached him that Śrīpādarāya of Muḷabāgilu had freed a person from *brahmahatyādōṣa* with the holy water from his conch. Sāḷuva Narasiṃha sought his help. Śrīpāda sprinkled him with water from his conch, and released him from the great sin.[395] Whether or not this story is true, it clearly points to the favourable nexus Śrīpāda was able to forge with the Vijayanagara state.

It is said that Śrīpādarāya's opponents ridiculed him for making false claims that he was endowed with powers to release men from the sin of slaying a brāhmaṇa with water from his conch. Śrīpādarāya challenged them to clean the dark spots caused on a white piece of cloth by the oil from the *gēru* fruit. The opponents failed. Now, Śrīpāda poured water from his conch and cleansed the white cloth, and brought the opponents into submission.[396]

The rest of Śrīpādarāya's life was spent in teaching, devotion, composition of poetry, and defeating rivals. In one story told of him, Śrīpāda figures as a glutton, like Ānanda Tīrtha, consuming huge quantities of raw fruits and vegetables. When rivals

394 Varadarajarao 1987: x-xi.
395 Ibid., viii-ix.
396 Ibid.

ridiculed him for this, he is said to have produced back from his belly all the food he had consumed. The fruits and vegetables remained fresh. The rivals were beaten once again.

A long life of ninety-eight years is assigned to Śrīpādarāya, which places his death in ca. 1502. Before his death, he nominated Hayagrīva Tīrtha as his successor. Vyāsarāya would have been the ideal choice, had he not already been pontiff of the maṭha at Abbūru when he had accepted Śrīpāda as his teacher.

An important achievement of Śrīpādarāya was forging for the *dvaita* tradition healthy ties of patronage and reciprocation with the Vijayanagara state. To what extent was his role significant in the rise of Sāḷuva Narasiṃha to the centre-stage of Vijayanagara polity can only be speculated. There is no evidence that helps us to reflect upon this question at some length. But Śrīpāda introduced Vyāsarāya to Sāḷuva Narasiṃha, which must be considered a decisive move. In the years to come, Vyāsarāya became an important mouthpiece, as it were, of the religion promoted by the state. It is a matter of regret indeed that he ended up as one of the two greatest masters of existing knowledge in the history of the *dvaita* system (the other being Vādirāja), without causing innovations in the system built by Ānanda Tīrtha and Jaya Tīrtha.

Śrīpādarāya's life, like Vādirāja's, stands out for the manner in which in contrasts with Koḍēkallu Basava's. Although a traveller, poet, and a leading representative of his system, traits that most respected saints shared, Śrīpādarāya raised no army, fought no battles, and performed no miracles that was striking enough for him to be recognized as a miracle-worker. Nor is he credited with public works like excavating tanks or causing agriculture to expand. Unlike Koḍēkallu Basava's engagement with Isupāśca and the other kings he met during his fabled voyage, Śrīpāda's ties with the state was cordial and patronizing. References to the peasant and mercantile classes do not occur in the stories told of him. He was, like Vādirāja, the figurehead of orthodox learning that laid stress on the ethic of submission and complacency.

The comparison between Koḍēkallu Basava on the one hand, and Vādirāja and Śrīpādarāya on the other, leads us to an important conclusion. There had occurred in the course of the late fifteenth and the early sixteenth century, a great divergence in the praxis of sainthood in the Deccan region. Two distinct tendencies had emerged and gained deep roots: the first centered on the ethic of enterprise, which involved acts and initiatives ranging from public works and agrarian expansion to warfare and murder; the other revolved around the ethic of complacency, which called for devotion, submission, and singing praise of the Lord. This was a distinction of no mean consequence. The image of the saint would henceforth oscillate around these conflicting ethics. It is to this divergence that we must now turn.

5 Miracles, Ethicality, and the Great Divergence

The discussions in chapter 4 ended with the suggestion that a great divergence began to take shape in the praxis of renunciation in the Deccan region in the late fifteenth century. We must now set out to explore and unpack this divergence.

Two prominent trends in renunciation made their appearance in this period. Each articulated itself in a form that was remarkably different from the other, although it is unlikely that this was done consciously to meet doctrinal, epistemological, or eschatological ends. There were, as a matter of fact, shared hagiographic motifs, similar emphases on doctrinal issues, and overlaps and exchanges between them. All the same, their boundaries were not too porous to be infiltrated by the other to an extent that would obliterate the uniqueness found embedded in them.

The two sets of traditions were not monolithic blocs, but internally differentiated tendencies engulfing a wide range of monastic traditions and practices of renunciation. We may, for the sake of convenience, call them the *dāsa* and the *siddha* ethic, respectively, for want of better expressions. However, these broad umbrella-categories must not blind us to the fact that the *dāsa*s comprised of saints who followed diverse traditions like *dvaita*, and the *teṅgalai* (southern) and *vaḍagalai* (northern) schools of *viśiṣṭādvaita*,[397] or that the *siddha*s consisted of Vīraśaivas, Ārūḍhas, Avadhūtas, Pañcācāryas, Nāthas (also called Avadhūtas), Dattas, Viraktas, etc., and adherents of diverse practices like *kaivalya*, *karasthala*, *iṣṭaliṅga ārādhane* (of which the *karasthala* was a variant), *prāṇaliṅga ārādhane*, *khaṇḍajñāna*, *kālajñāna*, *nītijñāna*, *bōdhajñāna*, and so on.

The defining features of these traditions were certainly not new and yet, they were very infrequently noticed before the fifteenth century. The great initiatives that began with Mahaliṅgadēva and Śivagaṇaprasādi Mahādēvayya, and carried forward in the court of Dēvarāya II at Vijayanagara by Jakkaṇa and Lakkaṇṇa Daṇḍēśa, brought the *siddha* ethic to the centre-stage, and facilitated its propagation. Although the days of Jakkaṇa and Lakkaṇṇa Daṇḍēśa saw the high-noon of Vīraśaiva doctrinal creativity, it was only towards the later half of the fifteenth century and the early sixteenth century that it developed a genuinely popular appeal. We have already seen how this took shape in northern Karnataka in the hands of Koḍēkallu Basava. In southern Karnataka, the process took the form of composing hagiographies and exegetical literature. Gubbiya Mallaṇārya wrote the monumental *Vīraśaivāmṛtapurāṇa* in 1530-31. It is by far the most ambitious exposition of Vīraśaiva doctrines after the *Śivatatvacintāmaṇi* of Lakkaṇṇa Daṇḍēśa. Seventeen years earlier, in 1513-14, he had written the *Bhāvacintāratna*, which claims to be a Kannada rendition of the story of Satyēndra Cōḷa. Some decades before Mallaṇārya, another prominent saint

397 The *viśiṣṭādvaita* tradition in Karnataka had its headquarters in Mēlukōṭe, which is not examined by us in this study for want of space.

of southern Karnataka, Tōṇṭada Siddhaliṅga, wrote the *Ṣaṭsthalajñānasārāmṛta* (ca. 1470), which was a treatise on the *ṣaṭsthala* system.

Around the year 1485, a major change occurred in the political landscape of South India. The Saṅgama state of Vijayanagara collapsed, and the throne usurped by Sāḷuva Narasiṃha. The Sāḷuvas ruled for two decades. During their last years, political control was effectively in the hands of the Tuḷuva chief, Narasa Nāyaka. He died in 1503. Two years later, in 1505, his son Tuḷuva Narasiṃha seized throne. Thus began the Tuḷuva rule, which lasted up to 1565.[398] The most famous ruler in this line was Kṛṣṇarāya[399] (r. 1509-1529). Under the Sāḷuvas and the Tuḷuvas, the Vijayanagara state became ardent promoters of Vaiṣṇavism. Royal support to the Śṛṅgēri maṭha declined. The focus of attention shifted to the Veṅkaṭēśvara temple in Tirupati. This shift was accompanied by a change in the doctrinal preferences of the Vijayanagara rulers. They moved away from *advaita* to patronize saints who offered a critique of Śaṅkara's influential system. Thus did saints like Vallabha gain in importance in the capital city of Vijayanagara; "it was Vallabha's victory over the Māyāvādīs that ultimately led to his formal authorization in matters doctrinal."[400]

This was in keeping with the larger assertion of Vaiṣṇava devotionalism across large parts of the subcontinent in the sixteenth century. Vallabha, Rāmānanda, Kabīr, Tulsīdās, Sūrdās, Kēśavdās, Rāidās, and others in the Gaṅgā valley, Mīrā in Rajasthan, and Caitanya in Bengal, were leading advocates of Vaiṣṇava devotionalism. Ceṟuśśēri, Tuñjattŭ Rāmānujan Eḻuttaccan, Pūndānaṃ Naṃbūdiri, and Mēlpattūr Nārāyaṇa Bhaṭṭadiri espoused its cause in Kerala. In Odisha, it began with Śāraḷādāsa in the mid fifteenth century and snowballed into a far-reaching historical phenomenon under the *pañcasakhās* (five comrades), Baḷarāmadāsa, Jagannāthadāsa, Acyutānandadāsa, Yaśavantadāsa, and Śiśu Anantadāsa, in the early sixteenth century. The *pañcasakhā*s, especially Jagannāthadāsa, developed strong ties of friendship with Caitanya, and were also supported by the Sūryavaṃśi Gajapati king, Pratāparudra. To the west of Odisha, in the Marāṭha country, Ēknāth, and later, Tukārāṃ and Bahinābāyi in the seventeenth century, were the chief advocates of Vaiṣṇavism. They belonged to the Vārkharī tradition that was given shape and direction in the thirteenth and the fourteenth centuries by Jñānēśvara, Muktābāyi, Nāmdēv, and Cōkhāmēlā.

Annamayya, based in Tirupati, was the leading sixteenth-century voice of Vaiṣṇava devotionalism in the Telugu-speaking region. In Karnataka, Uḍupi rose as the preeminent centre of Vaiṣṇavism under the charismatic leadership of Vādirāja.

---

398 Of no mean importance is the fact that the Bahmani state also began to disintegrate at about the same time, when in 1489, Yūsuf Ādil Khān established the Ādil Śāhi state at Vijayapura. The Bahmani state finally collapsed in 1527.

399 The Kṛṣṇadēvarāya of modern historiography.

400 Hawley 2015: 209. See ibid, 190-229 (i.e. chapter 5) for an engaging discussion on this shift.

The Haridāsas, including Vādirāja, Vyāsarāya, Śrīpādarāya, Kanakadāsa, and Purandaradāsa, became influential propagators of this emergent creed.

The great divergence between the *siddha* and the *dāsa* ethics unfurled across many domains. We will examine some of them briefly.

Let us begin with the question of place. The *siddhas* were always known after the place where they lived for a long time, or where they eventually came to rest. Thus, Koḍēkallu Basava, Diggi Saṅgamanātha, Vaḍabāḷada Nāganātha, Galagada Cannabasava, Sālōṭagi Cannabasava, Nāgāvi Īrappayya, Tinthiṇi or Varavi Mōnappa, Śirahaṭṭi Fakīrappa, Sāvaḷagi Śivaliṅga, Muḷagundada Māḷiprabhu, Gūgi Candā Sāhēb, Indūru Timmaṇṇa Dhanagāra, Mahōḷada Hegrāsasvāmi, and so on. This contrasts with the *dāsas*, who almost invariably were never identified between the fifteenth and the eighteenth centuries with a place. Kanaka's close association with the village of Kāginele is known from his songs in which 'Kāginele Ādikēśavarāya' occurs as a signature. But he was never known as Kāginele Kanakadāsa. No such place-name prefix occurs in the names of Vādirāja, Vyāsarāya, Purandaradāsa, Śrīpādarāya, or Annamayya either.

Complementing this fact is another interesting difference. The *dāsas* often affiliated themselves with important political and commercial centres, or centres of pilgrimage, such as Vijayanagara, Tirupati, Paṇḍharpur, and Uḍupi. Kanakadāsa is known to have travelled to Uḍupi and Tirupati. Purandaradāsa also was associated with these two places in addition to Panḍharpur. Vādirāja was pontiff of the Sōde maṭha at Uḍupi, and visited Tirupati. Śrīpādarāya lived for many years in Śrīraṅgaṃ, and is known to have maintained close ties with the Vijayanagara court in Haṃpi, besides travelling to Paṇḍharpur. These centres went on to develop their own *sthalapurāṇas* or *sthalamāhātymas*, i.e., sacred legends on the greatness of the place. Some of them even made their way into the great Sanskrit *paurāṇic* texts. For instance, an account of Tirupati occurs in the Sanskrit *Skandapurāṇa*. This contrasts with *siddha* centres like Koḍēkallu, Sāvaḷagi, Varavi, Śirahaṭṭi, Kaḍakōḷa, Diggi, etc., none of which ever produced a *sthalapurāṇa* or a *sthalamāhātyma*, although it was not difficult to find entry into the *Skandapurāṇa*, which was regarded as a scrapbook of sorts.[401]

The next question that warrants reflection is the extent to which the *dāsas* and *siddhas* were commemorated. This may be examined by comparing the degrees to which their presence was historically felt or remembered at places associated with them. The case of Śirahaṭṭi Fakīrappa and Kanakadāsa serve as exemplary instances.

Śirahaṭṭi is a sleepy little town in the Gadaga district of Karnataka, lying at a short distance from the Kappattaguḍḍa range. It is also the headquarters of the tālūk. The neighbouring town of Lakṣmēśvara, the good old Puligeṟe, has a longer history, and

---

401 The *Skandapurāṇa* is pejoratively called the *Kantalpurāṇaṃ* (scrap *purāṇa*) in Tamil, as it turned out to be a 'scrap-bag' into which any place seeking respectability could infiltrate. See Doniger 2013: 233-234.

a more powerful mercantile presence. We have seen that Mahaliṅgadēva belonged to this town, and that Ādayya built the Sōmēśvara temple here. Lakṣmēśvara also commands a greater agrarian hinterland than Śirahaṭṭi. Besides, it is better connected, as it lies on the Hāvēri-Gadaga highway, and is closer to Savaṇūru, where Abdul Raūf Khān established a chiefdom after obtaining a *mansabdāri* of 6000 rank from the Mughal ruler Auraṅgzēb in 1686.[402] Other important towns like Aṇṇigeṟe, Guḍagēri, and Saṃśi, and leading hubs of commerce, like Hubbaḷḷi (Hubli), Gadaga, and Hāvēri, are easily reached from Lakṣmēśvara. Yet, it is the relatively backward Śirahaṭṭi that has been the headquarters of the tālūk. This is due in large part to the importance Śirahaṭṭi has in the religious history of the region. The town is home to the shrine and tomb of Fakīrappa (d. ca. 1725).

The saint has a ubiquitous presence in the town. There is a cinema hall in front of the maṭha. It is named after Fakīrappa. The degree college (i.e., college for undergraduate education) in the town is also named after him. It is not uncommon to find shops and business establishments in Śirahaṭṭi bearing his name. Fakīrappa is to Śirahaṭṭi what Veṅkaṭēśvara is to Tirupati or Jagannātha is to Puri. He is, verily, the defining feature of the town.

A hundred kilometres to the south of Śirahaṭṭi is the village of Kāginele. It nestles in the midst of rich maize fields and areca nut orchards, and is fifteen kilometres south of the district headquarters, Hāvēri. The place is associated with the name of Kanakadāsa, known for his devotional songs (*kīrtane*). Kāginele's contrast with Śirahaṭṭi cannot be more striking. Kanakadāsa is nowhere to be seen in the town. An image of the saint is found in the Ādikēśava temple. This was installed sometime in the mid twentieth century by devotees from Nañjanagūḍu near Maisūru. There is no information on where in the village he lived, or where he was eventually laid to rest. Kanakadāsa's presence in Kāginele is too remote even to be considered marginal.[403]

The differences between Fakīrappa and Kanakadāsa are crucial for the purposes of our analysis. They were not constituted idiosyncratically or doctrinally, nor were they determined by the degrees of influences the two saints were able to exercise. They follow a clearly discernable pattern along the lines of the *siddha-dāsa* divergence that can be seen elsewhere in the region. Take the village of Tinthiṇi, for instance. It lies on the desolate rocky stretches of the Śōrāpura doab on the river Kṛṣṇa, but attracts a steady stream of pilgrims (ranging from one hundred to two thousand every day)

402 Devadevan 2010a.

403 Things have of course changed over the last decade. When I visited Kāginele in 1998, no one to whom I spoke knew of any site or remains associated with Kanakadāsa. That the saint was associated with their village was not part of their living memory, but a fact known to them only through his songs in which 'Kāginele Ādikēśavarāya' was used as signature. This state of affairs continued during subsequent visits in 1999, 2001, 2002 and 2004. During my next visit in 2006, 'memories' concerning Kanakadāsa had begun to circulate.

to the shrine of Mōnappa, where his tomb is worshipped. Life in Tinthiṇi gravitates towards this shrine. The annual fair, which is known after the Islamic fashion as *urus*, attracts 75,000 to 100,000 devotees.[404] Mōnappa's presence is equally ubiquitous in Varavi, where he lived for some years. Varavi is in the Gadaga district, only three kilometres away from Fakīrappa's Śirahatti. The pattern found in Śirahaṭṭi, Tinthiṇi, and Varavi also occurs in many other *siddha* centres established between the late fifteenth and the mid eighteenth centuries. The shrine hosting the tomb of Śivaliṅga in Sāvaḷagi, twenty kilometres northwest of Gōkāk in the Beḷagāvi district, provides one such instance. The shrine is the heart of Sāvaḷagi, and Śivaliṅga, the purpose and meaning of the village. Over 75,000 devotees arrive to attend the annual fair of Sāvaḷagi. Even in a city like Kalaburagi, which was politically powerful for many centuries and where the tomb of Bandēnavāz attracts a large number of pilgrims, the presence of Śaraṇabasava is overarching. His temple is a major landmark in the city, and one of its most prominent centres of pilgrimage. It draws a crowd of over 200,000 devotees during the annual fair. Similarly, Koḍēkallu Basava has a towering presence in Koḍēkallu, although his shrine stands no comparison to the respect that the tombs of Fakīrappa, Mōnappa, Śivaliṅga, and Śaraṇabasava command in Śirahaṭṭi, Varavi,

---

A rectangular stone column lying in a corner of the village near the lake had come to be identified as the saint's tomb. This column was originally regarded by the Muslim residents of the village as the tomb of a Sūfi saint called Ādaṃ Śippi. It was now being represented as the tomb of Kanakadāsa, although tomb-worship was alien to the dāsa traditions. This 'retrieval of memory' was part of the political mobilization of the Kuruba (traditionally shepherd) caste, to which Kanakadāsa allegedly belonged. (It is, however, suggested in Kalburgi 2010 Vol.4: 376-377, on firmer grounds that Kanakadāsa came from the Bēḍa (hunter) caste.) This mobilization was carried out under the guidance of the Bharatiya Janata Party, the influential political group representing the Hindu Right, which had joined the Janata Dal (Secular) to form a coalition government in February 2006, and which came to power on its own (with three seats short of a simple a majority) in May 2008. Similar mobilizations were attempted by other parties, such as the Congress (I). When the Congress (I) came to power in May 2013, it was a prominent leader of the Kuruba caste, Siddaramaiah, who was elected Chief Minister of Karnataka. He continues to occupy the position when these pages are being written. When I visited Kāginele again in 2009 along with the Kannada historian S. Purushottama, the Government of Karnataka had already set up a Kāginele Abhivṛddhi Prādhikāra (Kāginele Development Authority), and offices, administrative buildings, and a library had developed. Steps were under way to renovate Kanakadāsa's 'tomb'. Five years later, I had occasion to go to Kāginele once again. This time, I was travelling with the historian from Israel, Gil Ben-Herut. We reached there early in the morning on 22 June 2014, and found the beautifully renovated 'tomb' already under worship. The priest blessed us and offered us the prasāda of Kanakadāsa. By this time, the Muslims of Kāginele had set their eyes on the humble tomb of Saṅgayya I (the son of Koḍēkallu Basava) in the village, which resembled 'Muslim' shrines in its architecture. When I visited Kāginele again on 5 August 2015 along with the Kannada historian H.G. Rajesh, the priest of Saṅgayya I's shrine informed that Muslims had claimed it to be the tomb of Ādaṃ Śippi, and had filed a case to restore its control to them!

404 On Mōnappa, see Padashetti 1992 (a mediocre work, originally written as a PhD dissertation under M.M. Kalburgi's guidance).

Sāvaḷagi, and Kalaburagi, respectively. This is due in large to the secrecy that the Koḍēkallu tradition maintained as far as their literature, forms of knowledge, and rituals were concerned. Access to Fakīrappa, Mōnappa, Śivaliṅga or Śaraṇabasava was easier. In contrast, Koḍēkallu Basava seems to have inspired greater awe and fear than respect, if the picture drawn between the lines in the *Nandiyāgamalīle* is any indication. Yet, nearly 75,000 people arrive during the annual fair held in his honour.[405]

The shrine of Śrīpādarāya on the outskirts of Muḷabāgilu in the Kōlāra district (one hundred kilometres east of Beṅgaḷūru) is an important *dāsa* centre. It draws few devotees. Many in the town have never heard of Śrīpādarāya or know of the existence of his shrine in their neighbourhood. Less than 5000 people visited the shrine during the annual fair until recently (which has increased in the last two decades to over 50,000, courtesy, the intervention of the Rashtriya Swayamsevak Sangh and the group of Hindu Right organizations called the Sangh Parivar functioning under its aegis). And unlike the fairs of Śirahaṭṭi Fakīrappa, Tinthiṇi Monappa, or Sāvaḷagi Śivaliṅga, the fair at the Muḷabāgilu shrine is not in honour of Śrīpādarāya, but held in the name of the deity he worshipped. A *dāsa* centre's difference with a *siddha* centre cannot be more striking.

There are no commemorative shrines or installations for any of the *dāsa*s, no fairs held for them, no worship carried out for their relics and remains.[406] All that has remained are their literary works, most of them in the form of short songs called *kīrtane* or *dēvaranāma*, and memories—some of them bright, some faint—about their devotion preserved by the Vaiṣṇava monasteries. The songs and legends enjoyed no popularity, as they circulated only among the residents and followers of the monasteries. In a striking reversal of fortune in the late nineteenth century, the Sindhi- and Marathi-inspired professional theatre troupes in Kannada, and the emerging academic discipline of Kannada Literature, began to foreground the *dāsa*s, to the disadvantage of the *siddha*s. Plays on the *dāsa*s were written and performed. Songs were composed in their honour. Their literary works were published in cheap chapbook form as well as in the form of carefully researched critical editions. Their songs were taught in schools, and school textbooks carried chapters about their life and work. In consequence, the Anglophone academia and much of the literate population in today's Karnataka have some familiarity with the names of Kanakadāsa

405 The Hindu Right has a strong presence at the temple of Śaraṇabasava, but it has not yet succeeded in penetrating into the Koḍēkallu, Tinthiṇi, Sāvaḷagi, and Śirahaṭṭi maṭhas in significant numbers.

406 It is interesting to note that *dāsa* 'tombs' are identified and worshipped at some places in Karnataka today. These include the Vādirāja Bṛndāvana at Sōde and the Nava Bṛndāvana near the village of Ānēgondi (off Haṃpi), where nine such 'tombs' exist. Inasmuch as *dāsa*s were cremated and not buried, and the ashes and bones never preserved, the question of erecting tombs does not arise. We can say with certainty that stories of the *dāsa* 'tombs' are fairly recent in origin, certainly not older than the nineteenth century. The history of these 'tombs' awaits research.

and Purandaradāsa, if not a reasonable historical understanding, but they know scarcely anything about Koḍēkallu Basava, Kalaburagi Śaraṇabasava, Tinthiṇi Mōnappa, Śirahaṭṭi Fakīrappa, or Sāvaḷagi Śivaliṅga.

A third point of divergence between the *siddha*s and the *dāsa*s concerned the performance of miracles. Most *siddha*s performed miracles, most *dāsa*s didn't. This resonates with the contemporary development in Europe, where the Roman Catholic Church maintained belief in miracles performed by men and women, and conferred sainthood upon them, while the emergent Protestant traditions of the sixteenth century believed that the power to perform miracles was rested only in God.

Miracles, or magical powers, had a long history in south Asia. Early Buddhists from the sixth century BCE are said to have mastered this art, even as the puritans among them, including the Buddha, abjured it. Monks were instructed not to practice miracles in the presence of lay devotees.[407] The Pālī canon was strictly opposed to the display of supernatural powers.[408] According to one story in the Pālī *Vinaya*, a rich man in the city of Rājagṛha was in possession of a begging bowl made of sandalwood. He hung it on a long bamboo pole and declared that a *śramaṇa* or a brāhmaṇa who was an Arhat and possessed magical powers may take it. Six masters, including Pūraṇa Kāśyapa tried, but failed. At that time, the *bhiṣku*s Piṇḍōla Bhāradvāja and Maudgalyāyana (Moggallāna) happened to pass through the place, seeking alms. Piṇḍōla Bhāradvāja asked his companion to claim the begging bowl, as he was an Arhat and possessed supernatural powers. Maudgalyāyana refused, and instead urged Piṇḍōla Bhāradvāja to take the bowl, as he was also an Arhat in possession of magical powers. Piṇḍōla Bhāradvāja agreed, rose into the sky, took possession of the sandalwood bowl, and descended after circling the city of Rājagṛha three times. He was received with great respect and fanfare by the crowd, and the rich man offered him expensive food as alms in the bowl.[409] It is not surprising, therefore, that Maudgalyāyana is one of the most revered monks in early Buddhism, while Piṇḍōla Bhāradvāja—who took pride in his supernatural powers and made a public display of it—a saint criticized widely. It must be noted, here, that the object of criticism was not the possession of magical powers, but its public display. Thus, the Buddha's preeminent disciple and successor, Mahākāśyapa, is never criticized for learning of the master's demise through his magical vision and reaching Kuśīnārā by flight. There is, in fact, pride about his supernatural accomplishments, which comes through in the words he is said to have spoken to the fellow monk, Ānanda.

> He who could imagine that my three knowledges, my six superknowledges and my mastery of the powers could be hidden away, could just as well imagine that a sixty years old elephant could be hidden by a palm leaf . . . could just as well imagine that the flow of the Ganges river could be

407 Ray 1994: 65.
408 Ibid., 134; 139.
409 Ibid., 153.

checked by a handful of dust . . . could just as well imagine that the wind could be imprisoned in a net.[410]

In the Deccan region, instances of miracles begin to occur at least from the early twelfth century. We have seen in chapter 2 how, in the twelfth century, Ēkānta Rāmayya severed his head and put it back in front of the Jainas in order to uphold the supremacy of Śiva. Harihara recounted this miracle in his *Ēkānta Rāmitandeya Ragaḷe*.[411] The head was cut off from the torso, and carried to the major Śaiva centres of the day, such as Puligeṛe, Aṇṇigeṛe, Keṃbhāvi, Kūḍalasaṅgama, Sonnalige, and Haṃpi, before bringing it back to Abbalūru and putting it back after seven days. Rāmayya's contemporary Rēvaṇasiddha, who lived in Maṅgaḷavāḍa and was perhaps known to Basava, is reported in an inscription dated 1188 to have performed miracles. Among his miracles were walking of water and bestowing riches on a devotee. On one occasion, the earth is said to have shaken when some people objected to the use of the word '*siddha*' by Rēvaṇasiddha.[412]

What is worthy of note in the two instances is that emphasis is laid only on the powers a true devotee of Śiva commanded. No attempt is made to identify the saints as miracle-workers.

In Harihara's hagiographies on the *śaraṇas*, the performance of miracle is nearly conspicuous by its absence. Leading *śaraṇas* like Allama and Akkamahādēvi perform no supernatural acts. Neither does Basava. A handful of miracles occur in the presence of Basava, mostly to vindicate him of the charges levelled against him. Note that the miracles happen; Basava does not perform them. In rare instances, when Harihara mentions the miracles performed by a *śaraṇa*, there is no attempt to represent him as a miracle-worker. The *ragaḷes* on Śaṅkara Dāsimayya[413] and Musuḷeya Cauḍayya[414] are prominent examples. Miracle figures only as one of the attributes of *śaraṇa* devotionalism, and a largely minor one inasmuch as Basava, Allama Prabhu, and Akkamahādēvi had no use of it.

The picture is considerably altered by the fifteenth century. In texts like the four *Śūnyasampadanes* and Cāmarasa's *Prabhuliṅgalīle*, Allama makes a proud display of his supernatural powers. The ability to perform miracles is one of his defining traits. He is a master of *līlā*. Accounts on the life of Basava come to be saturated now with the miracles he allegedly performed. In Siddhanañjēśa's *Gururājacāritra*, Basava is identified as the one who "showed the eighty-eight famous holy miracles to Bijjaḷa,

---

410 Ibid., 106.
411 *Ēkāntarāmitandegaḷa Ragaḷe*, 231-380.
412 See Pavate 2009: 28-31, for the text of this inscription.
413 *Śaṅkara Dāsimayyana Ragaḷe*, 1.171-188. Note that the miracle is called a *līlā* (1.187).
414 *Musuɣeya Cauḍayyana Ragaḷe*, 81-134.

the Lord of the world".[415] By the sixteenth century, the performance of miracles had evolved into a marker of identity.

Miracles are less prominent and scarcely emphasized in the legends on the *dāsa*s between the fifteenth and the eighteenth centuries. A well-known story told of Kanakadāsa demonstrates what miracles meant to the *dāsa* traditions. According to this story, the priests did not allow Kanakadāsa into the Kṛṣṇa temple in Uḍupi, as he belonged to a low caste. The saint began to sing in grief, "Open the door and offer me (a chance of) service, Hari".[416] And Hari (i.e., Kṛṣṇa), the all-knowing and merciful, obliged. Kanaka was standing on the rear of the temple. The image in the sanctum, therefore, turned a full 180°, and the wall on the rear collapsed, offering the saint a glimpse of the lord. The image faces this wall today, and a window known as *kanakana kiṇḍi* (Kanaka's hole) exists. The window offers a faint glimpse of the god from the outside to devotees who are short on time to line up in the queue to have a vision of Kṛṣṇa from inside.[417]

In this story, the *dāsa* made no miracle. He only petitioned to his deity. It was Kṛṣṇa who caused the miracle. A *siddha* on the other hand would not petition the god. He would perform the miracle on his own, as Maṇṭēsvāmi did in Ādi Kalyāṇa.

In the epic of Maṇṭēsvāmi sung by the nīlagāras of the Maisūru region, the saint is said to have gone on a visit to Ādi Kalyāṇa, ruled by the king Basava. Basava had installed a bell without tongue and a trumpet without horn at the gate of the fort. The bell would toll, and the trumpet would sound, only when a *śaraṇa* greater than Basava visited the city. Basava organized feeding (*annadāna*) to the Jaṅgamas in Ādi Kalyāṇa everyday. Thousands of Jaṅgamas came from far and wide to partake of the feeding. Most of them were false Jaṅgamas. Basava had instructed the gatekeeper Kaṭugara Saṅgayya that good (i.e., clean) Jaṅgamas must be given entry into the city first, and that the dirty ones with leprosy and other diseases allowed only after the good ones had left. Now, Maṇṭēsvāmi was Maṇṭēsvāmi, the father of recalcitrant renunciation in the region. Violating established conventions was his pastime. He arrived at the gate, disguised as a leper. Kaṭugara Saṅgayya refused him entry, and beat him up when the saint insisted. Miraculously enough, it hurt Basava and his wife Nīlamma, who were inside the fort, and not Maṇṭēsvāmi on whom the gatekeeper's physical blow had fallen. And then, the great sounds emerged from the bell without a tongue and the trumpet without a horn. It was a clear sign to Basava that a *śaraṇa* greater than him had arrived. Basava and Nīlamma set out looking for him. Maṇṭēsvāmi

415 *Gururājacāritra*, 1.6.

416 "*bāgilanu teredu sēveyanu koḍo hariyē*". This is among the most famous of Haridāsa songs in Kannada. For the text, see Parthasarathy 2013: 1133.

417 I am not sure if a vision of the deity in the sanctum sanctorum is possible from the *kanakana kiṇḍi*. Not once have I been successful in seeing Kṛṣṇa from the hole, not even when few visitors lined up before the sanctum, blocking the vision.

decided to take the couple to the dirtiest areas outside the town. So he rushed to the street of Haraḷayya, who belonged to the Mādiga (tanner/scavenger) caste, and fell into the garbage pit near his house. Basava and Nīlamma located him. But when Basava held one of Maṇṭēsvāmi's legs and tried to pull him out of the pit, the leg ripped off from the body. Nīlamma advised him to place the leg on a white cloth. Next, Basava pulled the other leg, which also came off. Similarly, both hands were pulled out from the body. And so was the head from the torso. Finally, Basava gave the head to Nīlamma, tied the rest of the body into a bundle, and carried it to the city. On the way, Maṇṭēsvāmi transformed the bundle into a bag of meat and the head into a pot of wine. The Jaṅgamas, who had assembled for food, were in for a rude shock. They rushed out of the city and took a dip in the lake in its vicinity to cleanse themselves of the pollution caused by meat and wine. They also washed their clothes, and spread them out to dry. Maṇṭēsvāmi arrived at the lake and convinced them that these purification rites remained incomplete as long as the *liṅga*s worn by them were not immersed into the lake. The Jaṅgamas agreed, and dropped their *liṅga*s into the water. With his magical powers, Maṇṭēsvāmi caused the *liṅga*s to vanish. It caused great commotion among the Jaṅgamas. Now, upon instructions from Maṇṭēsvāmi, the Jaṅgamas began to clear the water from the lake in search of their *liṅga*s, but could not retrieve them. Some of them left after picking up whatever pebble they could lay hands upon. Others pretended that they would come back on the following day, and left the city. In this way, Maṇṭēsvāmi purged Ādi Kalyāṇa clean of false Jaṅgamas. Only the true *śaraṇa*s remained: Basava, Nīlamma, and eight others, viz., Holeyara Honnayya, Mādigara Cannayya, Maḍivāḷa Mācayya, Gāṇigara Dāsappa, Aṃbigara Cauḍayya, Īḍigara Kyātappa, Turukara Bīrayya, and Haḍaga Lampaṇṇa.[418]

The motif of making the *liṅga* vanish occurs even in the story of Śirahaṭṭi Fakīrappa. He is said to have performed this miracle once when he was denied entry into the Murugharājēndra maṭha at Citradurga,[419] and again at Ḍaṃbaḷa and Śirahaṭṭi, when traders refused him alms.[420]

A further point of divergence between the *dāsa*s and the *siddha*s is related to the question of caste. The *siddha* centres were located in areas where conflicts over control of resources were less acutely felt. Here, caste-based differentiations were hardly registered. Caste, or the inequalities and exploitations based on it, rarely figured in the hagiographies or literary compositions of the *siddha*s in the sixteenth century. Nor is a fight against caste or a critique of the system mentioned in many of their traditions. Among the rare instance where caste (*jāti*) occurs is a *khaṇḍajñāna*

418 *Maṇṭēsvāmi*, 2 ('Kalyāṇada Sālu').
419 Siddharama Svami 2002: 18-21.
420 Ibid., 51-54.

song of Koḍēkallu Basava's, where he declares that pollution (*sūtaka*) based on caste does not exist for the devotee (*bhakta*).[421]

On the other hand, in the *dāsa* centres, where control over resources led to greater conflicts, caste appeared more prominently, although instances were never too many in number. A remarkable occurrence is the denial of entry to Kanakadāsa into the Kṛṣṇa temple of Uḍupi. The sixteenth century was characterized by an overwhelming presence of Nāyakas (military entrepreneurs turned revenue farmers), who were mostly of bēḍa (hunter) or kuruba (shepherd) origins, and therefore, outside the contours of the caste system. Only now were they being enlisted into the order of castes. Leading political houses like the Tuḷuvas of Vijayanagara and the Oḍeyas of Maisūru were of kuruba extraction. These groups were prominent sources of patronage, a fact the brāhmaṇical institutions of Uḍupi and Tirupati could scarcely ignore. There was, therefore, an uneasy accommodation of these new groups. Most *dāsa* institutions swore by the *varṇāśrama* system, and adhered to the caste system scrupulously, in spite of the fact that the emphasis was more on the lineage (*kula*) than on caste as an endogamous group. Yet, room was made available for critiques of the caste system. Who is a holeya (a caste of agrestic slaves and bonded labourers), wonders Purandaradāsa, and offers the following answer: a holeya is the one who does not adhere to virtues, who does not listen to the story of Hari, who as a servant wishes ill of the king, who loves a whore, who does not repay his debts, who is wayward, who is unfaithful to his salt, who desires his wife cowardly, who does not give alms when he is rich, who kills by poisoning, who does not speak in a straightforward manner, who is haughty about his purity, who fails to keep his word, who helps no one, who spoils others' life by deceit, who speaks lie, who consciously stays away from his religious duties, who longs for others' wives, who does not respect teachers and elders, who does not remember Purandara Viṭhala.[422] Thus, the term holeya must be appreciated as a signifier of vice, not as a marker of caste conferred by birth. Purandaradāsa draws a similar picture of the holeya and the holati (feminine gender of holeya) in another of his songs: the holeya and the holati are not the ones found in the *holagēri* (the street of the holeyas); rather, the one who falls pray to his wife's charms and speaks harsh words to his parents is a holeya, the one who hates her husband after becoming arrogant for having given birth to a son is a holati, the one who learns lessons from a teacher and yet causes worries to the elders is a holeya, the one who submits to another man and constantly disappoints her husband is a holati, the one who turns unfaithful to his salt and fights his master is a holeya, the one who repeatedly accuses her husband for their present state of poverty is a holati, the one who sows his seeds in another woman is a holeya, the one who quarrels, faints of epilepsy, speaks ill, and conspires is a holati, the one who takes no pity for the weak and stays fearless

421 No. 25, Soppimath 1998.
422 Parthasarathy 2013: 1843.

is a holeya, the one who is always hatching conspiracies in her mind is a holati, the one who is disrespectful to the offerings of Hari is a holeya, the one who favours other faiths, and accuses others is a holati, the one who does not bow down to the feet of Nārāyaṇa is a holeya, the one who rejects Purandara Viṭhala Nārāyaṇa is a holati.[423]

The picture drawn by the above discussion seems to be suggesting that two distinct trends in renunciation, with their own internally constituted logic of functioning, arose in the Deccan region after the late fifteenth century. It is important to allay this essentialist picture, as it was not the *siddha* or the *dāsa* ethic *per se* that led to the unfurling of this differentiation. Rather, it was the political economy that determined the manner in which it found expression. Thus, when we say that the *dāsa*s generally did not have place-names prefixed to their names, we must point to the important exception of Kākhaṇḍaki Mahipatirāya, an important *dāsa*. He lived in the heartland of the *siddha*s in northern Karnataka, and worked more on the *siddha* lines that the region warranted, although he was a Vaiṣṇava saint. Jagannāthadāsa's father Byāgavaṭṭi Ācārya's is another example from northern Karnataka for a *dāsa* saint with a place-name prefix. On the other hand, the region to the south of the Tuṅgabhadra was more conducive to the *dāsa* ethic. A number of *siddha*s lived here. Few among them performed miracles. Stories of miracles are most enthusiastically narrated in the legend of Maṇṭēsvāmi. He, however, was a marginal saint confined to the nīlagāras of the region in and around the Maisūru district. Although his maṭha at Boppēgauḍanapura was close to the Oḍeya rulers of Maisūru, Maṇṭēsvāmi never enjoyed popularity on a scale even distantly comparable to that of Śirahaṭṭi Fakīrappa or Sāvaḷagi Śivaliṅga. This, in spite of the fact that replicas of his tomb are preserved and worshipped at a number of shrines in different parts of Karnataka (which, however, attracts few devotees). Miracle was not of much use to the political economy of southern Karnataka. Thus, an important miracle-worker, Tōṇṭada Siddhaliṅga, is known for his charisma, knowledge, and the long years of penances that he carried out, rather than for the miracles he is believed to have performed. Better known as Yeḍiyūru Siddhaliṅga after the place where he was buried, he is among the few *siddha* saints in southern Karnataka to have a place-name prefixed to his name.[424]

We have observed that the *dāsa*s of Karnataka were scarcely known beyond the monastic circuits before the late nineteenth century. This should not be taken as a distinctly *dāsa* trait. For Annamayya enjoyed wide popularity in the neighbouring Telugu-speaking region. And so did Ēknāth and Tukārāṃ in Maharashtra, and Tulsīdās in the Gaṅgā valley. The popularity of the Vaiṣṇava saints of the fifteenth and the sixteenth centuries depended on two factors. One, they attained renown and a following if they had, like the *siddha*s, intervened into the political economy

423 No. 402, Karanth 2008.
424 Gubbiya Mallaṇārya is another southern saint to be known after his village, Gubbi. It is all too rare to find place-name prefixes among the *siddha*s of south Karnataka.

in a momentous manner to usher in substantial positive changes in the lives of men and women towards whom those efforts were directed. Two, they were well known and held in great reverence if they had rendered the *Rāmāyaṇa*, the *Mahābhārata*, the *Bhāgavatapurāṇa*, or the *Bhagavadgīta* into the vernacular languages.[425] Thus, while very few outside the monastic circuits concerned knew of Kanakadāsa, Purandaradāsa or Śrīpādarāya before the nineteenth century, Kumāravyāsa (or Gadugina Nāraṇappa), who rendered the *Mahābhārata* into Kannada, was a household name among the region's literate population and also among such of the illiterates that had the privilege of listening to the public reading (*pravacana*) of the epic. Ceṟuśśēri, who wrote the *Kṛṣṇagātha* in Malayalam based on the tenth book (*daśama-skanda*) of the *Bhāgavatapurāṇa*, and Eḻuttaccan, who rendered the *Rāmāyaṇa* and the *Mahābhārata* into the language, enjoyed similar popularity in Kerala.[426] In Odisha, only two of the five comrades (*pañcasakhā*s) of the sixteenth century were popular among the masses, Jagannāthadāsa, who wrote the Odia *Bhāgavatapurāṇa*, and Baḷarāmadāsa, who composed the *Jagamōhana Rāmāyaṇa* (and the radical *Lakṣmīpurāṇa*). The names of the other three, Acyutānandadāsa, Yaśavantadāsa, and Śiśu Anantadāsa, were rarely invoked. It was the fifteenth century saint Śāraḷādāsa—the author of the Odia *Mahābhārata*—that was more widely known.[427]

It is against the historical template of *siddha-dāsa* divergence that we must place the larger developments in religious life and practices of renunciation between the early sixteenth and the late eighteenth centuries.

We must now briefly turn to the *siddha* knowledge systems. The *siddha*s had a long history of intellectual innovation. Emblematic of their ingenuity are the multiple traditions and forms of argumentation that went into the making of the Vīraśaiva literature promoted by Jakkaṇa and Lakkaṇṇa Daṇḍēśa. We are, however, not suggesting that unlike the *dāsa*s of the sixteenth century and after, the *siddha*s were endowed with a logical acumen and sharp argumentative powers. Not often do we come across instances of original reasoning in their works. The argument that Nijaguṇa Śivayōgi made in order to emphasize the distinction between the body and the self in one such case. This argument, which we have cited in chapter 3, centres on the confusion caused

---

425 One saint, who neither changed people's lives nor rendered works such as the *Rāmāyaṇa* into the vernacular, was Pūndānaṃ in Kerala. Although a popular figure today, we do not know how much renown he enjoyed between the sixteenth and the nineteenth centuries.

426 The *Bhāgavatapurāṇa* is also available in Malayalam and is attributed to Eḻuttaccan, but scholars are more or less united in their opinion the authorship is open to question.

427 I cannot, however, comment on when the saints Narasiṃha Mehatā of Gujarat, Mīrā of Rajasthan, or Sūrdās, Kabīr, Rāidās, Kēśavadās and others of the Gaṅgā valley attained their present popularity, i.e., whether they were widely known before the nineteenth century (and if so, which ones and why) or were smuggled into limelight in the nineteenth century in the course of writing histories of literature and religion or plays meant to be performed by professional theatre troupes.

by the two statements, "I am the body" and "the body is mine".[428] Even in such brilliant works as Mahaliṅgaraṅga's *Anubhavāmṛta* or the *Śūnyasaṃpādane*s, one looks for novelty of arguments or reasoning in vain. Where, then, did the *siddha* ingenuity lie?

An examination of the *siddha* corpus tells us that their intellectual pursuits were largely directed towards system-building. It involved the production of analytical as well as descriptive works that were in the form of almanacs, manuals, and ethno-histories. The fifteenth-century Vīraśaiva project had already gone to great lengths in explicating systems like the *ṣaṭsthala* and the *ēkōttaraśatasthala*. The essentials of Vīraśaiva knowledge categories were laid out in Lakkaṇṇa Daṇḍēśa's *Śivatatvacintāmaṇi*. Expanding upon these works, Gubbiya Mallaṇārya produced a comprehensive account of the Vīraśaiva categories of knowledge in his encyclopedic *Vīraśaivāmṛtapurāṇa*. These works constituted almanacs of knowledge categories. To this very class belongs Nijaguṇa Śivayōgi's *Vivēkacintāmaṇi*, a dictionary of categories in the knowledge concerning renunciation that also included such secular knowledge as mathematics, weights and measures, etc.

Nijaguṇa's *Paramānubhavabodhe* and Mahaliṅgaraṅga's *Anubhavāmṛta* laid out distinct paradigms of visions (*darśana*) for the renouncer and the prerequisites and practices enjoined upon a practitioner. An early work under this paradigm was Kallumaṭhada Prabhudēva's *Liṅgalīlāvilāsacāritra*. The four *Śūnyasaṃpādane*s also fall under this category of texts. These works must be categorized as manuals related to the cosmologies of renunciation.

Hagiographic literature formed a third class of writings. Harihara, Rāghavāṅka, and Pālkurike Sōmanātha had produced the earliest specimens of this class in the late twelfth and the early thirteenth century. Bhīma's fourteenth-century *Basavapurāṇa* and Cāmarasa's fifteenth-century *Prabhuliṅgalīle* expanded upon the conventions laid by Harihara and his peers. Between 1500 and 1700, *siddha* hagiographies snowballed into a widely sought-after form of literature, especially in Kannada. These included not only full-length accounts akin to Siṅgirāja's *Amalabasavarāja Cāritra* and Ṣaḍakṣaradēva's *Basavarājavijayaṃ* on Basava, Cannabasavāṅka's *Mahādēviyakkana Purāṇa* on Akkamahādēvi, and Rudra's *Karasthala Nāgaliṅgana Caritre* on Karasthala Nāgaliṅga, but also works that narrated the lives of hundreds of *siddha*s in the manner of anecdotes. Prominent among these were Siddhanañjēśa's *Gururājacāritra*, Śāntaliṅgadēśikan's *Bhairavēśvara Kāvyada Kathāmaṇisūtra Ratnākara*, and Adrīśa's[429] *Prauḍharāyana Kāvya*. These works qualify to be called ethno-histories of sainthood.

---

428 *Paramānubhavabōdhe* 3.3.2.

429 Tradition and modern scholarship identify this poet as Adṛśya, as this is the name recorded in most extant manuscripts. However, Kalburgi 2010 Vol. 4: 396-398 persuasively argues that this poet's original name was Mallēśa, that Mallēśa is a corruption of Maleyēśa (the lord, *īśa*, of the hills, *male*), and that the poet Sanskritized the name to Adrīśa (the lord, *īśa*, of the hills, *adri*), of which Adṛśya is a later-day corruption. Some manuscripts indeed record the name as Adrīśa. We accept this suggestion and call the poet Adrīśa.

What is conspicuously missing in the *siddha* literature is an ethnography of places or centres of pilgrimage. This is significant, and we shall return to this question later in this chapter.

Even as the *siddha* knowledge systems were making great strides towards new forms of articulation and canonization, the political order of southern Karnataka began to undergo systemic changes that transformed the dynamics of religion in a big way. Sometime in the mid 1540s, the Śaṅkarācārya of Śṛṅgēri went on a pilgrimage to Kāśī. When he did not return for a long time, his worried disciples decided not to keep the pontificate vacant for any longer, and appointed another seer as Śaṅkarācārya. And dramatically enough, Narasiṃha Bhārati returned in 1547, and upon reaching Kūḍali in the Śivamogga district (where the rivers Tuṅga and Bhadra meet), he learnt of the developments at Śṛṅgēri. The chief of Santēbennūru, Sītārāmappa Nāyaka, or perhaps one of his near relatives, approached Narasiṃha Bhārati, and urged him to settle down at Kūḍali. The seer agreed, and a maṭha was set up there, inaugurating a parallel establishment.[430]

This is too naïve a story to be accepted at face value, particularly because the relationship between Śṛṅgēri and Kūḍali has been bitter and hostile ever since. In all likelihood, the Santēbennūru chiefs succeeded in creating a rift among the seers at Śṛṅgēri, or at least managed to manipulate an existing friction in the great monastery to their own political advantage.

The earliest known record of the Santēbennūru chiefs comes from Hirē Māḍaḷu. It tells us that Hanumappa Nāyaka set up a *Śivaliṅga* and made gifts of cow (*gōdāna*) and land (*bhūdāna*).[431] There are two other records from Hirē Māḍaḷu, perhaps from the same period. Both are in Marathi.[432] One of them refers to an *ināṃ* grant made by Hanumappa Nāyaka to a certain Dādāji Rāvu.[433] The next known record of these chiefs is from the Kūḍali maṭha.[434] This is from the year 1558. It tells us that Hanumappa Nāyaka, the son of Sītārāmappa Nāyaka, dispossessed a certain Tirumala Dīkṣita of his possession rights over five villages, conferred by the king (*rāyadatta*). These villages were located in the Harakēri Hōbaḷi of the Śivamogga Hōbaḷi in Gājanūru, belonging to the Vēṇṭhe of Āraga. The Dīkṣita had allegedly picked up a quarrel with Vidyāraṇya Bhārati, the pontiff of Kūḍali. This unruly act incurred the wrath of the Santēbennūru chief. Hanumappa Nāyaka took away the villages from Tirumala and made them over to the pontiff. Four years later, in 1562, Hanumappa Nāyaka's

430 Nadig 2001: 262-63.

431 Doc. 19, Nadig 2008. A total of fifty-seven documents belonging to or alluding to the Santēbennūru chiefs are compiled in this volume, which include stone and copperplate inscriptions, letters, and *sanads*. In addition, nine *kaifiyats* are also included. In the notes below, Doc. refers to the documents and Kaif. to the *kaifiyats* in this volume.

432 Doc. 17 & 18, Ibid.

433 Doc. 18. Ibid.

434 Doc. 4. Ibid.

son Billappa Nāyaka (referred to in this record as Pillappa Nāyaka) sent the *gauḍa* (peasant leader) of Cikkagaṅgūru to Maluka Oḍeya, who held the *amaraṃ* rights over Dummi Sīme, to lodge a complaint against the atrocities of his *ṭhāṇādār*, Dilāvara Oḍeya (Dilāvar Khān). But the *gauḍa* was killed on his way by Dilāvara's men. What ensued is not clear, but Maluka was made to grant some land in the Cikkagaṅgūru Sthaḷa to the children of the deceased. More importantly, he was forced to hand over the *amaraṃ* rights over Dummi Sīme to Billappa Nāyaka.[435] It was not the state, nor any enforcing agency, which compelled him to do so. This tempts us to suspect that the transfer of rights was more in the nature of a confiscation made by a bullying Billappa Nāyaka. Three years later, in 1565, Billappa Nāyaka and his brother Keṅgappa Nāyaka appointed Liṅgaṇṇa, the brother of a certain Appābhaṭṭa, to the office of the *sēnabhōva* (secretary) of Santēbennūru Sīme-Sthaḷa.[436] This record identifies the Nāyaka brothers as agents (*kāryakke kartaru*) of Rāmarāya, the *de facto* Vijayanagara ruler.

The trajectory is aggressive and calculated enough. In 1547, they break up the Śṛṅgēri maṭha, in 1556, they make an *ināṃ* grant, in 1558, they are impudent enough to revoke a grant made by the king, in 1562, they obtain the *amaraṃ* "rights over Dummi Sīme by means not so fair, and in 1565, they are in the service of the state!

The last of these dates is important. It was around this date that a number of Nāyakas began to assert themselves, so much so that the first known reference to many Nāyaka households which were to exercise control over different parts of southern Karnataka in the seventeenth and the eighteenth centuries, are found from this period. The Nāyakas of Bāṇarāvi, near Baḷḷari, established their sway over the region in 1564.[437] Dādayya Nāyaka, the founder of the Harapanahaḷḷi line of Nāyakas, is first heard of in 1565.[438] The case of the Santēbennūru Nāyakas was no different.

A record from Kūḍali identifies a certain Dhūmarāja as the progenitor of the Santēbennūru line. He is said to have arrived from Vijayanagara to settle down at Basavāpaṭṭaṇa.[439] Popular legends consider him the general of the Vijayanagara army.[440] In his monograph on these chiefs, Abdul Sattar opines that 'Dhūmarāja' is a normative name that seems to have come into vogue because of the control these chiefs exercised over the Dhūmaguḍḍa hill.[441] But it is likely that Dhūmarāja is the same as Bhūmarāja, whom many Nāyaka families in the Baḷḷāri region identify as their progenitor.[442] According to the Santēbennūru *kaifiyat*, produced not earlier

435 Doc. 1, Ibid.
436 EC 7 (1), Cn 62.
437 Pujarhalli 2004: 61.
438 Sadashivappa 1996: 85.
439 Nadig 2008: 10.
440 Ibid., 8.
441 Sattar 1997: 5.
442 Pujarhalli 2004, *passim*.

than 1780, Hanumappa Nāyaka obtained Madakari Nāḍu in Uccaṅgi Vēṇṭhe as an *amaraṃ* from the Vijayanagara king, Rāmarāya. We are then told that he established a fort at Raṅgapura or Raṅganāthapura, and renamed it Santēbennūru.[443] The chiefs moved to Basavāpaṭṭaṇa at a critical juncture in their history, but had to soon relocate again to Tarikere in the mid seventeenth century. However, they continued to affiliate themselves with Santēbennūru.[444] The Ānandapuraṃ copper plates of Keḷadi Sōmaśēkhara Nāyaka refer to them as the Pāḷegāras of Tarikere.[445] The Tarikere *kaifiyat* says that they belonged to Uccaṅgidurga, from where they moved to Basavāpaṭṭaṇa after obtaining a *sanad* from the Sultān of Dilli (*sic*) to administer the region.[446] The Hodigere *kaifiyat* credits Hanumappa Nāyaka's son Keṅgappa Nāyaka with the construction of the Hodigere fort.[447] Interestingly enough, this *kaifiyat* states that a claim was made concerning the administration of Dummi Nāḍu by Puṭṭamallappa and Timmappa, the sons of a certain Īśvarayya, and that Keṅgappa Nāyaka ratified the claim after examining the documents they produced. Nevertheless, the Nāyaka placed the fort under the command of Rāma Nāyaka, Keñca Nāyaka, three hundred *vālekāra*s, and twenty-five *kāmāṭi*s. This seems to be echoing Billappa Nāyaka's confiscation of the *amaraṃ* rights over Dummi Sīme from Maluka Oḍeya in 1562.

That Rāmarāya granted the *amaraṃ* of Madakari Nāḍu to Hanumappa Nāyaka is sheer fiction. But the *kaifiyat*s point to two major aspects of the sixteenth century Nāyakas: physical mobility, and the building of forts. With the progressive weakening of the Vijayanagara state after the defeat in the battle of 1565, the Nāyakas became a force to reckon with. In the seventeenth and the eighteenth centuries, their rank and file expanded exponentially, so to speak, although only some of them, like the Keḷadi Nāyakas in Karnataka, and the Nāyakas of Madurai, Ceñji, and Tañjāvūr in Tamilnadu, were powerful enough to function as state-like polities. Monasteries, temples, and other religious establishments in southern and coastal Karnataka were to a large extent at the mercy of the Nāyakas. That the Nāyakas were powerful enough to make land grants to religious establishments, or build temples and monasteries, was indeed worthy of note. Most leading peasant proprietors were in control of sufficient resources to engage in such acts of munificence. What made the Nāyakas compelling was, inter alia, their power to break up such mighty religious centres as the Śṛṅgēri maṭha, although few instances of the actual exercise of such power are known. Who were the Nāyakas?

443 Kaif. 1.
444 They are, however, also known as Tarikere Nāyakas.
445 Doc. 41.
446 Kaif. 9.
447 Kaif. 3.

Burton Stein identifies them as representatives of a new form of 'supralocal chieftainship' in south India.[448] Placing them in the league of the 'big men' of the period, Stein characterizes their presence as unprecedented in the region's history.[449] More importantly, he locates the early seventeenth century decline of the Vijayanagara state in the conflict that the nexus between the state and these supralocal chiefs came to engender.[450] Stein's argument has been cited with approval on some occasions, mostly by revisionist historians, but it remains by and large neglected. There are two reasons for this neglect. One, much of Stein's work draws upon arguments made in secondary works rather than on documentary evidence from primary sources like inscriptions and literary texts. A systematic study of primary sources presents a picture very different from the one that Stein draws. Two, his discussion of precolonial polities of South India is based on the segmentary state model, which holds that peasant localities were autonomous in their origins and existence, and chose to acknowledge only the nominal or ritual sovereignty of the state. Historians challenging this thesis have almost exclusively focused on Stein's discussion of the Cōḻa state in order to present evidence to the contrary, ignoring his position on the Nāyakas. A year before Stein brought out his controversial work, Nicholas Dirks published an article on what he called a 'south Indian little kingdom'.[451] This was followed by a paper on a 'little king' three years later,[452] and by an influential monograph after five more years.[453] Dirks presented the Nāyakas as the greatest controllers of land in the Vijayanagara state, with an estimated 75% of all land being held by them as *amaraṃs*.[454] He refused to treat *amaraṃ* as a specific tenure involving revenue-farming rights, and argued instead that it represented a relationship of service and gift engineered by 'displays of ritual kingship' on the part of the state.[455] This involved a pattern, or rather, a vicious circle: service→hope or expectation of gifts like land, titles, emblems, honours, privileges, and so on→new opportunities to offer service.[456] This is too idealized a picture and is hardly of help to us in understanding statecraft and kingship, for it reduces political hierarchies to a mere play of hyper-reciprocity. According to Norbert Peabody, Dirks fails to take note of the fact that "the constitution of warrior rule through the management of land had vital economic concomitants involving distinct strategies of maximization", and that appreciating these polities in isolation may not do justice to their role in the making of "a field of overlapping polities,

448 Stein 1980: 369.
449 Ibid, 370.
450 Ibid.
451 Dirks 1979.
452 Dirks 1982.
453 Dirks 1987.
454 Ibid., 44.
455 Ibid., 42.
456 Ibid., 44.

paramount powers, and political dependencies" which characterized most political maneuverings in this period.[457]

Noboru Karashima argues that the Nāyakas were feudal lords who rose to prominence as part of the Vijayanagara state's administrative apparatus in the later half of the fifteenth century, when bureaucracy had begun to make way for feudal tendencies. He identifies four distinct conditions that, according to him, make a political formation feudal:

> (1) the basic direct producers are not slaves but peasants who own the means of production themselves; (2) local magnates who possess superior rights to land that the peasants cultivate, subdue the peasants under their control, and extract surplus produce by means of extra-economic coercion; (3) political power assumes a hierarchical structure which is sustained by land grants among the ruling class and also by a certain ideology; and (4) commodity production is not generalized but limited only to the surplus portion which is appropriated by the exploiting class.[458]

This description is sharp and rigorous, but at the same time, too broad for us to accept. It encapsulates tendencies that were not specific to the Nāyaka period, but were prevalent with varying degrees of intensity even in the twelfth, the ninth, and the seventh centuries. Besides, we believe that in the interest of methodology and to ensure common ground for the advancement of knowledge, a phenomenon like feudalism is best discussed with a clearly identified referent in mind, instead of relying upon descriptions whose points of emphases vary from historian to historian.

Karashima traces the origins of the Nāyakas to the new group of non-brāhmaṇa landholders who arose in south India in the thirteenth and the fourteenth centuries.[459] These lords were subsequently enlisted into the service of the Vijayanagara state, which transferred them to far-lying areas of their territory. The state exercised absolute control over them. The Nāyakas paid one-third of their income from the assigned territories to the states, besides maintaining an armed regiment, which had to be pressed into service when demanded by the king. Karashima believes that their role as leaseholders of temple land was one of the major sources of their authority and income, which eventually is said to have made some of them immensely powerful when the influence of the Vijayanagara state began to dwindle.[460] The importance which Karashima attaches to the leasing of temple land and to the transfer of Nāyakas is somewhat inflated, but otherwise, this is the most measured piece of scholarship on the Nāyakas produced in the last three decades.

---

457 Peabody 2003: 82.
458 Karashima 2002: 30-31.
459 Karashima 1992: 117-30.
460 Ibid., 136.

Velcheru Narayana Rao, David Shulman, and Sanjay Subrahmanyam present the Nāyakas as 'semi-autonomous actors' who rose to prominence in the Tamil country in the sixteenth century.[461] They posit that the Nāyakas migrated from the Telugu country and occupied the dryland belts of Tamilnadu, where they played an entrepreneurial role in expanding agricultural production, and created a new economy. While for Karashima, the role of the Vijayanagara state was crucial in the emergence of the Nāyakas, Narayana Rao, Shulman, and Subrahmanyam underplay this dimension. Instead, they argue that the Nāyaka system was brought into existence by the Kākatīya state.[462] That the Nāyakas were not created by the state but only enlisted into its service is more than proved by the presence of the Nāyar militia in Kerala and the Nāyaks in Odisha and Chhattisgarh, regions that were never administered by the Kākatīya or the Vijayanagara kings.

In his study of the Hāgalavāḍi Nāyakas, D.N. Yogeeshwarappa presents an alternate thesis. He observes that the Vijayanagara state was characterized by three distinct tendencies, feudal, integrative, and decentralized. The Nāyakas represent the first of these, the feudal tendency.[463] Yogeeshwarappa also seems to suggest that the subservient status of the Nāyakas under Vijayanagara rule did not prevent them from exercising a set of choices. Dismissing the view that the arrival of Yerimādi Nāyaka, the founder of the Hāgalavāḍi line, from Tuṃmaḷa in Andhra to the Tumakūru region of Karnataka was an administrative transfer ordered by the state, Yogeeshwarappa argues that this was indeed a migration, undertaken with the desire to take control of a politically less-active region and establish ones own fortunes there.[464] That in doing so they enlisted themselves into the service of the state points to a choice the Nāyakas were able to exercise in obtaining *amaraṃ*s from the king.

An interesting discovery of Yogeeshwarappa's is of some interest to us in the ensuing discussion. The vernacular academia does not make any specific distinction between the terms, Nāyaka and Pāḷegāra (Poligar in English sources). The two are often used interchangeably. The latter is also used extensively in Anglophone accounts without clearly identifying how it differs from Nāyaka. Yogeshwarappa suggests that Pāḷegāra (Pāḷegāḷḷu in Telugu and Pāḷaiyakkārar in Tamil) may be a word of Tamil origin.[465] He notes that it never figures as a title of self-representation in contemporary records from Karnataka. Except a solitary inscription of 1654 from the Maṇḍya district, in which one of the signatories is referred to as a Pāḷegāra, records

461 Narayana Rao, Shulman and Subrahmanyam 1992: 29.
462 Ibid., 36-37.
463 Yogeeshwarappa 1999: 7.
464 Ibid., 29-30.
465 Ibid., 5.

invariable refer to the self as Nāyaka. The word Pāḷegāra is reserved for the other, which, Yogeeshwarappa says, points to the low esteem this word commanded.[466]

Inasmuch as Nāyaka and Pāḷegāra were different appellations referring to the same group, it becomes possible to make a fresh assessment of the Nāyakas in the light of the available evidence concerning the Pāḷegāras. The Pāḷegāras were primarily military entrepreneurs, who controlled bands of mercenary troops (*pāḷya* in Kannada, *pāḷaiyaṃ* in Tamil) drawn from the peasantry and other dispossessed sections of the population. These troops were deployed in warfare and raids of plunder. The Pāḷegāras also supplied troops to rulers, chiefs, and warlords in their raids and military campaigns. In the course of the late seventeenth and the eighteenth centuries, this practice developed into one of the most lucrative enterprises in the region. Hundreds of Pāḷegāra entrepreneurs arose, building *pāḷya*s and recruiting mercenary troops into their service. The magnitude of this enterprise is borne out by the fact that more than one hundred *pāḷya*s exists in the city of Beṅgaḷūru alone. Most of them are named after the persons who established them, Munireḍḍi Pāḷya, Pāpareḍḍi Pāḷya, Gauḍara Pāḷya, Subēdār Pāḷya, Divānara Pāḷya, Mohammad Sāb Pāḷya, Maṅgammana Pāḷya, and Kāmākṣi Pāḷya, to name a few. Note that the last two are named after women.[467]

Some of the more powerful Nāyakas or Pāḷegāras enjoyed revenue-farming rights under the Tuḷuva and Aravīḍu kings of Vijayanagara, and continued to extract land revenue, transit tolls, and other forms of dues even after the collapse of these states. Among them were the Keḷadi and the Ballaṃ Nāyakas. Others, like the Santēbennūru Nāyakas, forcefully confiscated such rights. Yet others, like the Nāyakas of Hāgalavāḍi, Harapanahaḷḷi, and Bāṇarāvi, established their own pockets of influence where they controlled revenue. Thus, the position taken by Stein, Dirks, Karashima, Narayana Rao, Shulman and Subrahmanyam, and Yogeeshwarappa, concerning who the Nāyakas were, all give us a true but partial picture. What was common to the Nāyakas was their military entrepreneurship. Many of them commissioned works of literature, carried out public works like expanding irrigation networks in the dryland belts, caused expansion of agriculture and the spread of rural market networks, and nurtured agrarian commercialism to various extents. Yet, the ownership of *pāḷya*s was what defined them as a class apart.

While military entrepreneurship did not develop into deeply entrenched forms of military fiscalism before the late seventeenth century, the smaller Pāḷegāras were already creating deeply asymmetric relationships with temples and monastic establishments of southern Karnataka by the mid sixteenth century. Not many of them

466 Ibid., 8-9.

467 See Devadevan 2010b for a historical survey.

extended support to the religious establishments. Consistent patronage came only from a few prominent chiefs, like the Nāyakas of Keḷadi and the Oḍeyas of Maisūru.[468]

By the seventeenth century, chiefs had to face increasing demands for revenues and tributes from the Ādil Śāhis and the Marāṭhas from the north, and the Keḷadi Nāyakas and the Maisūru Oḍeyas from within the region. A good number of these chiefs were Nāyaka migrants from Andhra, who established forts and *pāḷya*s in overwhelming numbers. Of itinerant origins as they were, the Nāyakas were less deeply rooted in the production relations of southern Karnataka. Their fabled mobility enabled them to move from one headquarter to another with ease. We have seen how the Santēbennūru chiefs moved into Santēbennūru, and shifted to Basavāpaṭṭaṇa and later, to Tarikere. In times of threats, even a powerful house of Nāyakas was found to be on the move. The Keḷadi Nāyakas moved to Ikkēri, and later, to Bidanūru, when faced with Ādil Śāhi attacks—reason why they are also known as the Nāyakas of Ikkēri and Bidanūru. One line of the Keḷadi house settled down in Koḍagu. Similar movements were noticed in other houses also. A prominent Nāyaka line branched off into two, one settling down at Ballaṃ in the Hāsana district of Karnataka and the other moving to Ceñji in Tamilnadu.[469]

Temples and monasteries of fifteenth and sixteenth-century southern Karnataka were founded by the local elites. Most of these elites were brāhmaṇically oriented, some of them, Vīraśaiva. By the mid sixteenth century, the brāhmaṇas of southern Karnataka began to face a new predicament. Their dominant position in the contemporary milieu was for centuries underwritten by their monopoly over literacy and religion, and the influence they could thereby exercise over political establishments. A gradual decline in their position began to be felt after the sixteenth century. This was caused by the absence of strong polities like the ones hitherto represented by the Hoysaḷa and the Vijayanagara states. Newer polities, including important ones like the Keḷadi Nāyakas and the Maisūru Oḍeyas, recruited them, but on a substantially lesser scale. Most Nāyakas of southern Karnataka lacked an establishment of literate functionaries. Besides, owing to the growing mobility that the new political economy offered, brāhmaṇa migrants from the neighbouring Tamilnadu, Andhra, and Maharashtra were successful in finding employment here. The arrival of brāhmaṇas from neighbouring regions did not constitute a major threat in itself, at least up to the late eighteenth century. Rather, the growing presence of Muslims and the Marāṭhas posed the real challenge, as functionaries under them were expected to work with languages other than Sanskrit and Kannada, viz., Persian and Marathi. This opened up greater avenues of employment under the chiefs for brāhmaṇa as well as non-brāhmaṇa groups proficient in these languages. Few brāhmaṇas in southern Karnataka fitted this bill.

---

468 On religious patronage of the Oḍeyas, see Simmons 2014.
469 Ota 2008.

Under these circumstances, the more enterprising of the brāhmaṇical groups turned increasingly to building temples and monasteries with their energies directed largely towards land management and agrarian production. The Vīraśaivas of southern Karnataka also set out on a similar course.

As early as the late fifteenth century, Tōṇṭada Siddhaliṅga had brought revolutionary changes in and around Yeḍiyūru where he caused the orchard economy to expand significantly. According to legends, Siddhaliṅga was born to Jñānāmbe and Cannamallikārjuna (unlikely to be their real names) in the village of Haradanahaḷḷi in the Cāmarājanagara district to the south of Maisūru. The village was known for its trade in areca nut, coconut, and other cash crops. At the age of eight, Siddhaliṅga was sent to the Gōsala maṭha to become a renouncer. Siddhaliṅga lived there for many years, and studied under the pontiff, Gōsala Cannabasava. He also performed many miracles, which included feeding the stone image of a bull, and lighting a lamp with water when it had run out of oil. Eventually, he was appointed pontiff of the monastery. But Siddhaliṅga was a saint; and as the lives of the saints examined in chapters 3 and 4 seem to suggest, a saint was not saintly enough unless he travelled widely. Siddhaliṅga obtained the consent of Gōsala Cannabasava, and set out on a long voyage in the train of 701 devotees. During this voyage, he performed a number of miracles. At Tiruvaṇṇāmalai in Tamilnadu, Śiva appeared before him, and offered him a garland. In Kerala, Siddhaliṅga convinced people to give up black magic, and initiated them into Śiva worship. In Siddhagaṅga, which was known for its endemic water scarcity, he caused a stream to flow from a rock. Thus continued his travels and regular displays of supernatural powers. Finally, he arrived at the village of Kaggere on the banks of the river Nāgini. Here, a certain Naṃbiyaṇṇa invited him for food, but before the feast commenced, highwaymen attacked the village. The villagers fled to seek shelter under the chief of Niḍugallu. When they returned twelve years later, they found a cow pouring its milk on its own over an anthill. Surprised by this miracle, they removed the anthill to find Siddhaliṅga lost in meditation. Siddhaliṅga eventually woke up, blessed Naṃbiyaṇṇa and the other villagers, and moved to the nearby Yeḍiyūru, where he came to rest. The temple at Yeḍiyūru houses his tomb.

The Yeḍiyūru temple owns substantial orchard lands, where coconut cultivation yields an impressive income. The temple was one of the earliest establishments in southern Karnataka to engage in what Max Weber would call monastic landlordism.[470] In the sixteenth and the seventeenth centuries, many other temples and monasteries in the region became increasingly involved in land management. Most of them were under the control of brāhmaṇas. With

470 Weber 1958: 257. Weber uses the expression in the context of Buddhist monasteries in Sri Lanka. Romila Thapar borrows the idea to explain landlordism in Indian monasteries. See Thapar 2000a: 220.

employment under the state and access to revenue coming from their position as state functionaries on the wane, the brāhmaṇas ventured into landlordism as a safe and effective means of resource augmentation.

Copperplate inscriptions of land grants preserved at the Rāghavēndra maṭha in Nañjanagūḍu exemplifies this neo-brāhmaṇical landlordist tendency. The maṭha is in possession of sixteen inscriptions. All of them are charters of land grants. Their contents are summarized in Table 11.

Table 11. Copperplate Inscriptions of Land Grants in Possession of the Rāghavēndra Maṭha in Nañjanagūḍu[471]

Sl. No.	Date	Donor	Recipient	Name of the Village Granted	Provenance
1.	1490	Kṛṣṇarāya (spurious)[472]	Vibhudēndra Tīrtha (of the maṭha in Hampi?)	Cikkakūḷḷi	Kṛṣṇa Valley
2.	1575	Śrīraṅgarāya	Surēndra Tīrtha (of the maṭha in Hampi)	1. Pudukkuḍi and 2. Nāvalūr (renamed Rāmacandrapura)	Kāvēri Delta
3.	1576	-do- (spurious)[473]	Sudhīndra Tīrtha (of the maṭha in Hampi?)	1. Baccanahāḷu, 2. Khyāḍa, 3. Yaḍavāḷa, 4. Ciñcala, and 5. Araḷihaḷḷi	Tuṅgabhadra, Malaprabha and Kṛṣṇa Valleys
4.	1513	Rāmarāya (spurious)[474]	Surēndra Tīrtha (of the maṭha in Hampi)	1. Ānēhosūru, 2. Lēpagiri, 3. Śīrugāpura, 4. Mallāpura, 5. Honnamaṭṭe, and 6. Hērakallu	-do-
5.	Date lost	-do- (spurious)[475]	-do-	1. Ṭhoḷali, 2. Kammārakaṭṭe and, 3. Cikka Moraṭi	Upper Tuṅgabhadra valley

471 Source: Nj. 110 to Nj. 125, *Epigraphia Carnatica*, (revised edition) Vol. 3.
472 This is a spurious inscription because the date is too early for Krsnaraya (r. 1509-1529).
473 This record is spurious because the region where the grant was made was not under the control of Śrīraṅgarāya in 1576. A gift after purchase is of course possible, but the grant makes no allusion to purchase of land by the donor.
474 This is spurious because the engraver was Maṅgaṇācārya, son of Vīraṇṇa, who was also the engraver of the pervious record. The two records are separated by sixty-three years. Maṅgaṇācārya is also named as the engraver of the first record, dated 1490.
475 This is spurious because of the same reason mentioned in note 474 above.

Sl. No.	Date	Donor	Recipient	Name of the Village Granted	Provenance
6.	1543	Tirumalarāya	Emme Basava (of the Hastināvati region)[477]	Komrakere	Mid Tuṅgabhadra valley
7.	1580	Cavappa (spurious)[476]	Vijayīndra Tīrtha (of the maṭha in Kuṃbhakōṇaṃ)	1. Kokyūru, 2. Guḷḷūru, 3. Palla and, 4. Raghupakaṭle	Kṛṣṇa valley
8.	1614	Cinna Cavappa	-do-	One *māna* of land in Tañjāvūr	Kāvēri delta
9.	-do-	-do-	-do-	Two *vēlis* of land in Kuṃbhakōṇaṃ	Kāvēri delta
10.	1679	Muddaḷagādri Nāyaka	Yōgīndra Tīrtha (of the maṭha in Kuṃbhakōṇaṃ?)	Ārāṃbaṇṇa and a maṭha in Śrīraṅgaṃ	Tāmraparṇi valley and Kāvēri delta
11.	1698	Maṅgamma	Sumatīndra Tīrtha (of the maṭha in Kuṃbhakōṇaṃ)	Āyirdharma, and select hamlets, temples and maṭhas surrounding it	Kāvēri delta
12.	1680	Vaḍeyāri	Sudhīndra Tīrtha (of the maṭha in Kuṃbhakōṇaṃ?)	1. Nānmādipānallūr and 2. Kōḍikāla	-do-
13.	1699	Uttamaraṅgappa Kāḷakakōḷa Voḍeyāri	Sumatīndra Tīrtha (of the maṭha in Kuṃbhakōṇaṃ)	1. Part of the toll from Payaraṇipāḷyaṃ and 2. Part of the toll from i) Nattaguḷi, ii) Veḷande, iii) Tirukaḷappūr, iv) Virāndavarankūru and, v) Vālappanikōvil	-do-
14.	1746	Vijayavoppula Maḷavarāya	Vasudhēndra Tīrtha (of the maṭha in Kuṃbhakōṇaṃ)	Three hundred *guṇṭa*s of land in Ālaṃddoreya Kaṭṭaḍa	-do-
15.	1663	Doḍḍadēvarāja	Rāghavēndra Tīrtha (of the maṭha in Nañjanagūḍu)	Nallūru (renamed Dēvarājapura)	Maisūru
16.	1774	Sōmarāja	Varadēndra Tīrtha (of the maṭha in Nañjanagūḍu)	Details lost	Details lost

476 Cavappa belonged to the Tañjāvūr region in Tamilnadu, and is unlikely to have made a grant in the Kṛṣṇa valley, unless it was a gift after purchase. Since it is not stated to have been purchased by him before donation, this is a spurious record.
477 The recipient did not belong to the tradition of this maṭha. Evidently, the grant made over to him was confiscated by the Rāghavēndra maṭha.

The Rāghavēndra maṭha inscriptions have a very interesting story to tell. From the details in Table 11, it is seen that five of the first seven records were clearly spurious, while one recorded a grant made to another establishment. Three grants were made to the *maṭha* in Haṃpi. The Haṃpi *maṭha* is likely to have been the recipient of two more grants. Six grants were made to the *maṭha* at Kuṃbhakōṇaṃ. This *maṭha* might have received two more grants, although this is not clearly established from the purports. The *maṭha* at Nañjanagūḍu, where the records are now found, was endowed with only one grant. The last inscription points to the likelihood that a second grant came its way.

Although the picture is hazy, a reasonable conclusion may be drawn. A *maṭha* of Lord Rāma existed near the Vijaya Viṭṭhala temple in Haṃpi in the sixteenth century. It either moved to Kuṃbhakōṇam or merged with an existing monastery there after the defeat of Vijayanagara in 1565. A branch of this monastery was opened in Nañjanagūḍu in the seventeenth century under circumstances that are not known to us. This monastery held control over some of the lands originally given to the *maṭha* of Kuṃbhakōṇaṃ. Whether this was a peaceful arrangement, or involved conflict, can only be speculated upon. What is evident, though, is that the Nañjanagūḍu monastery forged many records in the name of Vijayanagara rulers like Kṛṣṇarāya, Rāmarāya, and Śrīraṅgarāya to lay claims over lands in the Tuṅgabhadra, Kṛṣṇa, and Malaprabha valleys.

Temples and monasteries under brāhmaṇa and Vīraśaiva control were now beginning to attach as much land to their establishment as possible. We have noticed earlier in this chapter how Santēbennūru Hanumappa Nāyaka confiscated five villages granted to Tirumala Dīkṣita by the Vijayanagara ruler in the Harakēri Hōbaḷi of the Śivamogga Hōbaḷi, and made it over to the new monastery established by him at Kūḍali. The Śṛṅgēri maṭha succeeded briefly in taking control of these lands, only to be restored to Kūḍali again. The five villages kept swapping hands between the two maṭhas for a long time, and remained a bone of contention between Śṛṅgēri and Kūḍali.

Although temples received grants, such instances were relatively fewer in number. By far, the most prominent recipients of grants after the mid sixteenth century were the maṭhas. In the fifty-five years of the sixteenth century beginning with the year 1545, as many as nine grants were made to maṭhas by, or during the reign of, the Keḷadi Nāyakas, viz. the Nirāsi maṭha of Nagara in 1545, the Virūpākṣa maṭha of Śaṅkaranārāyaṇa twice in 1563, the Umāmahēśvara Lakṣmīnārāyaṇa maṭha in 1563, the Hosakere maṭha in 1569, the Cauḷikere maṭha in 1578, the maṭha to the southwest of the Sōmanātha temple in Maṇigārakēri in 1580, a maṭha at Mūḍakere in 1585, and the Mahattina maṭha at Caṃpakasarasi in Ānandapura in 1592.[478] Instances began to multiply manifold in the seventeenth century.

478 Nos. 5, 13, 27, 21, 26, 28, 30, 41 and 43, Jois 1991.

Under the historical circumstances outlined in the preceding pages, the brāhmaṇical temples and monasteries of southern Karnataka became increasingly inward-looking, and conspicuously orthodox. With consistent if not extensive incomes coming from the lands they held, they directed their energies towards land management and the regulation of production relations that the agrarian regime precipitated.

We have seen in chapter 3 that peasant proprietors of the dryland belts to the south of the Tuṅgabhadra were also in control of the rural markets in earlier centuries. With increasing fiscalization of the economy on the one hand, and the arrival of the Nāyakas and the consolidation of their authority in the region on the other, there occurred a major change in this dynamics. The Nāyakas and other chiefs established a number of forts on the major trade routes. These forts were often garrisoned, and a body of troops stationed there. More importantly, they functioned as outposts for the collection of revenues, especially transit tolls (*suṅka*). Some inscriptions of the Keḷadi Nāyakas refer to these forts as *suṅka-durga*s, forts for transit toll collection.[479] Reference is also made to *suṅkada-ṭhāṇe*, toll station,[480] and to a *durga-ṭhāṇya* (*sic*), 'the fort station'.[481] Marketplaces (*pēṭe*s) were established close to these forts. Collection of transit toll was mostly in kind. The inscriptions refer to the toll on the transit of paddy as *durgada bhatta*, the fort's paddy.[482] The goods were sold in the marketplaces, and the proceeds remitted to the treasury. A sharp increase was seen in the cultivation of commercial crops like areca nut and coconut. This was especially true of the coastal and the Malenāḍu (the Western Ghat) areas.

Inscriptions of the Keḷadi Nāyakas contain richly detailed references to grant of lands where commercial crop cultivation figured prominently. In a grant made in 1642 by Vīrabhadra Nāyaka, mention is made of 8780 areca nut trees, of which 821 were saplings, 2001 young trees, and the remaining 5958, yielding revenue. Of these, 4798 trees were assessed at one rate, and the other 1160, at another rate.[483] A grant made in 1702 by Basavappa Nāyaka I, recorded on a set of copperplates found at Bhāratīpura, refers to the 500 trees belonging to the Śṛṅgēri maṭha and the 5500 trees held by the Tīrthahaḷḷi maṭha, in addition to several others, like the 1050 trees of Nellisaruhāna, the 1450 trees of Yeḍaguḍḍe, the 200 trees of Marēkoppa, and *vṛtti* tenures with 1810 trees in one instance, 110 in another, 30,000 in a third case, 9222 in a fourth, and so on.[484] The record doesn't tell us what trees they were, but since most trees mentioned in other grants are areca nut, and at times coconut, the trees mentioned here might

---

479 Nos. 72 and 78, Ibid.
480 No. 195, Ibid.
481 No. 206, Ibid.
482 Nos. 56, 78, 80, 89, 135, 141, 148, 201, 203, 304, 246, 259, etc in Ibid., are random instances.
483 No. 98, Ibid.
484 No. 212, Ibid.

be either of these. As brāhmaṇas and other elites like the Vīraśaivas turned to land management and attached land to their temples and monasteries in increasing numbers, the control that the peasant magnates once exercised over land began to weaken, leading to increased subjugation and exploitation of the peasantry. At the same time, a new class of merchants appeared in the region to become leading clients for the produce coming from the lands held by temples and monasteries. They procured the surplus from these lands, and sold them in the rural markets. As a result, the peasantry came to be dispossessed of its control over rural markets. The rural markets were now effectively under the grip of the Nāyaka and other chiefs, merchants, and the temples and monasteries.

The significance of temples and monasteries in the regimes of agrarian production and rural markets was less intensely felt in many parts of southern Karnataka, primarily due to the lesser intensity with which commercial crop cultivation occurred here. This, however, was not the case in the coastal and the Malenāḍu regions, where coconut, areca nut, pepper, and other crops were turning out to be decisive in the emerging economy of the seventeenth and the early eighteenth centuries. The active presence of the Portuguese from the sixteenth century onwards, and the arrival of the English East India Company in the seventeenth, created new demands for these crops. This demand was powerful because the European companies supplied the goods not only to Europe, but also to many parts of Asia, as they were engaged in brisk inter-Asia trade as well. The companies were also in need of rice. Coastal Karnataka, where paddy cultivation was extensive, could however meet very little of the demand for rice.

Understandably enough, it was in the coastal and the Malenāḍu regions that the subjection and exploitation of peasantry was most cruelly felt. Here again, the agrestic labourers on the paddy-growing wetlands had a relative advantage, as paddy cultivation was labour intensive and called for a constant supply of labour. On the other hand, agriculture in the orchards, where coconut, areca nut, pepper, and other crops were raised, was less labour intensive, and open to mercenary labour. The possibility of the peasantry being dispossessed from access to land was much greater here. Neo-brāhmaṇical landlordism emerged as a powerful historical force in these regions.

One far-reaching consequence of the rise of this neo-brāhmaṇical landlordism, with its ability to dispossess the peasantry of its control over the means of production and its potentials for drawing mercenary labour from within the region and beyond, was that it was able to build great centres of pilgrimage that attracted a steady clientele from far and wide. Such centres of pilgrimage came up in the coastal and Malenāḍu regions, where the new landlordism was most developed. Uḍupi, Gōkarṇa, Śṛṅgēri, Subrahmaṇya, Kollūru, and Śaṅkaranārāyaṇa were among the prominent centres of pilgrimage here. Note that nineteen of the forty-two western centres of pilgrimage named by Vādirāja in his *Tīrtha Prabandha* (Table 10) were from these areas. This contrasts with southern Karnataka, where neo-brāhmaṇical landlordism was not as widespread or powerful. No centres of pilgrimage (with the exception of the Jaina centre of Śravaṇageḷagoḷa) arose here, that could match the greatness of Uḍupi, Gōkarṇa, or Śṛṅgēri. Although important temples commanding landed wealth existed at Śrīraṅgapaṭṭaṇa, Nañjanagūḍu, and Mēlukōṭe, their potentials as centres of pilgrimage were rarely explored before the nineteenth century. Vādirāja mentions only two centres of pilgrimage from here, Harihara and the obscure Bidirahaḷḷi (Vēṇugrāma). Both were, strictly speaking, not in the south but on the banks of the Tuṅgabhadra, and shared greater historical ties with the north. Neo-brāhmaṇical landlordism was also not deeply entrenched in northern Karnataka in the fifteenth and the sixteenth centuries. Correspondingly, this region also drew a blank as far as centres of pilgrimage were concerned. The *siddha* centres were hubs of activity and commanded a wide following. But these were centres that had forged tributary relationships with a specific set of communities who paid tributes to the monasteries in exchange for the military, the medical, and the other 'magical' services they offered.

The precarious conditions forced upon the peasantry by the new political economy in the coastal and the Malenāḍu region had its logical corollary in the *dāsa* ethic of complacency that the brāhmaṇical establishments promoted. This ethic called for devotion and surrender to the supreme god. Uttering the god's name (*nāmasmaraṇe*) and singing his praise were the cornerstones of this mode of devotion. The story of the Kṛṣṇa image in Uḍupi turning backward and the rear wall of the temple falling apart, so the great devotee Kanakadāsa may have a glimpse of god, captures the submissiveness and the ethic of complacency that the temples and monasteries of the brāhmaṇical classes idealized and advocated. Action, especially in its radical, rebellious, and recalcitrant variants, was to be abjured. For, in the ultimate analysis, the world was a play of the god. Human agency as such did not exist, and volition on the part of human beings was only the substance of fairytales. Human destiny was predestined to be a scene in the god's cosmic play, and all human acts unfurled in the fullness of time as enactments of the divine *līlā*. Once this truth was understood, all that was called for was an emotionally involved appreciation of the god's greatness, and an intense longing for a vision of his face.

In the songs that the *dāsa*s composed in great numbers, an emotionally drawn picture of god occurs against a domestic setting. Its goal was directed towards generating responses of pity and sympathy for the submissive devotee. All that the songs expressed in so many words was that without Kṛṣṇa, the days were dark, the nights devoid of the colour of dreams, and life lacking in purpose, meaning, and fulfillment. Here are a few lines from one of the most popular *kīrtane*s of Vyāsarāya's:

> Kṛṣṇa, come quickly,
> Show your face.
>
> The yellow dress from Kāśī,
> Flute in the hand,
> Sandal (wood paste) applied on the body....[485]

485 Parthasarathy 2013: 545.

Here are lines from another of his songs:

(Say) Kṛṣṇa Kṛṣṇa Kṛṣṇa three times
to bring him to mind.
He will be pleased, grant release,
And bear all burden.

What if all Vēdas and Śāstras are read
And their essence known?
No match to the name of Makarakuṇḍaladhara....[486]

These ripples of submissive devotion initiated by Vyāsarāya turned into huge tides in the hands of Purandaradāsa and Kanakadāsa. Purandara sang:

Raṅga, come,
Pāṇḍuraṅga, come,
Śrīraṅga, come,
Narasiṃha, come,

Child, come,
My father, come,
Mukunda, the beloved of Indira, come....[487]

Here are lines from another of his song:

Can't you say, "Kṛṣṇā"?
No trouble at all, if you remember Kṛṣṇa.

When the human-birth comes,
When there is a tongue,
Can't you say, "Kṛṣṇā"....[488]

A third example from the same bard:

Come, mother Bhāgīrathi,
Show the people,
Show me bathing to the people....[489]

Purandara was almost obsessed with seeing and showing.

Come running, Vaikuṇṭhapati,
I want to see you till the mind is sated.

486 Ibid.
487 No. 760, Karanth 2008.
488 No. 12, Ibid.
489 No. 592, Ibid.

Do not harass, Merciful One,
I beg you, Raṅgayya....[490]

Purandara wrote a large number of songs. The concerns expressed in them are too diverse to be exhausted by a handful of examples. Yet, they share a set of common features. They are mostly set against a domestic backdrop, are dialogic in nature, carry an emotional appeal, long for the physical presence of Kṛṣṇa, and conspicuously lack in intellectual content. The songs of Kanakadāsa are no different, although they invoke the trope of wonder at least on some occasions, and come up with strategies of representation that are, sometimes, lively and original. His song on the elephant-faced god Gaṇēśa is a good example. It is in the form of an address to Gaṇēśa's mother:

Our mother Śāradā, Umāmahēśvarī,
Who is it that dwells in you?
Is it the proud Gaṇanātha,
The son of Kammagōḷa's enemy?

Who is he
With black features on the face,
Ears large as a winnowing sieve,
With sharp tusks?
Is it the chivalrous Gaṇanātha
The son of the three-eyed
With the broken moon?....[491]

The following lines from another of Kanaka's songs invokes a sense of wonder in a striking manner:

Are you in *māyā*, or is *māyā* within you?
Are you in the body, or is the body within you?
Is the void in the temple, or the temple in the void?
Is the eye in the intellect, or the intellect in the eye?
Or, are both the eye and the intellect in you, Hari?

Is sweetness in the sugar, or the sugar in the sweetness?
Or, are both sweetness and sugar in the tongue?
Is tongue in the intellect, or intellect in the tongue?
Or, are both tongue and the intellect in you, Hari?

Is the fragrance in the flower, or the flower in the fragrance?
Or, are both flower and fragrance in the nose?
Or, when the matchless Kāginele Ādikēśavarāya breathes?
Is nothing in me but all in you?[492]

490 Parthasarathy 2013: 445.
491 No. 1, Kavyapremi 1995.
492 No. 47, Ibid.

A third example from Kanaka's oeuvre where Kṛṣṇa is praised:

> Beloved, come,
> Our god has arrived.
>
> Our Raṅga became the red-eyed Mīna (fish)
> And slew Sōma the rogue, ho!
> He slew Sōma the rogue
> And gave the Vēdas to the Golden Bodied, ho!
>
> In the vast forest,
> Our Raṅga stood lifting the hill, ho!
> He stood lifting the hill
> And made the gods great, ho!
>
> Our Raṅga became a wild boar, Dear,
> And slew the Golden Eyed, ho!
> He slew the Golden Eyed
> And gave the earth to the Lotus Born, ho!....[493]

The integrity of the *dāsa* mental economy begins to strike us when we notice that the songs, and other writings of the *dāsa*s, had precious little to tell us about the body. Where the *siddha*s repeatedly invoked the body and almost never ceased from reflecting upon its composition and its relationship with the self, questions concerning the body never figured in the *dāsa* oeuvre. Other than the sensory urge to have a glimpse of Kṛṣṇa or hear about him, the body had little significance in the *dāsa* scheme of things. Why, after all, should the submissive ones have longed for a body? Unlike the *siddha*s, there was no enterprise the *dāsa*s had on hand, no public works to be carried out, no armies to be built, no wars to be fought. The question of reflecting upon the body simply did not arise. They pictured the playful Kṛṣṇa in their minds, and portrayed a self that was fully disembodied and existing as an ideal rather than substance.

In terms of intellectual content, the songs drew a near cipher. Even the Sanskrit commentaries of Vādirāja, like the *Mahābhārata Tātparya Nirṇaya Bhāvaprakāśikā*, the *Tantrasāraṭīkā*, the *Mahābhārata Lakṣālaṅkāra*, the *Taittirīyōpaniṣad Bhāṣyaṭīkā*, the *Kaṭhōpaniṣad Bhāṣyaṭīkā*, the *Talavakārōpaniṣad Bhāṣyaṭīka*, and the *Māṇḍūkyōpaniṣad Bhāṣyaṭīkā*, contained precious little in terms of intellectual innovation, although they were monumental pieces of learning. Occasional sparks of argumentative ingenuity were seen only in the works of Vyāsarāya, although the arguments were easily falsifiable from within the contemporary conventions of reasoning. The larger corpus of *dāsa* literature only explicated what Ānanda Tīrtha

493 No. 77, Ibid.

had ingeniously written three centuries ago, and what Jaya Tīrtha had attempted to systematize in the fourteenth century. The commentaries of Vādirāja and others were perhaps meant to serve as textbooks for the students of the monasteries.

One might suggest that the *dāsa*s abjured the production of knowledge in its entirety. Knowledge, for them, was not open to expansion or innovation, as it had already been brought into its final form by Ānanda Tīrtha and Jaya Tīrtha, whose works marked a great intellectual closure. Had Umberto Eco written a *Name of the Rose* set against the sixteenth and the seventeenth century world of the *dāsa*s, we do not know what shape it would have taken. But there certainly would be one line from the great novel that he would put in the mouth of an influential *dāsa* pontiff: "There is no progress, no revolution of ages, in the history of knowledge, but at most a continuous and sublime recapitulation".

The world of the *dāsa*s remained stable, lost in its orthodoxy, intellectual deficit, exploitation, submission, and complacency, until the nineteenth century. But the world of the *siddha*s underwent tremendous transformations after the seventeenth century. We must now turn to this story of transformations.

6 Sainthood in Transition and the Crisis of Alienation

The Marāṭha warlord Śivāji died in the year 1680. He, more than anyone else, had mastered the art of political conceit in the seventeenth century, and perfected strategies of guerilla warfare developed earlier in the century by Malik Aṃbar.[494] His was by far the greatest threat to the Mughals before the invasion of Nādir Śāh from Iran, as it involved guerilla strategies they had hitherto not confronted. Guerilla warfare consisted of avoiding direct encounters, but cutting off supply lines, and resorting to multiple attacks at vulnerable locations away from the battlefield.[495] Śivāji had deployed these tactics against the Ādil Śāhis with a remarkable measure of success. This had enabled him to make strong inroads into northern and northwestern Karnataka, especially after he treacherously killed the Ādil Śāhi general Afzal Khān on 10 November 1659. By the time of Śivāji's death, the Marāṭhas were in control of many strategic locations in coastal Karnataka, the Western Ghats, and the adjoining regions to the east. Efforts were afoot to consolidate these gains by deploying functionaries to collect revenue. These portfolios called for a class of literate personnel faithful to the Marāṭha cause. The avenues for employment thus generated were to attract the Citpāvan and Karāḍ brāhmaṇas, who migrated from the Koṅkaṇa region to various parts of Marāṭhavāḍā.[496] They also moved in considerable numbers into northern and northwestern Karnataka. Sārasvata and Dēśasta brāhmaṇas also found employment under the Marāṭhas.[497] A credit network centering on Pūnā emerged, with brāhmaṇa bankers controlling it.[498] By the mid decades of the eighteenth century, neo-brāhmaṇical landlordism evolved powerfully in many parts of northern and northwestern Karnataka. Marāṭhi brāhmaṇas were the major stakeholders in this enterprise.

In 1686, six years after the death of Śivāji, the Ādil Śāhī state of Vijayapura collapsed following a protracted struggle with the Mughals. Auraṅgzēb annexed the Ādil Śāhi territories to the Mughal state, and formed the new *suba* of Karnataka out of some parts of the annexed territories. As a token of gratitude for the services rendered to the Mughals by the late Abdul Karīm Khān, Auraṅgzēb rewarded the deceased's son Abdul Raūf Khān with a *mansabdāri* rank of 6000,[499] conferred the title Dilēr

494 On Malik Amber and his innovation of guerilla warfare, see Gordon 1998: 42-45.
495 Ibid., 45.
496 Ibid., 194.
497 Ibid., 144.
498 Ibid.
499 *Mansabdāri* was a system of revenue and military tenure created by the Mughal ruler Akbar (r. 1556-1605). See Richards 1993: 63-68.

Khān upon him, and placed him in charge of the new *suba*.[500] Raūf Khān established the city of Savaṇūru, twenty kilometres to the south of Lakṣmēśvara, and made it his headquarters. Vijayapura was deserted within a few decades. The revenue, which the Ādil Śāhis had commanded, was now distributed among the successor chiefs in different parts of the region. In northern Karnataka, claims were made on the Ādil Śāhi revenue by the Gōlkoṇḍa rulers, and later, by the Nizāṃs of Haidarābād from the east, and the Marāṭhas from the north and northwest. The Surapura chiefs, whose line began with Hanuma Nāyaka upon whom Koḍēkallu Basava had conferred 'kingship', was an important pretender to a share of this revenue. Raūf Khān of Savaṇūru was another claimant, and by far, the most successful. His *suba* yielded Rupees 20,040,000 every year, a little over a fourth of the Rupees 78,400,000 that the Ādil Śāhi state collected as revenue during the reign of Muhammad Ādil Śāh (r. 1626-1656).[501]

Increased cultivation of commercial crops from the seventeenth century, and their trade through the routes along the Western Ghats, made the ghats and the areas near them gain in importance. The early Marāṭhas seem to have understood the significance of this emerging phenomenon. Land revenue from the commercial crop orchards, and the income they yielded through proceeds and transit tolls, were too sizeable to be ignored. The Marāṭhas directed great energies towards the control of this region. It was, in all likelihood, for the same reason that Raūf Khān moved from Vijayapura to Savaṇūru.

If the areas adjoining the ghats offered rich markets for political entrepreneurship, literate brāhmaṇas, and mercantile and military labour, there is no reason why it should not have attracted a similar market for renunciation, more so when many renouncers in northern Karnataka were also military entrepreneurs. Tinthiṇi Mōnappa seems to have been aware of this possibility. He moved from Tinthiṇi in the Śōrāpura dōāb, to Varavi, near Lakṣmēśvara. His friend Cannavīra left Vijayapura, wandered extensively, and eventually settled down at Śirahaṭṭi, three kilometres away from Varavi, where he attained renown as Śirahaṭṭi Fakīrappa. From the village of Sāvaḷagi near Kalaburagi, the saint Śivaliṅga moved closer to the ghats, and settled down in a hamlet on the banks of the Ghaṭaprabha, twenty kilometres northwest of Gōkāk. The hamlet eventually came to be known as Sāvaḷagi after the village from where Śivaliṅga came.

The lives of these saints resembled those of the earlier *siddha*s in several respects. Like Ārūḍha Saṅgamanātha, Koḍēkallu Basava, Maṇṭēsvāmi, and others, they travelled widely. They performed miracles, encountered kings and brought them into submission, excavated tanks, caused rain. But there were three notable additions to their portfolio: they organized feeding in their monasteries, they blessed barren

500 Devadevan 2010a.
501 Ibid.

couples with children, and they forged real (and not imagined) relationships with saints of other tradition, including the Sūfis.

Representative of this new sainthood is the life of Śirahaṭṭi Fakīrappa (ca. 1650-1725), a saint whose life is suffused with stories of miracles. Fakīrappa was born in Vijayapura. It is said, after a trope concerning the birth of the *siddha*s that was well established by the seventeenth century, that his parents Śivayya and Gauramma had no children for a long time. Upon the suggestion of a friend, Gauramma approached the great Chisti saint of Vijayapura, Khvājā Amīn-ud-dīn Alā (1597-1675). The Khvājā blessed her with a child and instructed her to hand over the child to his hospice, whereupon she would be blessed with another child whom the family could own for itself. Thus was born the prodigious Cannavīra. But the couple failed to keep their word, and refused to give away the child to Amīn-ud-dīn. As a result, Cannavīra died. Realizing their lapse, Śivayya and Gauramma prayed for mercy. Amīn forgave them, and brought Cannavīra back to life. The child was handed over to the hospice, and the couple blessed with another child. Cannavīra grew up to become the preeminent disciple of Amīn-ud-dīn. He evolved into a great miracle-worker at a young age. The Ādil Śāhi Sultān of Vijayapura learnt of his supernatural powers, and decided to test the young prodigy.[502] At his bidding, Amīn ordered Cannavīra to offer *namāz* sitting on water. To the shock of the Sultān, Cannavīra took his mat, walked on the waters of the nearby lake, and offered *namāz* sitting on the waters.[503] The Sultān realized that Cannavīra was a boy with divine powers. He became a follower of the boy instantly. This was the commencement of a great career in miracle-working. Cannavīra soon came to be revered as Fakīrappa.[504]

As with the other saints whose lives we have examined so far, a long voyage occupied the next leg of Śirahaṭṭi Fakīrappa's life. He left Vijayapura after the demise of Amīn, who assured him that he would meet him again in the next birth, when he will be born at Gōnāḷa as Mōnappa in a family of oil pressers.[505]

---

502 The reference is perhaps to Ali II (r. 1656-1672).

503 In other accounts, this miracle is said to have been performed by Amīn-ud-dīn himself. See Hanif 2000: 36-41 for a brief account of Amīn. Also see Eaton 1978.

504 Fakīrappa (from Fakīr) is a common name among the Vīraśaivas in the region even to this day. Other Islamic names adopted by the Vīraśaivas include Pīraṇṇa (from Pīr) and Husēnavva (from Hussain).

505 The reference is to Tinthiṇi Mōnappa. On this saint, see the rather mediocre Padasetti 1992, which is the only existing study on him. While hagiography places the birth of Mōnappa after the demise of Amīn (insofar as he is treated as a reincarnation of the latter), the available historical evidence shows that the two saints were contemporaries. Tinthiṇi is on the river Kṛṣṇa, and lies twenty-five kilometres to the east of Koḍēkallu. It does not take more than five hours to travel from Tinthiṇi to Koḍēkallu by foot. It took me three hours and forty minutes to cover this distance in 2002. In 2013, when I was older by eleven years and heavier by nineteen kilograms, I walked in the opposite direction from Koḍēkallu to Tinthiṇi in four hours and twenty-five minutes.

In the course of this great voyage, Fakīrappa performed a number of miracles. When he reached the village of Baṇḍeppanahaḷḷi, a communal dispute among the villagers had begun to take the form of a riot. Fakīrappa intervened, and restored peace. This was apparently done with the help of a miracle. He lit a lamp with water instead of oil,[506] and asked Baṇḍeppa (seemingly the founder of the village) to place it at an assigned location for three days. The lamp continued to burn even after three days. The feuding villagers were convinced of Fakīrappa's divinity, and on his advice, built a monastery in the village.

The next miracle happened at Kauḍīmaṭṭi. Here, Fakīrappa chanced upon a young girl Kamala, who was about to commit suicide by throwing herself into a well. She had taken the decision following long years of torture by her mother-in-law, Kāḍamma. Fakīrappa persuaded her to return home. No sooner did Kamala reach home than news arrived that Kāḍamma's daughter Gauramma had committed suicide by jumping into a well. The news came as a rude shock to Kāḍamma. Even as she was trying to come to terms with it, Fakīrappa arrived on the scene. He informed Kāḍamma that her daughter was tortured by her in-laws, which forced her into suicide. It was a *kārmic* reaction to Kāḍamma's cruel behaviour towards her own daughter-in-law. Kāḍamma realized what the *siddha* was hinting at, and pleaded with him to absolve her of the sins committed and bring her daughter back to life. Fakīrappa acquiesced, and the deceased Gauramma sprang back to life.

We find *karma* invoked again in the next miracle. This story is about Sundaramma, a woman from an affluent family who showed no devotion towards god, had scant regard for elders, and constantly insulted the devout. The result was that she had no children. Sundaramma learnt of Fakīrappa's powers, and approached him with request for granting a child. Under the *siddha*'s magical influence, she abandoned vanity, became a deep believer in god, and was blessed with a son.

The journey of the miracle-worker continued. In Muddēbihāḷa the pontiff of the Hirēmaṭha insulted Fakīrappa and, in consequence, contracted chronic stomachache. He prayed to Fakīrappa for mercy, and was cured of the illness. In gratitude, the pontiff became a devotee of Fakīrappa, and renamed his monastery as Śivayōgi maṭha. Fakīrappa also helped a couple from the Śivayōgi maṭha to overcome their poverty by gifting them a cow, which brought forth two bullocks and helped them in agriculture. The couple prospered, and their wealthy descendants continue to pay tributes to Fakīrappa to this day. In Śirōḷa, our hero met a young widow, Girijamma, whose child had died of snakebite. Fakīrappa brought the child back to life. He was then approached by a childless woman Gaṅgamma with prayers to bless her with a son. Gaṅgamma's prayers were also answered favourably.

---

506 We have seen in chapter 5 that Tōṇṭada Siddhaliṅga is also credited with lighting a lamp with water.

Fakīrappa's next destination was Citradurga, where he stayed for a long time at the Murugharājēndra maṭha. When he approached the gates of the maṭha, he was denied entry, as he was not wearing a *liṅga*. Like Maṇṭēsvāmi before him, Fakīrappa tried to force himself into the maṭha, and like Kaṭugara Saṅgayya before them, the gatekeepers pushed him out forcibly. Impulsive that he was on the one hand, and a miracle-worker on the other, Fakīrappa made the *liṅga*s worn by the gatekeepers disappear, to their great dread. He then vanished from the scene, and miraculously appeared in front of the pontiff inside the monastery. The *liṅga*s of the gatekeepers were restored after they begged for forgiveness.

The pontiff accorded Fakīrappa a warm welcome. Fakīrappa took up the responsibility of maintaining the cattle pen in the maṭha, and seems to have put in place an arrangement for surplus production of milk, leading to additional revenues to the maṭha. He might also have deployed the bullocks effectively in the agricultural fields held by the monastery.

Anecdotes of several miracles are told about Fakīrappa during his Citradurga days. These supernatural acts were performed in front of the boys with whom Fakīrappa took the cattle out to graze. In one such story, he is said to have picked up a cobra that bowed down to him, and dropped it in an anthill. On another occasion, a tiger arrived on the scene when he was grazing his herd with the boys. The herd and the boys fled, but Fakīrappa remained where he was, with a smile on his face. The tiger came to him, and bowed down to his feet. The saint sat on the tiger and rode around for a while, making a display of his prowess. In a third story, Fakīrappa distributed sweetmeats and food of their choice to the boys from a bag he was carrying. According to this story, the cowherds carried lunch packets every day when they went out to graze the cattle. On one day, one of the boys came without his packet, as his mother was busy preparing sweetmeats and other delicacies to throw a feast at noon. The boy decided to go home for lunch. Fakīrappa and the other boys urged him to stay, and share the food they had brought. The boy refused, saying that he ate *roṭṭi* (bread of wheat or millet flour) everyday and was sick of it, and that he didn't want to miss a feast. As the boy left, Fakīrappa asked the other cowherds what their choice dishes were, and miraculously produced them one after the other from his bag. The friends now called out to the boy who had left for home, and told him what was happening. The boy returned, shyly. Fakīrappa produced a feast for him from his bag, and gave out a message: there is always happiness in sharing food with others and eating together. This, however, is not the message that the historian draws from the anecdote, as we shall see later in this chapter.

After a long stay at the Murugharājēndra maṭha, time came for Fakīrappa to depart. He left for Haidarābād, to have an audience with the Nizāṃ. Once again, he was denied entry, and once again, Fakīrappa miraculously entered the palace, this time ending up in the queen's apartment. The news of an infiltrator in the queen's apartment spread throughout the palace, and the Nizāṃ rushed to the spot with a dagger in his hand, and a convoy of troops behind him. To his surprise, it was not a grown up man that he saw there, but an infant in the queen's lap. The queen was found breast-feeding the baby. What miracle, the Nizāṃ wondered: a baby in his barren queen's lap, and she suckling it. When he asked for an explanation, the queen said that she had no cue of what was happening, and told him that a Fakīr appeared in her apartment, fell into her lap, metamorphosed into a baby and made her suckle. The Nizāṃ stood dumbfounded. Now, Fakīrappa resumed his original form. The Nizāṃ fell to his feet, pleaded for forgiveness, and offered him half his kingdom. Fakīrappa refused to take the kingdom, and instead, urged him to maintain law and order in his realm, and restore harmony between the communities that were engaged in conflict and violence.[507] He also asked for the dagger the Nizāṃ had brought to kill him. The Nizāṃ offered Fakīrappa the dagger. There is preserved in the Śirahaṭṭi maṭha a dagger that is carried by the pontiff every year during the annual fair. This is believed to be the one presented by the Nizāṃ. In all likelihood, the dagger was given by Raūf Khān, the Navāb of the nearby Savaṇūru, or by the head of the Jummā Masjid in Lakṣmēśvara with which Fakīrappa seems to have maintained healthy relations.

From Haidarābād, the miracle-worker went to Dilli where he met the Mughal ruler Akbar.[508] He assumed the form of a five-coloured parakeet and flew into the hall where Akbar was holding court. The king was surprised to see the bird, and asked his renowned courtier Bīrbal what omen it signified. A parakeet is always a great omen, Bīrbal replied. Now, Fakīrappa turned back to his original form. He asked Akbar to bring him the sacred stone and pendant that his *guru* Cannabasava had left in the palace. Your *guru* Cannabasava left a stone and a pendant in my palace? Akbar asked in disbelief. Yes, Fakīrappa replied; it is kept in a casket in the basement of the fourth room in the northern quarter. The king and his entourage rushed to the basement of the said room, and discovered a casket there. In the casket were a sacred stone and a pendant. Akbar agreed to give it to Fakīrappa if he performed one more miracle. Here we go, Fakīrappa said; the royal elephant of yours has fallen dead in the stable. The king rushed to the stable and found that Fakīrappa's words had indeed come true. He appealed to him to restore the mammoth back to life. Fakīrappa stroked the animal, and it rose from the ground as if it was waking up from a long sleep. Pleased with the *līlā*, Akbar bowed to the saint, gave him the stone and the pendant, and presented him with a battle shield.

---

507 The first full-length hagiography of Fakīrappa, composed in the traditional *ṣaṭpadi* metres, was completed by Dyāmpurada Canna as late as 1945. This period of widespread communal hatred unfurling against the backdrop of the impending partition of India is likely to have influenced the poet. It is under this historical circumstance that Fakīrappa's relationship with Amīn-ud-dīn came to be interpreted as exemplifying, and intended to send out the message of, harmony between the Hindus and the Muslims.

508 Note that we are reproducing a hagiography for purposes of historical analysis; Akbar died in 1605, at least half a century before Fakīrappa was born.

The Nizāṃ of Haidarābād gave him a dagger, and the Mughal king of Dilli, a shield. Whether or not these events, or something remotely resembling it, really occurred, is a question that need not deter us here, as the story is certainly not misplaced or devoid of meaning. For, isn't it figuring in an account of a warrior-saint's life? Daggers, swords, and shields are powerful symbols in the political imagination of a warrior-saint tradition, and the story of acquiring them through defiance is meant to be a political statement in its own right.

From Dilli, Fakīrappa returned to the countryside of northern Karnataka. There lived in the village of Sagarakannōṭa a widow called Avvaliṅgavva. She belonged to a family of peasants, and had two sons, Bharamagauḍa and Sōmanagauḍa. Following the demise of her husband, she lost her access to property, and was regularly ill treated by her brothers-in-law and their wives. A friend of hers advised her to approach Fakīrappa for help. Avvaliṅgavva prayed to Fakīrappa in her mind, and began to look out for the wandering saint. One night, Fakīrappa appeared to her in a dream, and advised her to move to Māgaḍi. Avvaliṅgavva obliged. Fakīrappa met with Avvaliṅgavva in Māgaḍi, and asked her to find work, as this would enable her to tide over her current state of poverty. He then went to Kadaḍi, where the village headman had passed away some days ago without leaving an heir behind. The villagers gathered around Fakīrappa, and requested him to find a suitable headman for their village. Fakīrappa informed them of Bharamagauḍa, Avvaliṅgavva's son, who he said would make an ideal and efficient village headman. The villagers agreed to the seer's proposal, and Bharamagauḍa was appointed the headman of Kadaḍi.

The next destination in Fakīrappa's tour was Dundūru, a village that faced acute water scarcity. Like a master water-diviner, he identified a place that would throw up sweet water, and caused a well to be excavated on the spot. He built a monastery in the village and planted a jasmine vine. The half-acre garden of jasmine found today at Dundūru is believed to have developed from the vine planted by Fakīrappa.

Aṅkuś Khān was the ruler of Lakṣmēśvara at this time.[509] One night, he was playing chess with his wife when the lamp began to run out of oil. As it was late in the night, there were few servants in the palace, and the ones on duty were unable to find oil. Aṅkuś Khān asked the guard to spread news in the town through tom-tom that whoever prevents the lamp from getting extinguished will be given a reward of their choice. Fakīrappa arrived at the palace in the company of Avvaliṅgavva and Sōmanagauḍa, and replayed the miracle he had performed earlier at Baṇḍeppanahaḷḷi. He asked Sōmanagauḍa to pour water from his jar into the lamp. No sooner was it done than the wick sprang back to life. Aṅkuś Khān was pleased. When he asked

509 Aṅkuś Khān was an influential and widely popular Ādil Śāhi official, who built the Jummā Masjid of Lakṣmēśvara in 1617. He is unlikely to have been alive when Fakīrappa arrived in the region towards the close of the seventeenth century or in the early years of the eighteenth century. Aṅkuś Khān enjoys a wide following in this region, and is revered as a Sūfi saint.

Sōmanagauḍa what reward he wanted, he received the most unexpected reply. The instruction Sōmanagauḍa had received from Fakīrappa was to ask for the Khān's kingdom. "Give me your kingdom", Sōmanagauḍa said. Ankuś Khān was now in a dilemma. Fakīrappa decided to intervene. "You have no children. Your wife is barren. Who do you think will succeed to your kingdom after your death? Hand over the kingdom to Sōmanagauḍa and accept him as your son." Aṅkuś Khān agreed to the proposal on the condition that Sōmanaguaḍa and his family adopt the title of Khān, and administer the kingdom by wearing a green headgear and an Islamic necklace. Sōmanagauḍa agreed to these terms, and became a ruler. To this day, his 'Hindu' descendants bear the title, Khān.

Continuing his journey across the villages and towns of the region, Fakīrappa reached Ḍaṃbaḷa. Here, a merchant's wife refused him alms, and as a result, the *liṅga*s worn by members of the family disappeared. Predictably enough, the liṅgas were restored after the people expressed remorse and begged for mercy. In a mosque in Ḍaṃbaḷa, Fakīrappa freed a group of saints from their addiction to poppy leaves.

During his stay at Ḍaṃbaḷa, an arrogant saint called Bhārati arrived there and challenged the chief, Veṅkappa Dēsāyi, to organize a debate with him. The chief was helpless. He knew of no scholars in his territory that had the genius to take on Bhārati. A debate was certain to be humiliating, and so it eventually turned out. Everyone who dared to confront Bhārati was defeated. It so happened that an imbecile brāhmaṇa boy was serving Fakīrappa with great devotion at this time. He was the butt of ridicule, not only for his limited intellect, but also for serving a wandering saint against the advice of fellow brāhmaṇas. Now, Fakīrappa decided to send the boy to debate with Bhārati, much to the consternation of the townsmen. The boy arrived at the venue, declared that he had no knowledge of Vēdas, Śāstras, Purāṇas, or any of the other such great sciences as grammar, logic, rhetoric, metrics etc., but was endowed with the blessings of the *guru*. With this solemn declaration, he began debate. And what a prodigy the boy turned out to be! He defeated Bhārati with hardly any effort.

At the end of his great journeys, Fakīrappa decided to settle down at Śirahaṭṭi. Here, he dug a little well to the north of the village, built a hermitage, made it his abode, and resumed his life of performing miracles. The hermitage eventually became a monastery. As in Ḍaṃbaḷa, he caused *liṅga*s of a merchant's family and his guests vanish when the merchant refused him alms. And again as in Ḍaṃbaḷa, the *liṅga*s were given back to them when the merchant fell at his feet in remorse.

Sometime after Fakīrappa had settled down at Śirahaṭṭi, an eminent peer of his reached Varavi, three kilometres from Śirahaṭṭi. His name was Tinthiṇi Mōnappa. He had set out on a journey from the village of Tinthiṇi near Koḍēkallu, where he had lived for many years. At Varavi, he founded another maṭha, and gained renown as Varavi Mōnappa. One day, he came to Śirahaṭṭi. Fakīrappa immediately identified his *guru*, for wasn't Mōnappa an incarnation of his *guru* Khvājā Amīn-ud-dīn? Mōnappa took Fakīrappa to Lakṣmēśvara to perform another miracle. An old woman called Piḍḍavve had died without repaying a loan she had incurred. Mōnappa and Fakīrappa approached the dead body and said, "You can't go away without repaying the loan. We bid you return and pay the money". What next? The dead body started breathing again. Piḍḍavve repaid the loan, and Mōnappa and Fakīrappa blessed her to live for some more years.

By this time, Fakīrappa had acquired a group of faithful devotees. He travelled to Kōḷivāḍa with some of them, and built a monastery there. It is said that when he reached the village, nobody came to welcome him or pay respects to him. Dyāmavva, the deity of the village, was upset by this, and prevailed upon the villagers to become devotees of Fakīrappa. She also performed a miracle and compelled a trader from Hubbaḷḷi to donate land for the monastery.

Few *siddha* accounts speak of a devotee blessed by a saint overstepping his advice. The story of Fakīrappa provides one such instance. Avvaliṅgavva was in a state of destitution. With the blessings of Fakīrappa, her first son Bharamagauḍa had become the headman of a village, and her second son Sōmanagauḍa, a ruler. Avvaliṅgavva was now on the verge of death. She desired to have a sprawling tomb built in her honour, and sought Fakīrappa's consent for the same. Fakīrappa tried to dissuade her from this misadventure. He prediced that her tomb would remain unkempt, deserted, and neglected by everyone. But Avvaliṅgavva decided not to oblige. She spent a fortune on building a tomb for herself. After her death, she was buried there. But eventually, Fakīrappa's prophecy came true. The tomb survives in Śirahaṭṭi to this day in a state of utter neglect.

Fakīrappa had lived a long life. He had performed countless *līlās*. It was now time for him to depart. One day, a band of street performers came to Śirahaṭṭi. Fakīrappa invited them to his monastery and asked them to perform. A fifteen-year old boy was the cynosure of the performance. Fakīrappa realized the boy's potentials and asked the bandleader to offer him to the monastery. The bandleader refused, as the boy was the most sought-after performer of the band. The band left Śirahaṭṭi, but made no progress, as no village appeared in sight even after walking on and on for many hours. The bandleader realized what had gone wrong. He returned to Śirahaṭṭi, begged Fakīrappa for forgiveness, and offered the boy to the monastery.

The following day, Fakīrappa summoned the elders of the village, and announced that the boy would be the next pontiff of the Śirahaṭṭi maṭha. The elders were hesitant, as they regarded a boy from a caste of performers unfit for the lofty position of a pontiff. "You are right", Fakīrappa said with sarcasm, "the boy is from an impure caste. Let us purify him in fire, as there is no greater purifier than fire". Accordingly, a bonfire was made, and, the boy put in the blaze to the dread of the elders. The next day, Fakīrappa summoned the elders again, and cleared the ash from the bonfire in their presence. And what did the elders see there? The boy, hale and healthy, unburnt, and unaffected by the fire! "The boy has been purified in fire. He is not of low origins anymore. He will be our successor", Fakīrappa announced. He then outlined the rituals, fairs, and ceremonies that should be performed in the monastery after his demise. He also ordained that the pontiffs would be known, in the consecutive order of succession, as Fakīra Siddharāma, Fakīra Śivayōgi, and Fakīra Cannavīra.[510]

Shortly after these arrangements were made, Fakīrappa assumed the form of a serpent, and disappeared into an anthill. His tomb is believed to be built over this anthill.

Fakīrappa was the paradigmatic miracle-worker of the late seventeenth and the early eighteenth century. He was among the three greatest saints renowned for supernatural powers that northern Karnataka had ever seen (the other two being Sāvaḷagi Śivaliṅga and Kalaburagi Śaraṇabasava). It was for this reason that he became widely influential in the subsequent times, and monasteries in his honour built extensively during the late eighteenth, the nineteenth, and the twentieth centuries. Today, there are forty-eight known maṭhas of Śirahaṭṭi Fakīrappa in Karnataka. At least four of them were apparently built during his lifetime, viz. the maṭhas at Śirahaṭṭi, Baṇḍeppanahaḷḷi, Dundūru, and Kōḷivāḍa. Table 12 gives a list of the known monasteries of Fakīrappa.

Śirahaṭṭi Fakīrappa's story is similar to the hagiography of the earlier saint, Koḍēkallu Basava, in several respects. The saint composed no poetry. Neither did he promote trade or develop a distinct *darśana* of his own. Yet, he was a warrior-saint, carried out public works extensively, shared a relationship with the rulers that was far from cordial, and actively engaged with the peasantry. However, the context of his initiatives, and their impacts, were markedly different. Fakīrappa was functioning in an age of rural scarcity and large-scale dispossession of the peasantry and other classes from their traditional access to land. Acts like excavating wells, causing rain, finding employment for his dependents, and helping them tide over poverty resonated very differently with the rural illiterate masses. In this connection, it must be stressed that the stories of Avvaliṅgavva and the couple from the Śivayōgi maṭha in Muddēbihāḷa do not seem to be adequately emblematic. For, Fakīrappa was a warrior-saint, and is likely to have recruited a large number of dispossessed peasants into his militia. Such instances are not recorded in the extant hagiography, presumably because the hagiography was compiled in the twentieth century, when the image of the saint-as-warrior with a band of troops was long-forgotten and patently unfamiliar to an institution that had chosen to preach peace between Hindus and Muslims. Yet, vestiges of the warrior past have survived. The pontiff of the Śirahaṭṭi maṭha meets his devotees once in a year on horseback, carrying the dagger in his hand. The pontiff at Sāvaḷagi also continues to this day to ride a horse with a sword in his hand during

510 The Śirahaṭṭi maṭha has had thirteen successors so far, conveniently named as Fakīra Siddharāma Svāmi I, Fakīra Śivayōgi Svāmi I, Fakīra Cannavīra Svāmi I, Fakīra Siddharāma Svāmi II, Fakīra Śivayōgi Svāmi II, Fakīra Cannavīra Svāmi II, Fakīra Siddharāma Svāmi III, Fakīra Śivayōgi Svāmi III, Fakīra Cannavīra Svāmi III, Fakīra Siddharāma Svāmi IV, Fakīra Śivayōgi Svāmi IV, Fakīra Cannavīra Svāmi IV and Fakīra Siddharāma Svāmi V.

festivals. In contrast to the Pāḷegāras of the south who also had militias with peasant recruits in them, Śirahaṭṭi Fakīrappa, Sāvaḷagi Śivaliṅga, and the other warrior-saints of the north presented a compelling personality: a holy man, making the dispossessed peasant fight, literally, to earn a living. This new saint was, therefore, simultaneously an embodiment of clairvoyance, credibility, and contingency.

Table 12. Places where Fakīrappa Monasteries Exist[511]

Sl. No.	Place	Tālūk	District	Sl. No.	Place	Tālūk	District
1.	Śirahaṭṭi	Śirahaṭṭi	Gadaga	25.	Navalagunda	Navalagunda	Dhāravāḍa
2.	Baḍni	-do-	-do-	26.	Rāṇēbennūru	Rāṇēbennūru	Hāvēri
3.	Svāgyāḷa	-do-	-do-	27.	Āladakaṭṭi	Hāvēri	-do-
4.	Lakṣmēśvara	-do-	-do-	28.	Hāvanūru	-do-	-do-
5.	Bannikoppa	-do-	-do-	29.	Maraḍūru	-do-	-do-
6.	Koñcagēri	-do-	-do-	30.	Haḷḷūru	Savadatti	Beḷagāvi
7.	Māgaḍi	-do-	-do-	31.	Sattigēri	-do-	-do-
8.	Yatnaḷḷi	-do-	-do-	32.	Harihara	Harihara	Dāvaṇagere
9.	Saṃśi	Kundagōḷa	Dhāravāḍa	33.	Handrāḷu	Koppaḷa	Koppaḷa
10.	Maḷali	-do-	-do-	34.	Tigari	-do-	-do-
11.	Gadaga	Gadaga	Gadaga	35.	Maisūru	Maisūru	Maisūru
12.	Lakkuṇḍi	-do-	-do-	36.	Baṇḍeppanahaḷḷi	Muddēbihāḷa	Vijayapura
13.	Savaṇūru	Savaṇūru	Hāvēri	37.	Kauḍīmaṭṭi	Śōrāpura	Yādagiri
14.	Koppa	-do-	-do-	38.	Śirōḷa	Mudhōḷa	Bāgalakōṭe
15.	Sirabaḍagi	-do-	-do-	39.	Bāḍigi Būdīhāḷa	Bīḷagi	-do-
16.	Kaḍakōḷa	-do-	-do-	40.	Baṅkāpura	Śiggāvi	Hāvēri
17.	Kōḷivāḍa	Hubbaḷḷi	Dhāravāḍa	41.	Nēginālḷa	Bailahoṅgala	Beḷagāvi
18.	Kurtakōṭi	Gadaga	Gadaga	42.	Agaḷavāḍi	Navalagunda	Dhāravāḍa
19.	Kirēsūru	Navalagunda	Dhāravāḍa	43.	Ennāpura	Ānēkallu	Beṅgaḷūru
20.	Dundūru	Navalagunda	-do-	44.	Śahāpura	Śahāpura	Yādagiri
21.	Śirūru	-do-	-do-	45.	Doḍḍa Jaṭaka	Nāgamaṅgala	Maṇḍya
22.	Kabanūru	Śiggāvi	Hāvēri	46.	Baṅkalagi	Sindagi	Vijayapura
23.	Oḍḍaṭṭi	Muṇḍaragi	Gadaga	47.	Baṇṭanūru	-do-	-do-
24.	Dhāravāḍa	Dhāravāḍa	Dhāravāḍa	48.	Cikkamuccalaguḍḍa	Bādāmi	Bāgalakōṭe

The era beginning with the mid seventeenth century was typified by widespread dispossession of the peasantry from their traditional access to land in the dryland belts of the Deccan. It threw up thousands of Avvaliṅgavvas, Bharamagauḍas, and Sōmanagauḍas across the region. This resulted from a decline in labour demand caused by a growing preference for commercial crops that were less labour intensive. Its inevitable corollary was that in the precarious labour market generated by the

511 Source: Siddharama Swami 2002: 228-229. Table 12 updates the information and rectifies the errors contained in the source.

commercial crop plantations, the peasantry had to remain glued to the paddy-producing wetlands, or the dryland belts where other grains like *jowar* (white millet) and *ragi* (finger millet) grew. This opened up a new chapter in reinforcing forced or bonded agrestic labour and strengthening the forces of exploitation. That this was accompanied by the rising acquisition of landed wealth by brāhmaṇa, Vīraśaiva, and other ritual and literary elites brought in the dimension of caste on a scale hitherto unknown in the history of the region.

This development also affected the prospects of sainthood. The new *siddha*s like Śirahaṭṭi Fakīrappa, Sāvaḷagi Śivaliṅga, and Tinthiṇi Mōnappa had to engage with this emerging situation. Mōnappa more than anyone else decried the institution of caste in his *vacana*s. In one of his *vacana*, Mōnappa says:

> The pearl is born in a shell,
> The diamond is born in a stone,
> Once the great *śaraṇa*s are born in fire / in the low caste
> Can one say, Basavaṇṇa, that my line or his line is great?[512]

Here, like many other *siddha* poets, Mōnappa plays on the word *hole*. The word signifies the fireplace. But it is used, through a corruption of the word, to indicate the holeya caste. The holeya was an agrestic labourer or slave who worked in the fields, *hola*. Mōnappa uses it to create a double entendre that is at once sharp and moving. Elsewhere, he says:

> The word does not vanish, the hole does not fill.
> Those who violate the norms and decrees
> Are pure holeyas by caste, Basavaṇṇa.[513]

Further,

> Caste customs exist when there is cooked rice,
> Vows and daily rituals, when there is water.
> When cooked rice and water deplete,
> What if the poor live in a palace?[514]

Mōnappa has more such *vacana*s, which criticize caste prejudices. One of them ridicules those who refuse cooked rice but consume with great relish the milk and the ghee (that a dirty animal yields).[515] What an irony that the milk from the flesh (of the cow) and sweet that the insect (i.e., the honeybee) yields are never disregarded,

512 Araganji 2001: 142.
513 Ibid., 144.
514 Ibid., 143.
515 Ibid., 144.

but the *śaraṇa*s born of fire are looked down upon as low caste.[516] Here, Mōnappa is echoing Kanakadāsa, who in the sixteenth century had sung: don't they offer the lotus, born in filth, to the flower-navalled one; don't the brāhmaṇas on earth drink the milk produced in the cow's flesh?[517]

These were simple words, without much reasoning or intellectual content behind them. Yet, they had a profound appeal in the illiterate world of the late seventeenth and the early eighteenth centuries, when raids, plunder, protracted warfare, recurring droughts, and scarcities, and the entrenchment of the neo-brāhmaṇical and Vīraśaiva landlordism led to large-scale dispossession on the one hand, and the reinforcement of caste prejudices on the other. One way, through which the dispossession of the peasantry was mediated, was by generating employment in the mercenary militias of the monasteries. It was a potentially lucrative employment, as it carried with it the prospects of securing wealth through loot and plunder. Another mode through which monasteries addressed the crisis of dispossession and scarcity was feeding (*dāsōha* or *annadāna*). Saints carried out regular begging tours, variously called *haṇḍi bhikṣā*, *taḷa bhikṣā*, etc., in the company of disciples and followers to gather resources for feeding. At times, they received endowments of land. Fakīrappa seems to have organized feeding in his monastery at Śirahaṭṭi. Feeding has been known in the monastery for much of its recorded history. What is unique about the *dāsōha* held in the Śirahaṭṭi monastery is that devotees had—and continue to have—the privilege of entering the kitchen, cooking their own food, and offering them to their kin and other followers. Sāvaḷagi Śivaliṅga was also involved in feeding. The *Sāvaḷagi Śrīśivaliṅgēśvarapurāṇa* says that he protected people during a severe drought.[518] Arrangements were made, among other things, for a granary when the maṭha at Sāvaḷagi was constructed.[519] The maṭha continued the tradition of feeding, and one of its pontiffs, the tenth seer from the village of Karīkaṭṭi, who assumed charge in 1885 and passed away in 1901, was known by the name, Annadāna Svāmi. The temple of Siddhaliṅga at Yeḍiyūru also held regular feeding for its devotees. It is in this context that the story of Fakīrappa producing choice food for his friends from him bag becomes meaningful. Feeding in times of distress was indeed the logic behind the miracle of rainmaking and the establishment of maṭhas by Fakīrappa and Sāvaḷagi Śivaliṅga at a number of locations throughout their journey.

Kalaburagi Śaraṇabasava (1746-1823) was as renowned for feeding as for the miracles he performed. Known for his powers of conferring children on barren women, he charged an exorbitant fee for the service, and raised it to the status of an industry. The rich were expected to pay one thousand rupees towards *dāsōha* for

---

516 Ibid., 143.

517 No. 120, Kavyapremi 1995.

518 *Sāvaḷagi Śrīśivaliṅgēśvarapurāṇa*, 12.20-23.

519 Ibid., 14.51.

being rewarded with a child.[520] Diggāvi Gurubasava and his wife from the village of Harasūru were among the couples that availed of this service.[521] Those unable to pay this huge amount had other choices open to them. Offering one thousand *roṭṭis* (breads made of millet flour) for *dāsōha* was one of them. Presenting one thousand pieces of firewood for the *dāsōha* kitchen was another. The poorest of devotees had the choice of presenting one thousand flowers for *pūja*, or making one thousand circumambulations around the monastery, or chanting the name of Śiva one thousand times as fee for being blessed with a child.[522]

At least since the sixteenth century, *annadāna* had begun to figure as a dominant aspect of the political economy of munificence. This is confirmed by inscriptional as well as literary references. For instance, as early as 1556, a Keḷadi Nāyaka inscription recorded a grant made for feeding of brāhmaṇas. The grant was made, when Keḷadi Sadāśiva Nāyaka was chief, by a certain Cikkadānayya to the feeding-house (*annatsatra*) of the *agrahāra* (brāhmaṇa settlement) of Tyāgarti to feed three brāhmaṇas everyday.[523] Instances increased in number in the subsequent period. Thirteen years later, in 1569, when Saṅkaṇṇa Nāyaka was the Keḷadi chief, a merchant called Timmaseṭṭi endowed land to the Sōmēśvara temple of Hosakēri for the daily feeding of six brāhmaṇas.[524] Another eleven years later, in 1580, the merchant Īśvaraseṭṭi, son of Gaṇapaseṭṭi, and (his wife?) Saṅkamaseṭṭiti, gave a grant to the newly built maṭha to the southwest of the Sōmanātha temple in Maṇigārakēri for feeding six people everyday.[525] Such instances multiplied in the seventeenth century. Feeding appeared as a prominent ideal in literary sources too. Hagiographies regularly spoke of Basava as an incarnate saint who organized feeding in Kalyāṇa. Here is how Śāntaliṅgadēśikan introduces Basava to his readers:

> In Kalyāṇa, when Basavēśvara Dēva was offering the desired food to ninety-six thousand over one lakh Caramūrtis and making arrangements to offer the desired food to the Viṭa-Jaṅgamas sporting with twelve-thousand sacred girls....[526]

We have noticed in chapter 5 how in the legend of Maṇṭēsvāmi, Basava was identified as a great benefactor of the Jaṅgamas, organizing *annadāna* for them regularly, and how Maṇṭēsvāmi intervened to rid Ādi Kalyāṇa free of the false Jaṅgamas.[527] This

---

520 Hiremath 1991: 177. The work under reference seems to be based on Hiremath's PhD dissertation, entitled *Śaraṇabasavēśvararu Hāgū Avara Parisarada Sāhitya* (in Kannada). I have not had access to this dissertation.
521 Ibid., 161.
522 Ibid., 177.
523 No. 8, Jois 1991.
524 No. 26, Ibid.
525 No. 30, Ibid.
526 *Bhairavēśvara Kāvyada Kathāmaṇisūtra Ratnākara*, 394.
527 *Maṇṭēsvāmi*, 2 ('Kalyanada Salu').

story emphasizes in so many words that the undeserving ones are not to be allowed to partake of the food offered during an *annadāna*. With lesser recalcitrance and drama, and with a greater measure of venomous resolve, Ādayya's wife Padmāvati makes the same point in the *Bhairavēśvara Kāvyada Kathāmaṇisūtra Ratnākara*. She was, as we have seen in chapter 2, a Jaina who fell in love with Ādayya and married him after converting to Śaivism. Once, her father Pārisaseṭṭi was hosting a group of Jaina saints. As there was a shortage of food, Pārisaseṭṭi and his wife took the saints to Padmāvati, who was preparing food to be offered to Śiva. She ignored the requests for food made by her parents. When they persisted, she said, "I cannot feed dogs with the food meant for the Lord". Finally, Pārisaseṭṭi held her back with force while his wife carried the food to the saints.[528]

Adrīśa, in his *Prauḍharāyana Kāvya*, tells us the story of a certain Viśvanātha who refused food to a sage, Bhīmamuni, and incurred his wrath to be born as a man-eater. Viśvanātha was then born as a brahmarākṣasa in the garden of king Candraśēkhara of Mahadadhipura in Kashmir. After many twists and turns, he attained release from the curse, and offered *annadāna*. This part of the story also speaks of the greatness of *jaladāna* (offering water) and *kanyādāna* (offering a virgin in marriage).[529] The story of Viśvanātha is followed by another anecdote, which underlines the greatness of offering food.[530] An account of a chief, strikingly named Annadānēśvara, is given in Siddhanañjēśa's *Gururājacāritra*.[531]

The institution of feeding was advantageous in the larger politics of munificence, as the regular and recurring act of performance involved in it carried greater resonance than making one-time endowments in the form of land, or capital in the form of cash and gold. It constantly invoked the donor and underlined his piety and benevolence. The results were therefore immediately gratifying for the donor, and in a manner of speaking, for the one who partook of the food as well. And in a land of endemic poverty, it was never difficult to find people who were in need of food.

Feeding was not a new phenomenon in the region. It had a long history, and we learn from inscriptions that it was widely practiced for several centuries. But the prominence it attained as a value in and after the sixteenth century was certainly unprecedented. This was by no means restricted to the Deccan region. In their influential study of the Nāyaka court-life of Tamilnadu, Narayana Rao, Shulman, and Subrahmanyam found *annadāna* pervasive enough to recognize it as a 'newly prominent institution'.[532]

---

528 *Bhairavēśvara Kāvyada Kathāmaṇisūtra Ratnākara*, 283.

529 *Prauḍharāyana Kāvya*, 8.

530 Ibid.

531 *Gururājacāritra*, 1.9.

532 Narayana Rao, Shulman and Subrahmanyam 1992: 203.

In the Deccan region, *annadāna* was also coeval with, and constitutive of, a series of crucial developments in the realm of the political economy. As monetization came to be deeply entrenched even in rural areas, demands for revenue from land was increasingly made. After the collapse of the Ādil Śāhi state in the late seventeenth century, military entrepreneurship expanded by leaps and bounds. Military labour, drawn from a peasantry rapidly undergoing dispossession and in need of alternate sources of livelihood, was mostly deployed in raids of plunder that often culminated in wide spread devastation of the countryside. These raids were primarily aimed at extracting tributes from local chiefs and military entrepreneurs. The Marāṭhas excelled in this business due to their superior use of guerilla manoeuvers.

As early as the late seventeenth century, agricultural production in the region had to encounter a new situation when the struggle between the Mughals, the Ādil Śāhi, the Kutb Śāhis, and the Marāṭhas had thrown up a large presence of military deputations. The need to ensure constant supply of grains to the military camps was putting greater strain on the peasantry. A series of drought and epidemics in the late seventeenth century also had a severe toll on agricultural production. Writes Eaton:

> Firstly, a devastating cholera epidemic, which was said to have killed 150,000 people of the Bijapur plateau, commenced the year fallowing Aurangzeb's conquest and lasted for three years. Then in 1696 the Bhima River flooded, drowning many and ruining a year's harvest in one of the Bijapur plateau's most productive regions. Worse still was the terrible famine that scourged the western Deccan in 1717 and plunged the economy of the area into severe instability. As a result of these calamities both the city and much of the Bijapur plateau suffered widespread death and desertion. A census taken by Aurangzeb after the fury of the cholera epidemic had abated (around 1690) showed that the city of Bijapur had lost over half of its former population in just the several years following the Mughal conquest.[533]

It was in this context that the feeding initiated in the *siddha* monasteries produced lasting images of the *siddhas* as humane, benevolent, gift giving, and life saving.

Although production slumped, monetization and rising prices ensured a steady flow of revenue.[534] As the eighteenth century progressed and military entrepreneurship increased, military supply lines also expanded exponentially. A partial estimate for the year 1786, based on very limited sources, has shown that 500,000 soldiers were stationed in Karnataka in that year.[535] This, in all likelihood, is only half the actual figure, as estimates for the number of soldiers with the Pāḷegāras of the south, the chiefs in the Western Ghats and coastal Karnataka, and the warrior-saints of the north, are not easily forthcoming. Very few forts yield information concerning the number of garrison soldiers. Considering these facts, an estimate of one million soldiers

533 Eaton 1978: 270.
534 Devadevan 2010a.
535 Devadevan 2010b.

in Karnataka at any given time in the late eighteenth century can by no means be overdrawn. Military evolved to become the greatest labour market after agriculture, and left deep marks of devastation in its trail.

And then came the inevitable, almost abruptly. As the eighteenth century came to a close and the nineteenth century commenced, the great militaries began to be disbanded everywhere in the region. Military entrepreneurship came to an end, almost with a whimper. This was occasioned by Lord Wellesley's policy of Subsidiary Alliance, one of the wisest policies to have come from the English East India Company. The Company forced the Nizāṃ of Haidarābād into submission, and defeated and killed the Maisūru ruler Tīpū Sultān in the Fourth Battle of Maisūru in 1799. Both states were made to sign the treaty of Subsidiary Alliance, under the terms of which the rulers had to disband their armies, and host cantonments of the Company's army at their own cost. Article II of the treaty, concluded with Maisūru on 8 July 1799, said:

> The Honourable East-India Company Behaudur agrees to maintain, and his Highness Maha Rajah Mysore Kistna Rajah Oodiaver Behauder agrees to receive a military force for the defence and security of his Highness's dominions; in consideration of which protection, his Highness engages to pay the annual sum of seven lacs of Star Pagodas to the said East-India Company, the said sum to be paid in twelve equal monthly instalments, commencing from the 1st July, A.D. 1799. And his Highness further agrees, that the disposal of the said sum, together with the arrangement and employment of the troops to be maintained by it, shall be entirely left to the Company.[536]

This was a humiliating arrangement for the Indian rulers, but a farsighted one indeed. With Subsidiary Alliance, the reign of endemic warfare of the eighteenth century was over. Its effects on the dispossessed peasantry were enormously harsh, though. The prospect of gaining wealth through organized campaigns of plunder had suddenly become a thing of the past. One million soldiers, supporting families whose cumulative population was at least five million by the lowest possible reckoning, were out of work in Karnataka. At the same time, access to land had become a more distant hope than before. Never in the bygone days was the angst of dispossession and alienation felt as chillingly in times of peace. Things changed very quickly in the coming decades, and soon, an unfamiliar world, the kind of which was never once imagined in the premodern history of the subcontinent, was beginning to take shape.

In the early decades of the nineteenth century, the British, and the Indian rulers, such as the Nizāṃ of Haidarābād and the Divān of Maisūru, initiated a series of public works, like building roads, bridges, and reservoirs. They also brought into existence a police force and a bureaucracy, in which the terms of employment were not based on hereditary rights. As newer projects like the establishment of

536 *Treaties and Engagements with Native Princes and States in India, Concluded for the Most Part in the Years 1817 and 1818*, ii.

schools, hospitals, printing presses, telegraph lines, and railway lines commenced, and the governments established offices, departments, and commissions to take care of a wide range of activities like health, public instructions, commerce, and communication, a new labour force emerged that had few things in common with the erstwhile forms of labour. A secular labour market had made its arrival. Work in this new labour market was not governed by principles of inheritance and succession. It was based on a process of recruitment that was, in principle, impersonal and bureaucratic. In other words, the labour in the secular labour market was abstract labour. The centuries-old equation between inheritance of profession, and the inheritance of land by way of service tenures and other personalized arrangements, began to wither away rapidly. This was the thin wedge of the political economy that eventually led to the liquidation of the old world, and ushered in the new.

The praxis of sainthood was not insulated from these developments. It began to go through a crucial phase of transition after the closing decades of the eighteenth century. Miracle-workers continued to thrive and, like their sixteenth, seventeenth, and early eighteenth century predecessors, built influential monasteries in different parts of the region. At the same time, a new class of stand-alone saints appeared. Most of them did not associate themselves with leading saints, lineages, or monasteries. Few among them built monasteries of their own. A handful of others were fortunate to have maṭhas built in their name after their demise. These saints may be called the *tatvapadakāra*s for want of a better name, as a number of them composed short songs in a genre called the *tatvapada*.

Śiśunāḷa Śarīf is the best known among the *tatvapadakāra* saints. Born ten miles to the south of Hubbaḷḷi in the village of Śiśunāḷa on 7 March 1819, Muhammad Śarīf was the son of Hajjūmā and Hazrat Imām Sāhēb. As with many *siddha*s, the story goes that the couple had no children for many years. They appealed to the saint Khādar Śah Vali of Hulagūru, who conferred upon them a son. Śarīf had his early education at the Kūli maṭha in the village, and passed the Mulki (matriculation) examination. He also spent many hours with manuscripts of the *Rāmāyaṇa*, the *Mahābhārata*, the *Dēvīpurāṇaṃ* (of Cidānanda Avadhūta), and the *Prabhuliṅgalīle*. He was also attracted towards popular performance genres like *bayalāṭa*, and took active part in them. He is said to have read the works of Sarvajña and Sarpabhūṣaṇa Śivayōgi with great enthusiasm and devotion.[537]

Śarīf might have been proficient in the Persian language, but he also learnt the Mōdi script, used extensively by the Marāṭha chiefs in their revenue and other records. Śarīf was obviously seeking employment with the new bureaucracy. He found a job as a Primary School teacher, and is said to have worked for some years in the schools

537 Gubbannavara 1999: xxx.

of Maṇḍiganāḷa, Kyālakoṇḍa, Pāṇigaṭṭi, Eribūdihāḷa, and Guñjaḷa.[538] It was around this time that he met the Smārtha brāhmaṇa, Gōvindabhaṭṭa, of the village of Kaḷasa. Impressed by his vast learning and reclusive bent of mind, Śarīf became his disciple.

Śarīf's conjugal life was short-lived. His wife Fātimā died a few months after delivering a baby girl. Now, Śarīf became fully absorbed in reading and meditation under Gōvindabhaṭṭa's tutelage. A widely popular anecdote is told about the brāhmaṇa *guru* and his Muslim disciple in which the people objected to Gōvindabhaṭṭa imparting religious training to a man without a sacred thread. An angry Gōvindabhaṭṭa carried out the investiture of Śarīf with due rites. It was on this occasion that Śarīf sang his popular song, *hākida janivārava, sadgurunātha...*, i.e. the great lord *guru* put the sacred thread on me.

After Gōvindabhaṭṭa's death, Śarīf settled down at Śiśunāḷa, and began to wander sporadically. But unlike the great saints of the preceding centuries, he did not travel widely across the subcontinent from Kāśi and Badari in the north to Kanyākumāri and Dhanuṣkōṭi in the south. His destinations were the towns and villages in parts of the old Dhāravāḍa district.[539] He went to Yalavigi, where he composed a *tatvapada* in praise of an orchard raised by a certain Rāmajōgi. He travelled to Śirahaṭṭi where he met the (eighth?) pontiff of the monastery of Fakīrappa, and sang a *tatvapada* in his honour. Thus were spent his days, in wandering, composing and singing songs, begging. The last decades of his life were plagued by severe poverty and threats from moneylenders who had given him loans on various occasions. Śarīf died on 7 March 1889, on his seventieth birthday.

The *tatvapada*s of Śarīf offer a glimpse of his world in particular and the world of the *tatvapadakāra* saints in general. It was a world becoming increasingly obscure and unintelligible. For several centuries, the inheritance of access to land and profession had in its reified manifestation enabled a self-understanding in which the self and the world, the soul and the body, and the sacred and the profane, were meaningfully intertwined into each other in a manner that nurtured a consciousness based on plenitude, with a great measure of cognitive if not ontological flexibility between the self and the other. The profane world with the strange bigotries of its men and women was not only open to contempt, criticism, reassessment, and reform, but carried within it potentials to provide similes and metaphors for the sacred. As in a number of *vacana*s attributed to Allama and Akkamahādēvi, the world could participate dialogically in the explorations concerning the divineness for the self. The new world was different. It had lost, to a substantial extent, its power of becoming similes and metaphors of the sacred. Unlike Koḍēkallu Basava or Maṇṭēsvāmi or

538 These may not have been the places where Śarīf actually worked. At a time when institutions imparting modern education did not exist in several leading towns and commercial centres of the region, it is unlikely that remote and thinly populated villages such as Maṇḍiganāḷa, Kyālakoṇḍa, Pāṇigaṭṭi, Eribūdihāḷa and Guñjaḷa were endowed with Primary Schools.

539 The old Dhāravāḍa districts were divided into the Dhāravāḍa, the Gadaga, and the Hāvēri districts by the Government of Karnataka in 1994.

Sāvaḷagi Śivaliṅga or Śirahaṭṭi Fakīrappa, the *tatvapadakāra*s were generally not seen travelling widely, performing miracles or composing literatures that tried to explore the self or the sacred and its relationship with the rest of the world. Rather, they already knew perfectly well what the self was, and where its sources and sacredness lie. Unlike the early hagiographies of Basava, Allama Prabhu, Akkamahādēvi, and Siddharāma, composed by Harihara, Rāghavāṅka, and Pālkurike Sōmanātha, where the saints are seen going through critical stages of conflict in their mind, or the later hagiographies by Cāmarasa and his successors, where the saints are in full control of the world around them which they change through their miracles, the *tatvapadakāra* saints are in a strange predicament. They already know what they are; they have access to the farthest corners of the sacred. The sacred is a given that they are endowed with, and the crises and conflicts in their lives contribute precious little to an understanding of the sacred, or to greater levels of self-awareness. What they do not really know are the mysteries of the mundane world with its burden of day-to-day engagements that are filled with uncertainty. Thus, the activities and relationships of the mundane world cease to serve as similes and metaphors of the self or the sacred. The *tatvapadakāra*s explored many a possibility of transforming the world around them into similes and metaphors, but the results are far from reassuring. Here, for instance, is one song by Śarīf where Rāmajōgi's orchard is deployed as a metaphor.

Look at the garden, my friends!
Look at the play of the great *guru*!

[The garden] of *dharma* that became a wonder
with its true knowledge of Brahman,
To destroy a million *karma*s.

Having become the field in a field / having become void in the void
And with branchless roots,
When the fruits weighing down
sways in the breeze,
[Look at the garden] of those who make it rise up one by one!

[Look at the garden] Rāmajōgi of the great village on earth,
With Yalavigi as its name,
Raised with love,
And where, in the tender forest,
Rāma dwells!

Areca nut, the coconut fruit,
The grace of the banana shoots that sway,
[Look at the garden] of the dark and beautiful song,
with its metre, class, and rhyme,
That our Lord of Śiśunāḷa built in the end![540]

540 No. 123, Gubbannavara 1999.

An attempt is made in the third stanza to present the orchard as a metaphor for the six yogic *cakras* that rise one after the other, but without much success. And an attempt is made in the last stanza to present the orchard as a song with the prescribed requirements of prosody, again with little success. Here is another popular song of Śarīf's in which the act of swallowing is placed in relief as a metaphor.

> The hen swallowed the monkey,
> Look, little sister?
>
> The goat swallowed the elephant,
> The wall swallowed the lime,
> The percussion swallowed the actress that came to play....
>
> The cavern swallowed the hill,
> The ant swallowed the cavern,
> The soul swallowed the feet of Gurugōvinda.[541]

Contrast these poor metaphors drawn from the world around him with Śarīf's firm and majestic expression of the knowledge of the self: "I am not what they call 'I'," he says. "I am not the human life. I am not the stuff that declares you to be Nārāyaṇa, Brahma, and Sadāśiva. I am not this human body, nor old age and death, not the pleasure of boon and glory, nor am I the curse of forgetting. I am not the mother, the father, or the son, I am not the Lord of the world. I am not caste and lineages, nor am I the pollution of love. I am not the learning or the Vēdas, I am not the one that is merely debating. I am not the one that dwelt in the self-awareness of *nāda*, *bindu*, *kaḷā*, *bhēda*, and *vastu*. I am not the difference between you and I, I am not the different forms. (Lord) Śiśunāḷa will not manifest unless I am wiped out, but I am not the stuff you can wipe out."[542] The late eighteenth-century saint Sōmekaṭṭe Cannavīra, who was not a stand-alone saint but had a monastery to identify with, would not have agreed more with these words of Śarīf's. Here is what Cannavīra had to say in one of his songs about the self: "You are Śiva, my dear, do you have an Other? Find out for yourself the difference between You and I. Learn for yourself, with your own reflection. Stay forever, by knowing the difference between knowing and forgetting. Find the abode of the supreme, and learn for yourself, my dear. Mingle in the essence of the world, and know it for yourself. You are the path for *nāda*, *bindu*, and *kaḷā*. Know the beginning and the end, and you will realize that you are the soul; the Ōṃkāra of the beginning is subjected to your consciousness, my dear. Look at what stands on top of the Tripuṭagiri hill, and dance, my dear. You will find it shining,

541 No. 253, Ibid.
542 No. 225, Ibid.

like the rays from a prism. You, yes my dear, You are Cannabasava, the teacher on your forehead."[543]

Śarīf's understanding of the self is echoed in a song of one of his contemporaries, Nīralakere Basavaliṅga, who was also not a stand-alone saint.

I am Brahman, I am the world.
There is nothing other than me, it's true.[544]
Who else, without me?
I am non-dual, it's true.

I am the one that was knowledge, it's true,
I am the one that was forgetfulness, it's true.
I am beyond *turīya*,
transcending knowledge and forgetfulness, it's true.

I am the one that was *aṅga*,[545] it's true.
I am the one that was *liṅga*, it's true.
I am the one that was *saṅga*[546]
between *aṅga* and *liṅga*, it's true.

I am the one that was the eye, it's true.
I am the one that was the scene, it's true.
I am the one that was the vision
between the eye and the scene, it's true.

I am the one who was the teacher, it's true.
I am the one who was the holy disciple, it's true.

I am the one who was the secret
between the teacher and the student, it's true.

I am the one that became I, it's true.
I am the one that became you, it's true.
Nīralakerevāsa, bright as a million suns,
I am the one without a sign, it's true.[547]

543 *Sōmekaṭṭe Cannavīra Svāmigaḷa Kṛtigaḷu*, 23.94. The word *niṭila*, forehead, in the last line appears to have been used to fulfill the requirements of the second-syllable rhyme (which rule, however, is violated in the first line of the last stanza). What Cannavīra perhaps intended was *nikhila*, universal.
544 '*nija*', one's own. This is among the earliest instances in Kannada where the word is used to mean 'truth'.
545 '*aṅga*', body.
546 '*saṅga*', union.
547 No. 94, *Nīralakere Basavaliṅga Śivayōgigaḷa Svaravacanagaḷu*.

The stand-alone *tatvapadakāras* had appeared at a time when dispossession from traditional access to land and profession was rife. Existing identities, based on caste or religion, were centered mostly on the logic of inheriting access to land and profession. This logic was now undergoing disintegration. But caste was yet to undergo its great modern transformation, and Hinduism was still in an incipient form. Under these circumstances, the only identity that was immediately accessible to people of the Deccan region was the places to which they belonged. In the context of dispossession, the longing for a place might have been all the more tantalizing. The *siddha* saints had explored this possibility for nearly four centuries by appending place-names like Vaḍabāḷa, Diggi, Koḍēkallu, Tinthiṇi, Śirahaṭṭi, Sāvaḷagi, and so on as prefixes to their names. This became a generalized practice among the *siddhas* in the nineteenth century. Saint after saint came to attach place-name prefixes to their names: Śiśunāḷa Śarīf, Nālatvāḍada Vīrēśa Śaraṇa, Garagada Maḍivāḷappa, Hosaḷḷi Būdisvāmi, Nāgarahaḷḷi Śaraṇabasava, Naragundada Vīrappajja, Navalagundada Nāgaliṅga, and so on. Table 13 gives a list of nineteenth and twentieth-century *tatvapadakāras* from the Haidarābād Karnataka region.[548] Note how place-names figure invariably as prefix in all cases.

The disintegrating identities of caste and religion, derived from the inheritance of access to land, affected the *dāsa* saints too. As it turned out, they were also to adopt place-name prefixes in considerable numbers in their attempt to explore alternate sources of identity. Unlike Kanakadāsa, Purandaradāsa, Vādirāja, and Śrīpādarāya in the fifteenth and the sixteenth centuries, Karnataka now had *dāsas* named Maisūru Veṅkaṭaramaṇadāsa, Bāgēpalli Subrahmaṇyadāsa, Harapanahaḷḷi Rāmācārya, and Kūḍligi Madhvācārya. Table 14 gives a list of these *dāsa* poets.

While the new order with hereditary access to land and profession on the decline produced a number of stand-alone saints, the monasteries also became deeply rooted in landedness and expanded their influence over the peasantry by bringing them under their grip as followers in increasing numbers. It was possible to deploy the surplus labour released by the armies disbanded after the Subsidiary Alliance towards this end. Many monasteries developed a hierarchy of followers. The monasteries also won over large sections of the population as devotees by extending the networks of feeding among the dispossessed. We have seen how a saint like Kalaburagi Śaraṇabasava mobilized resources for this purpose.

---

548 The districts of Bīdara, Kalaburagi, Yādagiri, Rāyacūru and Koppaḷa, which were earlier under the Nizāṃ of Haidarābād, are together known as Haidarābād Karnataka.

Table 13. Nineteenth and Twentieth-Century *Tatvapadakāras* from the *Haidarābād* Karnataka Region[549]

Sl. No.	Name of the Tatvapadakāra	Sl. No.	Name of the Tatvapadakāra
1.	Marakundi Basavaṇṇappa	33.	Kōnāpurada Rāmappa
2.	Niḍuvañci Bhadrappa	34.	Kvānaḷḷi Honnappa
3.	Dhummanasūra Siddhaprabhu	35.	Mahagāvi Vīrāsāb
4.	Kohinūra Hussanasāb	36.	Niṃbōḷi Tippaṇṇa
5.	Bhūtāḷe Śillappa	37.	Kalkaṃbada Rukm-ud-dīn Sāb
6.	Bōrgi Rehamānsāb	38.	Dēvāṅgada Aṃbārāya
7.	Keñcā Maḍivāḷaśeṭṭi	39.	Dēvāṅgada Ānandarāya
8.	Huḍugiya Gurupādappa	40.	Kūḍalūru Basavaliṅga
9.	Maṅgalagi Nannādsāb	41.	Gūgallu Parappayya
10.	Aṣṭūru Narasappa Māstar	42.	Gabbūra Haṃpaṇṇa
11.	Muddinavāḍi Azīz Paṭēl	43.	Nīralakere Basavaliṅga
12.	Rāmapurada Bakkappa	44.	Santēkallūru Ghanamaṭhada Nagabhuṣaṇa
13.	Bidanūru Gaṅgamma	45.	Aravali Bijali Vastādi (i.e. Ustād)
14.	Harasūru Aṇavīrappa	46.	Gabbūra Ayyappajja
15.	Kaḍakōḷada Maḍivāḷappa	47.	Dēvadurgada Cannamalla
16.	Cennūra Jalālsāb	48.	Veṅkaṭāpurada Khēmaṇṇa
17.	Khainūra Kṛṣṇappa	49.	Hosapēṭeya Ayyappa Panthōji
18.	Ainole Karibasavayya	50.	Tāḷapaḷḷi Veṅkayya
19.	Telugabāḷa Rēvaṇṇa	51.	Baḷagānūra Marisvāmi
20.	Kaḍlēvāḍada Siddhappa	52.	Dēvadurgada Ādi Amāteppa
21.	Mōṭanaḷḷi Hassansāb	53.	Gabbūra Mārtāṇḍappa
22.	Bēnūru Khāki Pīr	54.	Gōnuvāra Baḍēsāb
23.	Dēvāṅgada Guṇḍappa[550]	55.	Rāmadurgada Shēikh Abdul Bābā
24.	Rastāpurada Bhīma	56.	Rāyacūru Hanumantavva
25.	Kāḷagi Maśāksāb	57.	Rāyacūru Yaramāreppa
26.	Jāvaḷagi Guruvarēṇya Śaraṇa	58.	Mañjarlāda Khādarsāb
27.	Mādana Hipparagā Siddharāma	59.	Jahīrābādina Tippaṇṇatāta
28.	Rājōḷada Murugharājēndra	60.	Hosūru Tippaṇṇa
29.	Siragāpurada Baṇḍeppa	61.	Kalmalāda Tāyaṇṇa
30.	Kauḷūru Siddharāma	62.	Hērūru Virupaṇṇa
31.	Jaṃbagi Śaraṇappa	63.	Vaḍaki Tātayya
32.	Sāvaḷagi Muhammadsāb	64.	Tāḷakēri Basavarāja

549 Source: Sabarad 2000.

550 Dēvāṅga is the name of a village in the Āḷande tālūk of Kalaburagi district, and should not be mistaken for the weaver caste, also called Dēvāṅga.

Table 14. Nineteenth and Twentieth-Century *Dāsa* poets with place-name prefixes[551]

Sl. No.	Name of the dāsa poet	Sl. No.	Name of the dāsa poet
1.	Ēri Nārāyaṇācārya	35.	Bāgēpalli Subrahmaṇyadāsa
2.	Karajagi Dāsappa	36.	Mānvi Guṇḍācārya
3.	Liṅgasugūru Yōgīndrarāya	37.	Gōkāvi Bhīmācārya
4.	Modalakallu Śēṣadāsa	38.	Citradurgada Rāmacandrarāya
5.	Kōsigi Svāmirāyācārya	39.	Heḷavanakaṭṭe Giriyamma
6.	Tirupati Pāṇḍuraṅgi Huccācārya	40.	Harapanahaḷḷi Bhīmavva
7.	Harapanahaḷḷi Kṛṣṇācārya	41.	Mudnūru Hanneraṅgadāsa
8.	Cikkōḍi Ācārya	42.	Askihāḷa Gōvindadāsa
9.	Maisūru Veṅkaṭaramaṇadāsa	43.	Kallūra Subbaṇṇācārya
10.	Kuñcūru Hanumantācārya	44.	Gadvālada Subbaṇṇadāsa
11.	Burli Hanumantaraṅgarāya	45.	Santēbennūru Rāmadāsa
12.	Surapurada Prēmadāsa	46.	Mānā Madurai Dāsa
13.	Savadi Rāmacandrappa	47.	Liṅgasugūru Svāmirāyācārya
14.	Kinnāḷada Śrīnivāsadāsa	48.	Gōrābāḷa Hanumantarāya
15.	Kākhaṇḍaki Rāmācārya	49.	Citradurga Śrīnivāsarāya
16.	Varavaṇi Rāmarāya	50.	Doḍḍaballāpurada Rāghavēndradāsa
17.	Surapurada Ānandadāsa	51.	Bāgēpalli Sēṣadāsa
18.	Maḍakaśirāda Bhīmadāsaru	52.	Hoḷēnarasīpurada Bhīmarāya
19.	Bennūru Rāmācārya	53.	Saragūru Veṅkaṭavaradācārya
20.	Harapanahaḷḷi Rāmācārya	54.	Galagali Avva
21.	Harapanahaḷḷi Śrīpatidāsa	55.	Narēgalla Rāmaṇṇa
22.	Surapurada Bhīmācārya	56.	Kamaladāni Nārāyaṇarāya
23.	Puṇe Rāghavācārya	57.	Aihoḷe Bhīmarāya
24.	Mēlnāṭi Lakṣmaṇārya	58.	Huyilagōḷa Nārāyaṇarāya
25.	Surapurada Gōpati Viṭhaladāsa	59.	Savaṇūru Dūrappadāsa
26.	Keṃbhāvi Dāsācārya	60.	Niḍaguraki Jīvūbāyi
27.	Aḍakalaguṇḍa Bhīmācārya	61.	Gadvāla Satyācārya
28.	Hōḷi Śēṣagirirāya	62.	Harapanahaḷḷi Veṅkaṭadāsa
29.	Sagara Kṛṣṇācārya	63.	Karajagi Tīrthappa
30.	Surapurada Hējīb Kṛṣṇarāya	64.	Honnāḷi Dāsa
31.	Keṃbhāvi Surēndrarāvu Kulakaraṇi	65.	Kūḍligi Madhvācārya
32.	Śaṅkhavaraṃ Veṅkaṭarāghavācārya	66.	Savaṇūru Bādarāyaṇadāsa
33.	Bīranūru Kṛṣṇācārya Jōṣi	67.	Santekelūru Varadēśadāsa
34.	Huṇasīhoḷi Bhīmarāvu Kulakaraṇi	68.	Ciṭṭūru Śrīnivāsarāya

551 Source: Parthasarathy 2013: 1856-1859.

Śaraṇabasava also practiced agriculture, and encouraged devotees to take to the farm.[552] During his visit to Parvatābād, he found the area affected by draught and scarcity of food. A famine was looming large over the horizon. The saint made an appeal for donation of grains and other foodstuffs, set out on begging tours, and launched feeding, which is said to have averted the famine.[553] Śaraṇabasava also encouraged several other saints and landlords to practice *dāsōha* on a large scale. One such saint who initiated feeding was Daṇḍarāya Śaraṇa of Avarādi.[554] Ādidoḍḍappa Śaraṇa of Kalaburagi was another.[555] Others include Mallikārjunappa Gauḍa of Bidanūru, and Balavanta Śaraṇa of Nāganūru.[556] Balavanta Śaraṇa was the son of Dhūḷavva and Śaraṇappa, a child conferred upon the couple by Śaraṇabasava with the bidding that the boy will grow up to become a leading practitioner of *dāsōha*.

Śaraṇabasava is said to have incurred debts while generating resources for feeding.[557] Not always did he succeed in repaying the loan. Among the moneylenders who failed to recover their loans was a certain Kallappa of Moraṭagi. After many appeals and threats, he employed a goon of Marāṭha origins, Rāmji Dāda, for recovering the loan. What followed is understandably banal. Rāmji reached Śaraṇabasava's monastery with a group of gangsters, was overwhelmed by Śaraṇabasava's charisma and the piety he practiced, and was persuaded by the saint to give up his rowdy life and commence feeding. In the meantime, Kallappa's loan had been repaid, quite predictably, through a miracle.[558]

The practice of feeding instituted by the monasteries, whether by design to create a huge following, or by a genuine concern for the suffering masses, was of no mean historical consequence. It shielded the region from the devastations of famine that turned out to be so frequent in the nineteenth century. Not that famines were unknown in South Asia before the nineteenth century or that they never resulted in widespread devastation. However, the emerging world of dispossession from hereditary access to land and profession is sure to have made the situation graver than before. Millions died in the great famines of the nineteenth century in Bengal, Odisha, and Andhra. The famine of 1866 wiped out a third of Odisha's population.[559] Not one case of famine was reported from Karnataka for much of the nineteenth century, except from the Baḷḷāri region, contiguous with the famine-prone Rāyalasīma district of Andhra, and Mysūru in the south.

---

552 Hiremath 1991: 176.

553 Ibid., 93.

554 Ibid., 97-99.

555 Ibid., 99-101.

556 Ibid., 102-104.

557 Ibid., 92.

558 Ibid., 102-103.

559 On the demographic and economic consequences of this famine, see Mohanty 1993. Mohanty estimates that death toll in the 1866 famine was "higher than one million", Ibid., 57.

In its report submitted in 1880, the Indian Famine Commission of 1878 recorded that the Deccan region was subjected to a severe famine in 1792, and again in 1803. Whether this region included Karnataka is not made clear. However, no other case of famine was reported until 1878 (when the report terminates) for the Karnataka region. One instance of scarcity is reported for the Deccan in 1845, again without clearly indicating if Karnataka was part of it. The scarcity was occasioned by scanty rainfall in 1844. In contrast, scarcity was reported in northern Deccan in 1825 and 1834. Besides, in the Baḷḷāri region, which was more arid and infertile than many other parts of Karnataka and where fewer monasteries existed, a famine was reported in 1854, and another in 1866. It is also worthy of note that although Karnataka is known for its droughts, which in some places like Citradurga occurs every alternate year, the Famine Commission noticed 'principal droughts' in the Deccan only in 1802 and 1876. The first of these led to a famine in 1803, but the drought of 1876 had no such implications in northern Karnataka. In Maisūru, though, the 1876 drought led to a famine in 1877. Note that few monasteries existed in the Maisūru region, and fewer practiced feeding. In sharp contrast to the situation in Karnataka, the Madras Presidency, including coastal Andhra, witnessed famines in 1783, 1792, 1807, 1813, 1824, 1833, 1866 and 1877. Scarcity affected Haidarābād in 1833 and 1854, and famine visited the region in 1792, 1803, 1866 and 1877.[560]

At a time when large parts of South Asia were reeling under famine and scarcity, the drought-prone regions of northern Karnataka present us with a situation that can only be regarded a miracle. And why not? The great miracle-workers of the region had performed the humble miracle of organizing feeding in times of plenty as well as in times of distress. As a result, the droughts and scarcities are only likely to have taken away hundreds of lives, not millions as in the Bengal and Madras presidencies.

It was in the world of famines and scarcities in the Madras presidency that Christian missionaries were most active. Here, they arranged for feeding, of course on a far lesser scale than the *siddha* monasteries of northern Karnataka. They also established schools, hospitals, and churches, and carried out missionary work under their banner. Thousands of people were converted to Christianity. At about the time of the 1866 famine, a certain Mahimā Gōsāyī was active in Odisha, redefining the practice of sainthood, and more significantly, mobilizing resources to feed people in the *ṭuṅgi*s he set up at different places for the purpose. The following that he won over in the course of this work were to eventually congeal into a new faith called Mahimā Dharma, which now has over half a million followers in Odisha.[561]

Northern Karnataka did not witness the emergence of any new religious faith such as the Mahimā Dharma. Nor did Christian missionaries succeed in winning

560 *Report of the Indian Famine Commission, 1880, Part – 1*, p. 21-22. Also see Digby 1878.

561 For an introduction to the Mahimā Dharma, see Eschmann 1978 and Bahinipati 2009. For advanced discussions, Banerjee-Dube 2001 and Banerjee-Dube and Beltz 2011.

over converts in this region. The presence of Christianity continues to be feeble here. Attempts to carry out missionary work were of course not unknown. Between 1837 and 1851, five missions of the London Missionary Society were established in the Dhāravāḍa region, one each in Dhāravāḍa (1837), Hubbaḷḷi (1839), Beṭagēri (1841), Malasandra (1841), and Guḷēdaguḍḍa (1851).[562] "The native population", observed the missionary, Joseph Mullens, "...have a...hold upon the Hindu religion and the law of the caste. It was long therefore before the gospel began to tell upon them, and drew its converts".[563] And it was a group of goldsmiths and coppersmiths that they succeeded in converting.[564] Among the 'Nudi Lingaits', Mullens noticed the German Missionaries of Dhāravāḍa and the London Missionaries of Beḷagāvi 'making the most rapid progress'.[565] Here is his description of the extent of progress made:

> On one occasion, a Lingait priest, with two hundred of his followers came to visit Mr. Albrecht at Dharwar. The visit occurred on a Sunday morning, and the whole company attended public worship, behaving in the most proper and orderly manner. They brought with them a number of Christian books which they had previously received and assured the missionary not only that they constantly studied them, but were convinced that they were true, while their own books were false. They even asserted also their full belief in the Lord Jesus and called themselves his disciples. A year or two later Mr. Würth of Hoobly, travelling through the country, came upon another band of these disciples with their guru. They had never seen a missionary but had received a large number of Canarese tracts, one or two theological treatises, and a Canarese New Testament. They also professed their faith in the Lord's divinity and quoted passages to prove it.

And then comes the anti-climax.

> Many of the Lingaits continued to visit the missionaries; and at length in the year eighteen hundred and forty-eight, four were baptized. One of these was a priest and from the influence he possessed proved very zealous and useful in bringing his former disciples and companions to the missionary. In the same year, three young men, Lingaits, two of whom were priests, came in to Dharwar from a village a hundred miles distant. They had received some tracts at second-hand and were greatly struck with their contents. A young christian [*sic*] came into their village, read over the books with them, and induced them to go with him into a temple at some distance that they might worship God together in secret. By degrees as they continued to study these books, they obtained a clear knowledge of the gospel and seemed thoroughly to be converted men. They were soon after baptized. Similar baptisms of Lingaits have also taken place in Belgaum.[566]

This, then, was the 'rapid progress' made: success in converting four people at one mission, three at another, and so on. Northern Karnataka was not in need of

562 Mullens 1854: 41.
563 Ibid.
564 Ibid.
565 Ibid., 42.
566 Ibid., 43-44.

the Christian missionaries. They had their own miracle-working saints and their monasteries that offered them food in times of distress, and eminently addressed their spiritual needs.

We have now come to the end of what we have chosen to call a prehistory of Hinduism. This prehistory commenced with the emergence of religious identities in the eleventh and the twelfth centuries, passed through many a vicissitude from knowledge, travel, and warfare, to penance, miracles, and feeding, and in the end reached a strange world of alienations and dispossessions. It was this new world that gave birth to Hinduism. The manner in which it happened is very important in the light of the prehistory we have traced. We must therefore end this study with a prolegomenon that point to signposts of this process, and opens up fresh avenues for understanding what Hinduism is.

7 Epilogue

In the preceding chapters, we have traced a prehistory of Hinduism. This is only one of the many possible prehistories of its kind. The geographic region identified for study, and the limited number of traditions of renunciation chosen for analysis, restrict its scope and details. It is not an exhaustive account of the traditions within the region either, as we have not said a word about many important religious centres such as Śrīraṅgapaṭṭaṇa, Mēlukōṭe, and Mantrālaya, or about influential saints such as Sarvajña, Sarpabhūṣaṇa Śivayōgi, and Kaḍakōḷada Maḍivāḷappa. Several other prehistories of Hinduism can indeed be written, both within the region and beyond. Such accounts have the potential to yield historical information that is as yet unknown to the Anglophone academia. They offer fresh perspectives and possibilities of understanding that are, to say the least, intriguing in their own strange ways. More importantly, they point to the intellectual limits of the existing historical, Indological, and anthropological scholarship concerning religious life in South Asia.

In the light of what the foregoing discussions tell us, we may venture to outline a frame of reference through which a fresh assessment of the development of Hinduism in the nineteenth and the twentieth centuries can be carried out.

There are a number of focal points in the story told in the preceding chapters. Two of them are of decisive significance for understanding how Hinduism was constructed. The first is the saint, occurring in various guises to engender the ethics of enterprise and complacency. Religious life in premodern India tended to gravitate towards him—and, at times, her—to a considerable extent, although this was hardly the sole feature of religion, as far as its practitioners were concerned. The second point of focus is class relations, figuring largely on an occupational plane in the form of complex and deep-rooted relationships between the peasantry, the trading and artisan groups, and the political elites. What happens to these two focal points in the course of the nineteenth and the twentieth centuries is central to our understanding of the development of Hinduism.

Before entering into this discussion, an important aspect of the political economy of the preceding century, brought into relief in chapters 5 and 6, needs to be emphasized again. During the later half of the eighteenth century, the peasantry in the Deccan region faced large-scale dispossession from their traditional access to land due to extensive monetization of landed wealth. In a technical sense, this must be understood as an instance of alienation, involving a de facto dispossession from the means of production. Eighteenth century sources tell us that dispossession from land (and, therefore, from the means of production) led increasingly to slavery or bonded labour in its agrestic form. Classical economic theory, especially in its Marxist variant, identifies dispossession from the means of production as a central feature of the capitalist economy. We must, with a measure of caution, make an attempt to revise this position. For, instances of dispossession were fairly common in the Deccan region for well over a millennium before the eighteenth century, and had begun to occur on an increased scale after the sixteenth century. However, the dispossessed had the (inevitable) choice of taking to begging, or getting absorbed as slaves or bonded labour, both agrestic and domestic.[567] One of the earliest examples of this kind comes from the story of Niṃbiyakka, narrated by Harihara in the late twelfth century. When Niṃbiyakka and her father lost all their possessions, they decided to take to begging. But modesty forbade them from begging in the place of their birth. So the two travelled to another city, where under the shelter of anonymity, they commenced a new life as beggars. Then came the worse, when the father was afflicted with a disease. With no other choice of survival available to them, the father urged Niṃbiyakka to save his life by becoming a *tottu*, a slave offering sexual services to her master.[568] A dutiful daughter that she was, Niṃbiyakka promptly submitted.[569] In the following centuries, *tottus*, slaves, and bonded labourers became a regular feature of the labour market. However, a new possibility had opened up by the eighteenth century. The dispossessed could become a stand-alone saint. Cidānanda Avadhūta, whom we have mentioned on a couple of occasions before, is an exemplar of this new possibility.

Cidānanda's life is recounted in the *Cidānandāvadhūta Cāritra*, a hagiography by his disciple Ayyappa. According to this work, the Avadhūta is born Jhaṅkappa to the couple, Annamma and Lakṣmīpati, in the village of Hiriya Harivāṇa near Ādavāni. Following the partition of the family property among the brothers, Lakṣmīpati's fortunes begin to decline. He moves to the village of Hebbāḷa near Gaṅgāvati with his wife and son to find work. Soon, Lakṣmīpati and Annamma pass away, and Jhaṅkappa is orphaned. He is raised by Paṃpakka, the daughter of a village functionary, Nāgappa.[570] Within a few years, the boy is initiated into renunciation as Cidānanda. He travels widely, and becomes a master of *haṭhayōga* and *rājayōga*. He also turns out to be a poet of great merit. Among his works are the *Dēvīpurāṇaṃ* and the *Jñānasindhu*. Although his story resembles the accounts of earlier saints like Koḍēkallu Basava, Śirahaṭṭi Fakīrappa, Tinthiṇi Mōnappa, and Sāvaḷagi Śivaliṅga in its broad outlines, the differences are too significant to be overlooked. Firstly, Cidānanda is said to be the legitimate son of Annamma and Lakṣmīpati, and not a child conferred by a saint. Secondly, very little is said about the miracles he performed. Thirdly, Cidānanda built no monastery, nor did he identify with an existing one. He stood alone, dispossessed of land and family, encountering alienation in its stark form. Cidānanda was truly a stand-alone saint in its archetypal manifestation.

---

567 The choice was indeed inevitable, for hasn't Sartre told us that "we are condemned...to make a choice"?

568 *Tottu* is a form of domestic slavery involving sexual services as well. It is interesting that in Harihara's *Mahādēviyakkana Ragaḷe* (3.76), the king, Kauśika, offers to be Akkamahādēvi's *tottu*, if she agrees to marry him!

569 *Niṃbiyakkana Ragaḷe*, 49-68.

570 *Cidānandāvadhūta Cāritra*, 1.

It was possible for the dispossessed to become a saint even in earlier times, as the life of Ānanda Tīrtha's brother Viṣṇu Tīrtha in the thirteenth century suggests. This trend continued into the nineteenth and the twentieth centuries. Nīralakere Basavaliṅga was one such saint, who was sent to a monastery at a young age when his parents could not raise him due to poverty. An alternative possibility was to attach oneself to a monastery in some capacity or the other. This pattern is typified by the life of Bidanūru Gaṅgamma, who ended up in a monastery to become the mistress of its pontiff, who sired her son Kaḍakōḷada Maḍivāḷappa to the consternation of the town's orthodoxy.[571] However, the stand-alone saint, without a monastery to support him or her, was clearly a new development.

It was in this context of dispossession, disbanding of armies (discussed in chapter 6), and the rise of the stand-alone saint that a historically far-reaching development began to unfurl across different parts of South Asia in the nineteenth century. This was the genesis of a secular labour market. Under the aegis of Indian rulers and chiefs (who presided over the 'princely states') as well as under the British administration, initiatives were undertaken to set up schools, colleges, hospitals, industries like cotton mills, paper mills, and printing press, railway and telegraph lines, etc. The state was beginning to play an increasing role in the development and control of infrastructure such as roads, bridges, irrigational installations, and other public utilities on a scale hitherto unknown in the subcontinent's history. The functioning of the state was thoroughly reorganized along modern bureaucratic lines. These developments led to the emergence of a new labour market that was secular in nature, and not determined by lineage, caste, and religion, at least in theory. In any case, the new labour market was not organized around principles of hereditary succession. The secular labour market, with its homogenizing abstract labour, was the cornerstone that eventually dismantled the old world and ushered in the new. The making of modern South Asia is generally attributed to forces like colonialism (and colonial modernity), nationalism, the arrival of the printing press, the great decennial census operations, introduction of modern education, and the development of newer forms of knowledge. None of these explanations appear to be persuasive. Modern South Asia was brought into existence by the secular labour market and its abstract labour, in the making of which colonialism and the other forces at best played roles of varying significance. We have seen that Śiśunāḷa Śarīf was a schoolteacher before becoming a saint. Aṣṭūru Narasappa Māstar and Hosapēṭeya Ayyappa Panthōji were also schoolteachers. Dēvadurgada Ādi Amāteppa was a revenue official of the Nizāṃ of Haidarābād, perhaps a member of the Nizāṃ's Local Fund Committee. None of these positions was inherited.

571 The pontiff was Mallikārjunappa Gauḍa of Bidanūru, a peer and associate of Kalaburagi Śaraṇabasava.

With hereditary labour coming under increasing disfavour, the longstanding relationship between the inheritance of access to land on the one hand, and the inheritance of labour on the other, came to be liquidated. Simultaneously, and perhaps in consequence, absolute ownership of land with clearly defined, and legally sanctioned titles began to emerge as the norm. The prevailing practice of multiple tiers of control over land and multiple shades of access to its proceeds began to gradually wither away, culminating in the great land reforms of the later half of the twentieth century. The dissolution of the land-labour relationship also led to the weakening of the centrality once enjoyed by lineage groups (*kula*, *vaṃśa*, etc.); for the inheritance of land did not ensure inheritance of labour anymore. This is the reason why most South Asians today are able to remember their grandfather and some of his activities, and in many cases, recall at least the name of their great grandfather if not his acts, but have absolutely no knowledge about the generations preceding him. This is a far cry from the world brought to us by the inscriptions, literary works, and texts like the *vaṃśāvali*s and *kaifiyat*s, where the acts of many generations in the family line are recorded. Modern South Asians have mastered the art of speaking about five thousand years of their nation's past, but cannot trace the genealogy of their own families beyond their great grandfather!

The brāhmaṇas and the scribes were the most powerful groups that stood to benefit from this process. Two factors contributed to the advantageous position they enjoyed. One, in the predominantly illiterate world of South Asia, they had a near-total monopoly over the use and abuse of writing. Two, they did not constitute castes in their own right, but were literacy-driven classes. Different group of castes with their own theories and practices represented the class of brāhmaṇas and scribes in their respective regions, so that the Mādhvas of coastal Karnataka had precious little to share with the Naṃbūdiris of Kerala, who in turn had few things in common with the Mohāpātras of Odisha or the Dēśpāṇḍes of Maharashtra. The Hinduism that was in the making served the class interests of these literate groups.

The new secular labour market did not gravitate towards a lineage group. Rather, it drew upon a community of the working class, so to speak. The identities which this class sought to forge were, therefore, not lineage based, but community oriented. The model for such a community was provided by the production relations governing the new urban working class, with its hierarchies, associations, cooperation, and divisions of labour. It is also likely that the British military cantonments of the nineteenth and the early twentieth centuries produced images of a close-knit, cohesive, and homogenizing community, which reinforced the idea of the community modelled after working class production relations. These developments made it possible for the idea of community-based identities to be gainfully articulated. This was how nationalisms and sub-nationalisms, in their secular, religious, ethnic, and linguistic variants, found expression in South Asia. And this was how caste, imagined as a community based on principles of endogamy and exogamy, came to be redefined as the central institution of the South Asian world. The great religious community of Hinduism was also created in this context of community-based identities.

How was Hinduism created? We may bring our study to a close by making a set of preliminary remarks that address this question. The theory and history of Hinduism, and its practice, were brought into existence by the upwardly mobile, literate, and mostly male intelligentsia of the nineteenth century. This intelligentsia consisted of the upper class and the white collared sections of the middle class. The lower class and the lower rungs of the middle class were not privy to this historical enterprise. The peasantry was also conspicuous by its absence.

This class character informed the histories of Hinduism that came to be written. It was a largely text-based history, in which religious works of antiquity in Sanskrit, like the Vēdas, the Upaniṣads, the Purāṇas, the *Rāmāyaṇa*, and the *Mahābhārata*, occupied the central place. Śaṅkara's system of *advaita* became the theoretical fulcrum of this new religion. Hope, inaction, and prayer were its ideals. (Note that hope, inaction, and prayer in the form of petitioning were also the ideals of the Moderate phase of the Indian National Congress.) Knowledge sprang from the written word in its new guise as the printed book. This meant that the living saint as a repository of knowledge was no longer of any use. Thus, saints and their genealogies came to be sidelined in the histories of Hinduism. If the names of selected saints (such as Śaṅkara, Rāmānuja, Kabīr, and Tulsīdās) were regularly invoked, it was because they had allegedly gained a clear understanding of the ancient *vaidic* wisdom, or had fought against oppression and inequality that stained the otherwise spotless fabric of the wonder called Hinduism. Contrary to contemporary understandings concerning forms of secular knowledge, these histories did not understand ethics, morality, and spiritual knowledge as processes subject to change, revision, and rejection, but as eternally true revelations contained in the scriptures. This order of things did not warrant the presence of the living saint, for what the saint had to say was now made available in the printed book, the new repository of knowledge. Inasmuch as the focus was on knowledge and values, and not on labour or enterprise, the histories of Hinduism had no reason to provide space for the peasantry, who embodied labour and enterprise as substance as well as metaphor. Thus was created the foundations of a new religion, which cherished spiritual knowledge and values in their written form, and sidelined the ideals of labour and enterprise. In other words, Hinduism was created by the abolition of the saint and the peasant. This mode of representing Hinduism attained full-blown proportions in the twentieth century.

Alienation from traditional access to land and profession had severe psychological implications. It created a deep sense of void, and lasting images of loss: loss of possession, belongingness, and meaning. Paradigms of self-awareness that were deeply engrained in the psyche for many centuries were overthrown by the secular labour market and the great anxieties and uncertainties it precipitated. Alienation was now absolute. With possibilities of exercising control over the means of production becoming a distant dream, a lasting sense of vacuum and victimization crept in. The new identities that came to be forged by the existential need for self-awareness were profoundly informed by this sense of victimization, and a craving for retributive justice. Nationhood was one such identity. Caste as a closed endogamous group was another. The making of Hinduism in the late nineteenth and the early twentieth centuries was determined by the same existential imperative.

It is not surprising, therefore, that the earliest attempts to articulate Hinduism by the Indians were often made in response to Christian missionary initiatives. Advocates of Hinduism carried out spiteful propagandas against Christianity and its missionaries. The sense of void and victimization caused by being uprooted from the inheritance of access to land and profession shaped the modern Indian's unconscious, and made alienation a defining feature of the modern individual. By a reified extension, a desire for retributive justice also became a necessary component of the unconscious. In its conscious forms of articulation, Christian missionaries appeared as the target of attack. Conscious attempts in this direction are too many and too familiar to be enumerated. However, inasmuch as alienation in general functioned unconsciously in the efforts to articulate Hinduism, one notices that grievances against the Christians were recorded even from the most unlikely quarters. Swami Vivekananda was among the tallest representatives and exponents of Hinduism in the nineteenth century. His eclectic approach to other religions is well known, as is his deep admiration for Christianity. Yet, he took time to make the following remarks at the World's Parliament of Religions in Chicago:

> Christians must always be ready for good criticism, and I hardly think that you will mind if I make a little criticism. You Christians, who are so fond of sending out missionaries to save the soul of the heathen – why do you not try to save their bodies from starvation? In India, during the terrible famines, thousands died from hunger, yet you Christians did nothing. You erect churches all through India, but the crying evil in the East is not religion—they have religion enough—but it is bread that the suffering millions of burning India cry out for with parched throats. They ask us for bread, but we give them stones. It is an insult to a starving people to offer them religion; it is an insult to a starving man to teach him metaphysics. In India a priest that preached for money would lose caste and be spat upon by the people. I came here to seek aid for my impoverished people, and I fully realised how difficult it was to get help for heathens from Christians in a Christian land.[572]

In his *Hinduism: Doctrine and Way of Life*, C. Rajagopalachari, expressed his reverence for Christianity by alluding to how the modern world had moved away from its values.

> It is indeed a miracle that earnest Christians preserve both their faith and their psychological health under the conditions of current national and international activities. The State permits, aids and abets the wholesale infringement of what is daily read and formally taught as the word of Christ. Yet, almost all the citizens of the State profess religion and believe themselves to be

572 Paranjape 2015: 16.

> Christians. They duly celebrate Christian rites and festivals. The reign of relentless private competition, the right to make maximum private profit at the expense of others and the exploration of every advantage got by accident or acquired by enterprise, so that the differences between man and man may grow in geometric progression, are all plain denials of Christ.[573]

Yet, Rajagopalachari did not fail to express his grievance against Christian missionaries in India for the harm done to Hinduism.

> The claim may to outsiders seem strange, especially to those whose knowledge of Hinduism has been derived from the information supplied by the Christian missionaries of an older generation. As we are not, however, living in the times of the proselytizing Christian missions whose one function was to show that Hinduism was good for nothing, it may be hoped that the claim made in this book will receive a fair examination at the hands of sincere thinkers.[574]

Thus, grievance and a sense of victimization were to be seen not only among the ideologues of Hindutva, like Vinayak Damodar Savarkar and Madhav Sadashiv Golwalkar, but also among sober spokesmen of Hinduism, as exemplified by the critiques of Vivekananda and Rajaji.

In the twentieth century, Islam became the chief target against which the unconscious longing for retributive justice found its conscious expression. The rest—from the partition of the subcontinent in 1947 to the demolition of the Babri Masjid in 1992, the Gujarat communal pogram of 2002, and the lynching that occurred at Dadri when these pages were being written—is history.

The making of Hinduism was not a smooth process, though. Action oriented themes were beginning to register their presence as early as the late nineteenth century in opposition to the advocacy of hope, inaction, and prayer. Representatives of this tendency—Swami Vivekananda, Dayananda Saraswati, Bal Gangadhar Tilak, Mohandas Karamchand Gandhi—were to draw inspiration from the *Bhagavadgītā*. The *Gītā* itself was poorly understood, and continues to be so. But two of its sayings became great religious slogans: i) one has a right only over action, never over the fruits of action,[575] and ii) I (Lord Kṛṣṇa) appear whenever *dharma* is debilitated and *adharma* triumphs; I return in every age to protect the virtuous, destroy the wicked, and establish *dharma*.[576] Vivekananda was one of the earliest exponents of action-oriented Hinduism. The Arya Samaj, which the Hindu orthodoxy of the day strongly reproached, was another powerful advocate of action. The living saint had a substantial role to play in this alternative understanding of Hinduism. Nevertheless,

---

573 Rajagopalachari nd: 16.

574 Ibid. 19.

575 "*karmaṇyēvādhikārastē, mā phalēśu kadācana*", *Bhagavad Gītā*, 2.47.

576 "*yadā yadā hi dharmasya glānir bhavati bhārata, abhytthānaṃ adharmasya tadātmānaṃ sṛjāmyahaṃ; paritrāṇāya sadhūnāṃ vināśāya ca duṣkṛtāṃ dharmasaṃsthāpanārthāya saṃbhavāmi yugē yugē*", Ibid., 4.7-8.

his presence was not decisive or central to the process. Nor was his a monastic sainthood. There was no emphasis on the genealogies either. Against this backdrop emerged the Extremist faction of the Indian National Congress, which embodied a saintly countenance while at the same time advocating action. Tilak and Aurobindo were the trendsetters in this regard. Things changed remarkably when Gandhi took charge of the national movement. With him, the image of the saint (with a monastery, but without a lineage of teachers) became central once again. Gandhi brought his saintly image to bear upon the peasantry, whom the Moderates and the Extremists had consistently ignored. Only with the participation of the peasantry did the national movement attain the shape of a mass movement. In consequence, the rank and file of Hinduism expanded exponentially. The peasantry's ethic of labour and action had to be incorporated into Hinduism now. It was not a one-way traffic though. The religious practices of the peasantry were substantially altered in the process. It is from this class character of Indian nationalism and its relationship with Hinduism that the source of tension between Gandhi on the one hand and the Extremists and the Hindu hardliners on the other arises.

Similar tensions mark the history of the Rashtriya Swayamsevak Sangh (RSS), the most important and influential organization of the Hindu orthodoxy. This is manifested in the deep differences between Madhav Sadashiv Golwalkar, who became the second chief (*sarsanghchalak*) of the RSS in 1940, and Madhukar Dattatreya Deoras, who succeeded him in 1973. Golwalkar was an advocate of 'constructive work', which included initiatives in community development, vocational training, and employment, the promotion of indigenous (*dēśi*) goods and products, and rescue and rehabilitation works in times of natural disasters, wars, and insurgency. Besides, it also involved training in martial art and self-defense in the *śākhās*, and establishing educational institutions where the curriculum was focused on 'character building' and the cultivation of a 'Hindu national consciousness'. There was a battle to be waged against 'enemies of the nation'—precisely the Muslims and the communists—but this was postponed to an indefinite future, to be realized in the fullness of time. The insider critic, Sanjeev Kelkar, aptly summarizes the message it sent out to the activist:

> It offered them a target larger than their life but demanded only moderate sacrifice and moderate courage. It gave them a sense of power, of being together and being a part of an organisation. It gave them confidence to face the disadvantages in life at a time when India was poor, starved and had locked itself into a state of stasis. This brand of patriotism and heroism did not demand the courage of revolutionaries.[577]

Golwalkar abjured publicity, rarely appeared before the media, and presented a saintly image that promoted his vision of 'character building'. Deoras was sharply opposed

577 Kelkar 2011: 56.

to this order of things, and shared a very difficult relationship with Golwalkar. As soon as he took charge as *sarsanghchalak*, he worked out a new plan of action for the RSS. He insisted on direct political action, and appeared frequently in the media. The Anti Congress movement (or the JP movement) that was taking shape in the country in the early 1970s under the leadership of Jayaprakash Narayan, provided a platform for bringing the Hindu right into the political mainstream. In the course of the next two decades, the RSS succeeded in reaching out to the peasantry and the backward castes. Groups that had remained outside the fold of the Hinduism that arose in the late nineteenth century were now vigorously mobilized into the service of Hindu nationalism. The *siddha* monasteries became important loci of organizing Hindu activism and militancy at the local level.

From the early 1980s, the Sangh Parivar began to address the question of Hinduness or Hindutva at the level of legends, symbolism, rituals, and everyday practices. Its intensity increased in the 1990s and the first fifteen years of the twenty-first century. It involved many calculated strategies, measures, and initiatives. Devotion to Rāma, and reclaiming his place of birth, Ayōdhyā, as a sacred centre for all Hindus, was one such initiative, and by far the most scandalous of all. It found expression through Ramanand Sagar's popular television serial, *Rāmāyaṇ*, the Bharatiya Janata Party leader Lal Krishna Advani's *rath yatra* of 1990, and the *kār sēva* that culminated in the destruction of the Bābri Masjid at Ayōdhyā on 6 December 1992. Another programme of the Sangh parivar was to intervene and cause changes in the rites and ceremonies related to marriage and conjugal life. Women in Odisha were introduced to the *maṅgalsūtra*—hitherto alien to the region—as the arch symbol of marriage. The practice of applying vermillion (*sindūra*) at the spot above a woman's forehead, where the hair is parted, was unknown to Kerala. The Sangh Parivar successfully introduced it in the state in the late 1990s. Other means adopted to develop Hinduism as a popular religion at the level of practice include the generalization of festivals like Dīpāvaḷi (Divāli), Vināyaka Caturthi, Navarātri, Karvā Chauth, Rakṣābandhan, Hōlī etc. Ceremonies like the Satyanārāyaṇa Pūja, Akṣaya Tṛtīya, and Guru Pūrṇimā were now performed widely, yōga, astrology, and *Āyurvēda* were redefined as legacies of the Hindu intellect, *satsaṅg*s and sessions of *bhajan*s and *kīrtan*s were performed day after day in temples and *āśrams*, the neo-conservative opposition towards conversions to Christianity and Islam reinforced through propaganda, and new centres of pilgrimage invented in different parts of the country, including some, like Vaiṣṇōdēvi and Amarnāth, in the strife-ridden Jammu and Kashmir. Like a Christian visiting a Church or a Muslim offering *namāz*, the Hindus were expected to become absorbed into the newly-defined religious universe of their own with the consciousness that this was ordained upon them by their religion. These efforts were successful to a large extent.

Only now are we witnessing the real beginnings of Hinduism as faith, canon, practice, and identity. We are on the threshold of a new era. This is one of the great moments in the religious history of the Indian subcontinent in particular and humankind in general, when close to a sixth of humankind, with its large number of assorted traditions, beliefs, practices, rites, rituals, and legends, are being united, and directed towards a common destiny. It is a tragedy that this project, like the great enterprise of Ādayya and Ēkānta Rāmayya, is proceeding along ethically misbegotten lines. It is moving on the lines directed by the venomous Rashtriya Swayamsevak Sangh and the virulent Sangh Parivar that it has brought into existence. Inevitably enough, this great unification is governed by hate, suspicion, mistrust, intolerance, and finally, deep violence, both physical and psychological. There is certainly no hope in the foreseeable future, because although progressive forces of our times have the power to unite and give Hinduism a new shape, purpose, direction, and meaning, Hinduism will still continue to be a reified face of the unconscious, craving for retributive justice, an unconscious created by far-reaching historical forces that in the course of the late eighteenth, the nineteenth and the twentieth centuries dispossessed men and women in the subcontinent of their traditional inheritance of access to land and profession. Hinduism was born of an historically-created alienation. The many and varied results of this alienation not only remain with us today, but have also grown from strength to strength. A 'progressive', 'humane' and 'peace-loving' Hinduism cannot therefore be free from the deep psychological longing for retributive justice, even if peace and nonviolence is what it overtly preaches. A ray of hope will appear over the horizon, only when the alienation characterizing our lives and times, is historically liquidated. Only then will a new Hinduism come into existence.

Bibliography

The primary sources discussed in this book, and cited at appropriate places in the footnotes, are too extensive to be fully included in this bibliography. Only secondary sources and primary sources that are either independent collection of inscriptions (not part of epigraphy serieses like *Epigraphia Carnatica* and *South Indian Inscriptions*) or anthologies of short poems (generally not exceeding hundred quartains, sestets and octaves in length) are listed.

Abraham, Meera. 1988. *Two Medieval Merchant Guilds of South India*. New Delhi: Manohar Publications.

Abu-Lughod, Janet L. 1989. *Before European Hegemony: The World System A.D. 1250-1350*. New York: Oxford University Press.

Adiga, Malini. 2006. *The Making of Southern Karnataka*. Hyderabad: Orient Longman.

Ahmed, Aijaz. 1992. *In Theory: Nations, Classes, Literatures*. New York: Verso.

Ahmed, Aziz. 1969. *An Intellectual History of Islam in India*. Chicago: Aldine.

Aiyangar, S. Krishnaswami. 1991 [1921]. *South India and Her Muhammadan Invaders*. New Delhi: Asian Educational Services.

Alam, Muzaffar and Sanjay Subrahmanyam. 2008. *Indo-Persian Travels in the Age of Discoveries, 1400-1800*. New Delhi: Cambridge University Press.

Ali, Daud (ed). 1999. *Invoking the Past: The Uses of History in South Asia*. New Delhi: Oxford University Press.

Altekar, Anant Sadashiv. 1934. *The Rashtrakutas and their Times*. Poona: Oriental Book Agency.

Appadorai, A. 1936. *Economic Conditions in Southern India (1000-1500)*. 2 Vols. Madras: University of Madras.

Appadurai, Arjun. 1981. *Worship and Conflict Under Colonial Rule: A South Indian Case*. Cambridge: Cambridge University Press.

Araganji, Dhulendra. 2001. *Śrī Maunēśvara Mahātme*. (in Kannada). Gadag: Paru Prakashana.

Arasaratnam, S. 1978. "Indian Commercial Groups and European Traders, 1600-1800: Changing Relationships in Southeastern India". *South Asia*, 1 (2): 42-54.

Aruni, S.K. 2004. *Surapura Samsthāna: Historical and Archaeological Study of A Poligar State in South India*. Delhi: Bharatiya Kala Prakashan.

Asad, Talal. 1993. *Genealogies of Religion: Discipline and Reason of Power in Christianity and Islam*. Baltimore and London: The Johns Hopkins University Press.

Assayag, Jackie. 2004. *At the Confluence of Two Rivers: Muslims and Hindus in South India*. New Delhi: Manohar.

Bahinipati, Priyadarshi. 2009. *The Mahimā Dharma: Interpreting History, Trends and Tradition*. Bhubaneswar: Gyanajuga Publication.

Balagangadhara, S.N. 1994. *The Heathen in His Blindness: Asia, the West, and the Dynamic of Religion*. Leiden: Brill.

Banerjee-Dube, Ishita. 2001. "Issues of Faith, Enactments of Contest: The Founding of Mahima Dharma in Nineteenth-Century Orissa". In Hermann Kulke and Burkhard Schnepel (eds), *Jagannath Revisited: Studying Society, Religion, and the State in Orissa*. New Delhi: Manohar, pp. 149-177.

Banerjee-Dube, Ishita and Johannes Beltz (eds). 2011. *Popular Religion and Ascetic Practices: New Studies on Mahima Dharma*, New Delhi: Manohar.

Bapu, Prabhu. 2013. *Hindu Mahasabha in Colonial North India, 1915-1930*. Oxon: Routledge.

Bartley, C.J. 2002. *The Theology of Rāmānuja: Realism and Religion*. London and New York: Routledge.
Basavanal, S.S. 1968. *Basavaṇṇanavara Ṣaṭsthalada Vacanagaḷu*. (In Kannada). Bangalore: Government of Karnataka.
Bayly, C.A. "State and Economy in India over Seven Hundred Years". *The Economic History Review – New Series*, 38 (4): 583-596.
Bayly, Susan. 1989. *Saints, Goddesses and Kings: Muslims and Christians in South Indian Society, 1700-1900*. Cambridge: Cambridge University Press.
Ben-Herut, Gil. 2012. "Literary Genres and Textual Representations of Early Vīraśaiva History: Revisiting Ekānta Rāmayya's Self-Beheading". *International Journal of Hindu Studies*, 16 (2), pp. 129-187.
__________. 2015. "Figuring the South-Indian Śivabhakti Movement: The Broad Narrative Gaze of Early Kannada Hagiographic Literature". *Journal of Hindu Studies*, 8 (3), pp. 274-295.
Bhusanuramatha, S.S. (ed). 1988. *Vijaya Kalyana*. (in Kannada). Hampi: Kotturusvami Matha.
Breckenridge, Carol A, and Peter van der Veer (eds). 1993. *Orientalism and the Post-Colonial Predicament: Perspectives on South Asia*. Philadelphia: University of Pennsylvania Press.
Briggs, George Weston. 2007 [1938]. *Gorakhnāth and the Kānphaña Yogīs*. New Delhi: Motilal Banarsidass.
Bronner, Yigal. 2010. "The Poetics of Ambivalence: Imagining and Unimagining the Political in Bilhaṇa's *Vikramāṅkadevacarita*". *Journal of Indian Philosophy*, 38 (5), pp. 457-483.
Carman, John Braisted. 1994. *Majesty & Meekness: A Comparative Study of Contrast and Harmony in the Concept of God*. Michigan: Wm. B. Eerdmans.
Chakrabarty, Dipesh. 2000. *Provincializing Europe*. Princeton: Princeton University Press.
Chakravarti, Uma. 1987. *The Social Dimensions of Early Buddhism*. Delhi: Oxford University Press.
Champakalakshmi, R. 1996. *Trade, Ideology and Urbanization: South India 300 BC to AD 1300*. New Delhi: Oxford University Press.
__________. 2011. "The *Maṭha*: Monachism as the Base of a Parallel Authority Structure". In Idem. *Religion, Tradition, and Ideology: Pre-colonial South India*. Oxford Collected Essays. New Delhi: Oxford University Press, pp. 286-318.
Champakalakshmi, R. and Sarvepalli Gopal (eds). 1996. *Tradition, Dissent and Ideology: Essays in Honour of Romila Thapar*. New Delhi: Oxford University Press.
Chattopadhyaya, Brajadulal. 1994. *The Making of Early Medieval India*. New Delhi: Oxford University Press.
Chaudhuri, K.N. 1985. *Trade and Civilization in the Indian Ocean: An Economic History from the Rise of Islam until 1750*. Cambridge: Cambridge University Press.
__________. 1990. *Asia before Europe: Economy and Civilisation of the Indian Ocean from the Rise of Islam to 1750*. Cambridge: Cambridge University Press.
Chekki, Dan A. 1997. *Religion and Social System of the Vīraśaiva Community*. Westport: Greenwood Press.
Chidanandamurthy, M. 1966. *Kannaḍa Śāsanagaḷa Sāṃskṛtika Adhyayana*. (In Kannada). Mysore: Prasaranga, University of Mysore.
__________. 1978. "Kannada Language and Literature during the Chalukyas of Badami (c. 540-750 A.D.)". In M.S. Nagaraja Rao (ed), *The Chalukyas of Badami (Seminar Papers)*. Bangalore: The Mythic Society.
__________. 2007 [2003]. *Basavaṇṇanavaru*. (In Kannada). Revised edition. Bangalore: Sapna Book House.
Collins, Steven. 1998. *Nirvana and Other Buddhist Felicities: Utopias of the Pali Imaginaire*. Cambridge: Cambridge University Press.
Das Gupta, Ashin. 1994. *Merchants of Maritime India, 1500-1800*. Aldershot: Variorum.

Dasgupta, Surendranath. 1991 [1922]. *A History of Indian Philosophy*, Vol. 4. Delhi: Motilal Banarsidass.
Desai, P.B. 1968. *Basaveshwara and His Times*. Dharwar: Karnatak University.
Deshpande, Madhav. 1993. *Sanskrit and Prakrit: Sociolinguistic Issues*. Delhi: Motilal Banarsidass.
Devadevan, Manu V. 2007. *Kalyāṇada Mithika Itihāsa*. (In Kannada). Report submitted to the Department of Culture, Government of India.
_________. 2009a. *Pṛthviyallodagida Ghaṭavu: Karnāṭakada Ninnegaḷu*. (In Kannada). Heggodu: Akshara Prakashana.
_________. 2009b. "Bhāṣe Pramāṇavādāga". (in Kannada). *Kannada Sahitya Parishat Patrike*, 87 (1-4): 106-113.
_________. 2009c. "Shadow Lines: The Advent of Territoriality in South Asia". *Phalanx*, 4, pp. 1-17.
_________. 2010a. "The Ravaging Hand: Abdul Karim Khan and the Decline of Bijapur". *Deccan Studies*, 8 (1), pp. 59-72.
_________. 2010b. "Pāpareḍḍigaḷa Prapañca". (in Kannada). *Hosathu*, December 2010.
_________. 2010c. *The Historical Evolution of Literary Practices in Medieval Kerala (ca. 1200-1800 C.E.)*. Unpublished PhD dissertation, submitted to the Mangalore University.
Digby, William, 1878. *The Famine Campaign in Southern India (Madras and Bombay Presidencies and Province of Mysore) 1876-78*. 2 Volumes. London: Longmans, Green, and Co.
Dirks, Nicholas B. 1979. "The Structure and Meaning of Political Relations in a South Indian Little Kingdom". *Contributions to Indian Sociology*, 13 (2), pp. 169-206.
_________. 1982. "The Pasts of a Palaiyakarar: The Ethnohistory of a South Indian Little King". *The Journal of Asian Studies*, 41 (4), pp. 655-83.
_________. 1987. *The Hollow Crown: Ethnography of an Indian Kingdom*. Cambridge: Cambridge University Press.
_________. 2001. *Castes of Mind: Colonialism and the Making of Modern India*. Delhi: Permanent Black.
_________. 2006. *The Scandal of Empire: India and the Creation of Imperial Britain*. New Delhi: Permanent Black.
Doniger, Wendy. 2009. *The Hindus: An Alternative History*. New York: The Penguin Press.
_________. 2013. *On Hinduism*. New Delhi: Aleph.
Duff, Alexander. 1840. *India and India Missions: Including Sketches of the Gigantic System of Hinduism, Both in Theory and Practice; Also Notices of Some of the Principal Agencies Employed in Conducting the Process of Indian Evangelization, &c. &c.* second edition. Edinburgh: John Johnstone, Hunter Square.
Dumezil, Georges. 1988. *Mitra-Varuna: An Essay on Two Indo-European Representations of Sovereignty*. Translated by Derek Coltman. New York: Zone Books.
Dumont, Louis. 1960. "World Renunciation in Indian Religions". *Contributions to Indian Sociology*, 4, pp. 33-62.
Dutta, Ranjeeta. 2014. *From Hagiographies to Biographies: Rāmānuja in Tradition and History*. New Delhi: Oxford University Press.
Eaton, Richard M. 1978. *Sufis of Bijapur: 1300-1700*. Princeton: Princeton University Press.
_________. 2005. *A Social History of the Deccan, 1300—1761: Eight Indian Lives*. The New Cambridge History of India I.8. Cambridge: Cambridge University Press.
Eaton, Richard M. and Phillip B. Wagoner. 2014. *Power, Memory, Architecture: Contested Sites on India's Deccan Plateau, c. 1300-1600*. New Delhi: Oxford University Press.
Eschmann, Ancharlott. 1978. "Mahimā Dharma: An Autochthonous Hindu Reform Movement". In Ancharlott Eschmann, Hermann Kulke and Gaya Charan Tripathi (eds), *The Cult of Jagannath and the Regional Tradition of Orissa*. New Delhi: Manohar, pp. 375-410.
Evans-Wentz, W.Y. 1950. *The Book of the Tibetan Dead*. London: Oxford University Press.
Farquhar, J.N. 1967 [1920]. *An Outline of the Religious Literature of India*. Delhi: Motilal Banarsidass.

Flood, Gavin D. 1996. *An Introduction to Hinduism*. Cambridge: Cambridge University Press.

Foekema, Gerard. 2003a. *Architecture Decorated with Architecture: Later Medieval Temples of Karnataka, 1000-1300 AD*. New Delhi: Munshiram Mahoharlal.

_________. 2003b. *Calukya Architecture: Medieval Temples of Northern Karnataka Built During the Rule of the Calukya of Kalyana and Thereafter, AD 1000-1300*. 3 Vols. New Delhi: Munshiram Manoharlal.

Fort, Andrew O. 1998. *Jīvanmukti in Transformation: Embodied Liberation in Advaita and Neo-Vedanta*. Albany: State University of New York Press.

Foucault, Michel. 2005. *The Hermeneutics of the Subject: Lectures at the College de France, 1981-82*. Edited by Frederic Gros, Francois Ewald and Alessandro Fontana. Translated by Graham Burchell. New York: Palgrave-Macmillan.

Freschi, Elisa. 2015. "Free Will in Viśiṣṭādvaita Vedanta: Rāmānuja, Sudarśana Sūri and Veṅkaṭanātha". *Religious Compass*, 9 (9), pp. 287-296.

Fritz, John M, George Michell and M.S. Nagaraja Rao. 1984. *Where Kings and Gods Meet: The Royal Centre at Vijayanagara, India*. Tuscon: University of Arizona Press.

Frykenberg, Robert E. 1989. "The Enigma of Modern "Hinduism" as a Concept and as an Institution: A Reappraisal with Special Reference to South India". In Günther D. Sontheimer and Hermann Kulke (eds). *Hinduism Reconsidered*. South Asian Studies No. XXIV. New Delhi: Manohar, pp. 29-49.

Frykenberg, Robert E. and Pauline Kolenda (eds). 1985. *Studies in South India: An Anthology of Recent Research and Scholarship*. Madras: New Era Publications.

Fuller, Chrisopher John. 2004. *The Camphor Flame: Popular Hinduism and Society in India*. revised and expanded edition. Princeton, New Jersey: Princeton University Press.

Gai, G.S. (ed). 1996. *Inscriptions of the Early Kadambas*. New Delhi: Indian Council of Historical Research.

Galewicz, Cezary. 2009. *A Commentator in Service of the Empire: Sāyaṇa and the Royal Project of Commenting on the Whole of the Veda*. Publications of the De Nobili Research Library, Vol. 35. Wien: the De Nobili Research Library.

Ganesh, K.N. 2009. "Historical Geography of *Natu* in South India with Special Reference to Kerala". *Indian Historical Review*, 36 (1), pp. 3-21.

Geertz, Clifford. 1973. *The Interpretation of Cultures: Selected Essays*. New York: Basic Books.

Gonda, J. 1956-57. "Ancient Indian Kingship from the Religious Point of View". *Numen* 3 (1): 36-71, 3 (2): 122-155, 4 (1): 24-58 & 4 (2): 127-164.

Goodding, Robert A. 2011. "A Theologian in a South Indian Kingdom: The Historical Context of the *Jīvanmuktiviveka* of Vidyāraṇya". In Steven E. Lindquist (ed), *Religion and Identity in South Asia and Beyond: Essays in Honor of Patrick Olivelle*. London and New York: Anthem Press, pp. 83-100.

Gopal, B.R. 1981. *The Chalukyas of Kalyana and the Kalachuris*. Dharwad: Prasaranga, Karnatak University.

_________ (ed). 1985. *Corpus of Kadamba Inscriptions* Vol 1. Sirsi: Kadamba Institute of Cultural Studies.

Gordon, Richard. 1975. "The Hindu Mahasabha and the Indian National Congress, 1915 to 1926". *Modern Asian Studies*, 9 (2), pp. 145-203.

Gubbannavara, Shivananda. 1999 [1981]. *Barako Pada Barako*. (In Kannada). Bangalore: Kannada Sahitya Parishat.

Guenther, Herbert V. 1995 [1963]. *The Life and Teachings of Nāropa*. Boston and London: Shambala.

Gururajachar, S. 1972. *Some Aspects of Economic and Social Life in Karnataka: A.D. 1000-1300*. Mysore: University of Mysore.

Hall, Kenneth R. 1980. *Trade and Statecraft in the Age of the Cōḻas*. New Delhi: Abhinav Publications.

_________ (ed). 2001. *Structure and Society in Early South India: Essays in Honour of Noboru Karashima*. New Delhi: Oxford University Press.

Hardy, Adam. 2001. "Tradition and Transformation: Continuity and Ingenuity in the Temples of Karnataka". *The Journal of the Society of Architectural Historians*. 60 (2), pp. 180-199.

_________. 2007. *The Temple Architecture of India*. Chichester: John Wiley & Sons.

Hawley, John Stratton. 1981. *At Play with Krishna: Pilgrimage Dramas from Brindavan*. Princeton, New Jersey: Princeton University Press.

_________. 1991. "Naming Hinduism". *Wilson Quarterly*, 15 (3), pp. 20-34.

_________. 2015. *A Storm of Songs: India and the Idea of the Bhakti Movement*. Cambridge, Massachusetts and London: Harvard University Press.

Hegde, Rajaram. 2003. "The Dynamics of Devotional Cults: Saivism in Medieval Karnataka". *Journal of Karnataka Studies*, 1, pp. 86-112.

Heitzman, James. 1997. *Gifts of Power: Lordship in an Early Indian State*. New Delhi: Oxford University Press.

Hiremath, S.M. 1991. *Śaraṇabasavaprabhe*. (in Kannada). Gadag: Vidyanidhi Prakashana.

Hocart, A.M. 1970. *Kings and Councillors: An Essay in the Comparative Anatomy of Human Society*. Chicago: University of Chicago Press.

Inden, Ronald. 1990. *Imagining India*. London: Basil Blackwell.

_________. 2006. *Text and Practices: Essays on South Asian History*. New Delhi: Oxford University Press.

Inden, Ronald B, Jonathan S Walters and Daud Ali. 2000. *Querying the Medieval: Texts and the History of Practices in South Asia*. New Delhi: Oxford University Press.

Indvadi, Venkatesha. 1999. *Maṇṭēsvāmi Paraṃpare*. (In Kannada). Hampi: Prasaranga, Kannada University.

_________ (ed). 2004. *Maṇṭēsvāmi Kāvya: Sāṃskṛtika Mukhāmukhi*. (In Kannada). Hampi: Prasaranga, Kannada University.

Jackson, William J. 2007. *Vijayanagara Visions: Religious Experience and Cultural Creativity in a South Indian Empire*. New Delhi: Oxford University Press.

Jaffrelot, Christophe. 2010. *Religion, Caste & Politics in India*. Delhi: Primus.

Jameson, Fredric. 1991. *Postmodernism Or, the Cultural Logic of Late Capitalism*. London and New York: Verso.

Jayaprakash, Banjagere. 2000. *Kannaḍa Rāṣṭrīyate*. (In Kannada). Bangalore: Krantisiri Prakashana.

_________. 2005. *Uliya Uyyale*. (In Kannada). Bangalore: CVG Publications.

Jestice, Phyllis G. (ed). 2004. *Holy People of the World: A Cross-Cultural Encyclopedia*, Volume 1. Santa Barbara, California: ABC-Clio.

Jois, Keladi Venkatesh. 1991. *Keḷadi Arasara Śāsanagaḷu*. Dambal-Gadag: Shri Jagadguru Tontadarya Samsthanmath.

Kailasapathy, K. 1968. *Tamil Heroic Poetry*. Oxford: Clarendon Press.

Kalburgi, M.M. 1973. *Kavirājamārga Parisarada Kannaḍa Sāhitya*. (In Kannada). Dharwar: Karnatak University.

_________. 2010. *Mārga*. 6 Vols. revised edition. (In Kannada). Bangalore: Sapna Book House.

Kalgudi, Basavaraj.1988. *Madhyakālīna Bhakti Mattu Anubhāva Sāhitya Hāgū Cāritrika Prajñe*. (In Kannada). Bangalore: Karnataka Sahitya Academy.

Karanth, S.S. (compiled). 2008 [nd]. *Purandaradāsara Padagaḷu*. (in Kannada). Hubballi: Sri Vaibhavalakshmi Prakashana.

Karashima, Noboru. 1984. *South Indian History and Society: Studies from Inscriptions, A.D.850-1800*. New Delhi: Oxford University Press.

_________. 1992. *Towards a New Formation: South Indian Society under Vijayanagar Rule*. New Delhi: Oxford University Press.

_________. 2002. *A Concordance of Nāyakas: The Vijayanagara Inscriptions of South India*. New Delhi: Oxford University Press.

_________. 2009. *Ancient to Medieval: South Indian Society in Transition*. Oxford Collected Essays. New Delhi: Oxford University Press.

Kaul, Shonaleeka. 2010. *Imagining the Urban: Sanskrit and the City in Early India*. Ranikhet: Permanent Black.

Kavyapremi. 1995. *Kanakadāsara Hāḍugaḷu*. (in Kannada). Dharwad: Samaja Pustakalaya.

Kelkar, Sanjeev. 2011. *Lost Years of the RSS*. New Delhi: Sage.

King, Richard. 1999. *Orientalism and Religion: Postcolonial Theory, India and "the Mystic East"*. New Delhi: Oxford University Press.

Kosambi, D.D. 1955. "Dhenukākaṭa". *Journal of the Bombay Branch of the Royal Asiatic Society*, 30, pp. 50-71.

Kulke, Hermann. 1993. *Kings and Cults: State Formation and Legitimation in India and Southeast Asia*. New Delhi: Manohar.

Kuppuswamy, G.R. 1975. *Economic Conditions in Karnataka: A.D.973-A.D.1336*. Dharwar: Karnatak University.

Kurtkoti, Keertinath. 1998. *Pratyabhijñāna* (In Kannada). Dharwad: Manohara Granthamala.

_________. 2003. *Adhyayana Mattu Pārāyaṇa* (In Kannada). Dharwad: Manohara Granthamala.

Laine, J. 1983. "The Notion of 'Scripture' in Modern Indian Thought". *Annals of the Bhandarkar Oriental Research Institute*, 64 (1-4), pp. 165-179.

Lal, Mohan. 1992. *Encyclopedia of Indian Literature: Sasay to Zorgot*. New Delhi: Sahitya Akademi.

Liceria, Sister M., A.C. 1972. Social and Economic History of Karnataka, c. AD 1000-1300. Unpublished PhD dissertation submitted to the Patna University, Patna.

Lorenzen, David N. 1972. *The Kapalikas and Kalamukhas*. New Delhi: Thomson Press.

_________ (ed). 2004. *Religious Movements in South Asia, 600-1800*. New Delhi: Oxford University Press.

_________. 2006. *Who Invented Hinduism: Essays on Religion in History*. New Delhi: Yoda Press.

Ludden, David. 1985. *Peasant History in South India*. Princeton: Princeton University Press.

Mahalingam, T.V. 1988. *Inscriptions of the Pallavas*. New Delhi: Indian Council of Historical Research and Agam Prakashan.

Mallappa, T.N. 1974. *Kriyasakti Vidyaranya*. Bangalore: Department of Publications and Extension Lectures, Bangalore Univesity.

Marr, John Ralston. 1985. *The Eight Anthologies—A Study in Early Tamil Literature*. Madras: Institute of Asian Studies.

Marx, Karl. 1909-10. *Capital: A Critique of Political Economy*. 3 Vols. Translated by Ernest Untermann. Edited by Frederick Engles. Chicago: Charles H. Kerr and Co. Co-operative.

Masson, J. Moussaieff. 1980. *The Oceanic Feeling: The Origins of Religious Sentiment in Ancient India*. Dordrecht: D. Reidel Publishing Company.

Mckay, Alex. 2015. *Kailas Histories: Renunciate Traditions and the Construction of Himalayan Sacred Geography*. Leiden: Brill.

Merleau-Ponty, M. 1962. *Phenomenology of Perception*. Translated by Colin Smith. London and New York: Routledge.

Michael, R. Blake. 1992. *The Origins of Vīraśaiva Sects: A Typological Analysis of Ritual and Associational Patterns in the Śūnyasaṃpādane*. Delhi: Motilal Banarsidass.

Michell, George. 2002. *Pattadakal*. Monumental Legacy. New Delhi: Oxford University Press.

_________. 2011. *Badami.Aihole.Pattadakal*. London: Deccan Heritage Foundation.

Mill, James. 2010 [1817]. *The History of British India, Volume 1*. New York: Cambridge University Press.

Mirashi, Vasudev Vishnu. 1981. *The History and Inscriptions of the Sātavāhanas and the Western Kshatrapas*. Bombay: Maharashtra State Board for Literature and Culture.

Modak, B.R. 1995. *Sayana*. Makers of Indian Literature. New Delhi: Sahitya Akademi.
Mohanty, Bidyut. 1993. "Orissa Famine of 1866: Demographic and Economic Consequences". *Economic and Political Weekly*, 28 (1-2), pp. 55-57 & 59-66.
Mugali, R.S. 2007 [1953]. *Kannaḍa Sāhitya Caritre*. (In Kannada). Mysore: Geeta Book House.
Mullens, Joseph. 1854. *Missions in South India*. London: W.H. Dalton.
Nadig, Santhebennur Sumateendra. 2001. "Santēbennūru Nāyakaru". In Rajaram Hegde and Ashok Shettar (eds), *Malekarṇāṭakada Arasu Manetanagaḷu*. (in Kannada). Hampi: Prasaranga, Kannada University.
_________. 2008. *Santēbennūru Nāyakaru*. (in Kannada). Bangalore: Directorate of Karnataka State Archives.
Nagaraj, D.R. 1999. *Allamaprabhu Mattu Śaiva Pratibhe*. (in Kannada). Heggodu: Akshara Prakashana.
_________. 2004. "Critical Tensions in the History of Kannada Literary Culture". In Sheldon Pollock (ed), *Literary Cultures in History: Reconstructions from South Asia*. New Delhi: Oxford University Press, pp. 323-382.
Nandi, Ramendranath. 1973. Religious Institutions and Cults in the Deccan (c. A.D. 600-A.D. 1000). New Delhi: Motilal Banarsidass.
_________. 1986. Social Roots of Religion in Ancient India. Calcutta: K.P. Bagchi and Company.
_________. 2000. *State Formation, Agrarian Growth and Social Change in Feudal South India (c. A.D. 600 – A.D. 1200)*. New Delhi: Manohar.
Nandimath, S.C. 2001. *Theology of the Śaivāgamas: A Study of the Doctrines of Śaiva Siddhanta and Veerasaivism*. Thiruvananthapuram: International School of Dravidian Linguistics.
Narasimhachar, D.L. 2015 [1971]. *Pīṭhikegaḷu Lēkhanagaḷu*. (in Kannada). Mysore: D.V.K. Murthy Prakashana.
Narasimhacharya, R. 2005 [1907-29]. *Karṇāṭaka Kavicaritre*. 3 Vols. (In Kannada). Bangalore: Kannada Sahitya Parishat.
Narayanan, M.G.S. 1996. *Perumals of Kerala: Political and Social Conditions of Kerala Under the Cēra Perumals of Makotai*. Calicut: Published by the author.
Narayanan, M.G.S. and Kesavan Veluthat. 1978. "Bhakti Movement in South India". In S.C. Malik (ed), *Indian Movements: Some Aspects of Dissent, Protest and Reform*. Simla: Indian Institute of Advanced Study.
Narayana Rao, Velcheru, David Shulman and Sanjay Subrahmanyan. 1992. *Symbols of Substance: Court and State in Nayaka-Period Tamil Nadu*. New Delhi: Oxford University Press.
Nietzsche, Friedrich. 1974. *The Gay Science: With a Prelude in Rhymes and an Appendix in Songs*. Translated by Walter Kaufmann. New York: Random House.
Nilakanta Sastri, K.A. 1955. *The Colas*. Madras: University of Madras.
_________. 1966. *A History of South India from Prehistoric Times to the Fall of Vijayanagar*. Madras: Oxford University Press.
Olson, Carl. 2015. *Indian Asceticism: Power, Violence, and Play*. New York: Oxford University Press.
Orr, Leslie C. 2000. *Donors, Devotees and Daughters of God: Temple Women in Medieval Tamilnadu*. New York: Oxford University Press.
Ota, Nobuhiro. 2008. "A Study of Two Nayaka Families in the Vijayanagar kingdom in the Sixteenth Century". *Memoirs of the ToyoBunko*, 66, pp. 103-129.
_________. 2015. "Who Built 'the City of Victory'? Representation of a 'Hindu' Capital in an 'Islamicate' World". In Crispin Bates and Minoru Mio (eds), *Cities in South Asia*. Routledge: Oxon and New York, pp. 27-44.
Padashetti, M.M. 1992. *Tinthiṇi Mōnappayya: Ondu Adhyayana*. (in Kannada). Gadaga: Virashaiva Adhyayana Samsthe.
Pandey, Gyanendra. 1990. *The Construction of Communalism in Colonial North India*. New Delhi: Oxford University Press.

Papan-Matin, Firoozeh. 2010. *Beyond Death: The Mystical Teachings of* 'Ayn al-Quḍāt al-Hamadhānī. Leiden: Brill.
Paranjape, Makarand R. 2015. *Swami Vivekananda: A Contemporary Reader*. New Delhi: Routledge.
Parthasarathy, Aralu Mallige. 2011 [1988]. *Śrī Vādirāja Saṃpuṭa*. (in Kannada). Bangalore: Sneha Book House.
_________ (ed). 2013. *Haridāsara 10000 Hāḍugaḷu*. (In Kannada). Edited with the assistance of Ha. Ra. Nagaraja Acharya. Bangalore: Sri Haridasa Sangha.
Pavate, Shivakumar. 2009. *Maṅgaḷavāḍa Mattu Itara Lēkhanagaḷu*. (In Kannada). Mysore: Akhila Bharata Sharana Sahitya Parishat.
Paz, Octavio. 1961. *The Labyrinths of Solitude: Life and Thought in Mexico*. New York: Brave Press.
Peabody, Norbert. 2003. *Hindu Kingship and Polity in Precolonial India*. Cambridge: Cambridge University Press.
Pennington, Brian K. 2005. *Was Hinduism Invented? Britons, Indians, and the Colonial Construction of Religion*. New York: Oxford University Press.
Perlin, Frank. 1987. "Money-Use in Late Pre-Colonial India and the International Trade in Currency Media". In John Richards (ed), *The Imperial Monetary System of Mughal India*. Delhi: Oxford University Press.
Pinch, William R. 1996. *Peasants and Monks in British India*. Berkeley and Los Angeles: University of California Press.
_________. 2006. *Warrior Ascetics and Indian Empires*. Cambridge: Cambridge University Press.
Polanyi, Karl. 2001. *The Great Transformation: The Political and Economic Origins of Our Time*. second edition. Boston: Beacon Press.
Pollock, Sheldon. 1984. "The Divine King in Indian Epic". *Journal of the American Oriental Society*, 104 (3): 505-528.
_________. 1985. "The Theory of Practice and the Practice of Theory in Indian Intellectual History". *Journal of the American Oriental Society*, 105 (3): 499-519.
_________. 1989. "Mimamsa and the Problem of History in Traditional India". *The Journal of American Oriental Society*, 109 (4): 603-610.
_________. 1993. "Ramayana and the Political Imagination in India". *The Journal of Asian Studies*, 52 (2): 261-297.
_________. 1995. "Literary History, Indian History, World History". *Social Scientist*, 23 (10-12): 112-142.
_________. 1998a. "The Cosmopolitan Vernacular". In *Journal of Asian Studies*, 57 (1): 6-37.
_________. 1998b. "India in the Vernacular Millennium: Literary Culture and polity, 1000-1500". In "Early Modernities," special issue. Edited by Samuel Eisenstadt and Wolfgang Schluchter. *Daedalus*, 127 (3): 41-74.
_________ (ed). 2004. *Literary Cultures in History: Reconstructions from South Asia*. New Delhi: Oxford University Press.
_________. 2005. *The Ends of Man at the End of Premodernity*. Amsterdam: Royal Netherlands Academy of Arts and Sciences.
_________. 2007. *The Language of the Gods in the World of Men: Sanskrit, Culture and Power in Premodern South Asia*. New Delhi: Permanent Black.
Popper, Karl. 2002 [1959]. *The Logic of Scientific Discovery*. London and New York: Routledge.
Poulantzas, Nicos. 1973. *Political Power and Social Classes*. London: New Left Books.
Pujarhalli, Virupaksha. 2004. *Baḷḷāri Jilleya Pāḷeyagāraru*. (in Kannada). Hampi: Prasaranga, Kannada University.
Raghavan, V. 1940. *The Number of Rasas*. Adyar, Madras: The Theosophical Publishing House.
Raghavavarier, M.R. and Kesavan Veluthat. 2013. *Tarisāppaḷḷippaṭṭayaṃ*. (In Malayalam). Kottayam: Sahityapravarthaka Sahakaranasangham.
Rajagopalachari, C. nd. *Hinduism: Doctrine and Way of Life*. New Delhi: The Hindustan Times.

Ramachandran, Puthusseri. 2007. *Kēraḷacaritrattinṟe Aṭisthānarēkhakaḷ*. (In Malayalam). Thiruvananthapuram: State Institute of Languages.

Ramanujan, A.K. (trans). 1973. *Speaking of Śiva*. Harmondsworth: Penguin.

__________ (trans). 1981. *Hymns to the Drowning*. Princeton, New Jersey: Princeton University Press.

__________. 1999. *The Collected Essays of A.K. Ramanujan*. Edited by Vinay Dharwadkar. New Delhi: Oxford University Press.

Ramaswamy, Vijaya. 1996. *Divinity and Deviance: Women in Vīraśaivism*. New Delhi: Oxford University Press.

Ramesh, K.V. (ed). 1984. *Inscriptions of the Western Gangas*. New Delhi: Agam Prakashan, Indian Council of Historical Research.

Ray, Himanshu Prabha. 1986. *Monastery and Guild: Commerce under the Sātavāhanas*. Delhi: Oxford University Press.

Ray, Reginald A. 1994. *Buddhist Saints in India: A Study in Buddhist Values and Orientations*. New York and Oxford: Oxford University Press.

Report of the Indian Famine Commission, Part 1, Famine Relief. 1880. London: George Edward Eyre and William Spottiswoode.

Richards, John F. 1993. *The Mughal State*. (The New Cambridge History of India I.5). Cambridge: Cambridge University Press.

Roy, Kumkum. 2010a. "Women and Men Donors at Sanchi: A Study of Inscriptional Evidence". In Idem. *The Power of Gender & the Gender of Power: Explorations in Early Indian History*. Oxford Collected Essays. New Delhi: Oxford University Press, pp. 38-52.

__________. 2010b. "The Artful Biographer: Sandhyākāranandi's *Rāmacaritam*". In Idem. *The Power of Gender & the Gender of Power: Explorations in Early Indian History*. Oxford Collected Essays. New Delhi: Oxford University Press, pp. 358-369.

Rubiés, Joan-Pau. 2000. *Travel and Ethnography in the Renaissance: South India Through European Eyes, 1250-1625*. Cambridge: Cambridge University Press.

Sabarad, Basavaraj (ed). 2000. *Haidarābād Karnāṭakada Tatvapadagaḷu*. (In Kannada). Hampi: Prasaranga, Kannada University.

Sadashivappa, Kum. Ba. 1996. *Harapanahaḷḷi Pāḷeyagāraru*. (In Kannada). Bangalore: Kannada Sahitya Parishat.

Saletore, B.A. 1934. *Social and Political Life in Vijayanagara Empire*. 2 Vols. Madras: B.G. Paul & Co.

Salje, W. 1998. "On Changing Others' Ideas: The Case of Vidyāraṇya and Yogavāsiṣṭa". *Indo-Iranian Journal*, 41 (2), pp. 103-124.

Sattar, P. Abdul. 1997. *Tarikereya Pāḷeyagāraru*. (in Kannada). Pandavapura: Sri Lokapavani Prakashana.

Sahlins, Marshall. 1985. *Islands of History*. Chicago & London: The University of Chicago Press.

Said, Edward. 1979. *Orientalism*. New York: Vintage Books.

Sax, William (ed). 1995. *The Gods at Play: Lila in South Asia*. New York: Oxford University Press.

Schouten, J.P. 1995. *Revolution of the Mystics: On the Social Aspects of Vīraśaivism*. Delhi: Motilal Banarsidass.

Sen, Tansen, 2004. *Buddhism, Diplomacy, and Trade: The Realignment of Sino-Indian Relations, 600-1400*. New Delhi: Manohar.

Settar, S. 1986. *Inviting Death: Historical Experiments on Sepulchral Hill*. Dharwad: Institute of Indian Art History, Karnatak University.

__________. 1990. *Pursuing Death: Philosophy and Practice of Voluntary Termination of Life*. Dharwad: Institute of Indian Art History, Karnatak University.

__________. 2012. *Somanathapura*. Second edition. Bangalore: Ruvari.

Settar, S. and Günther D. Sontheimer (eds). 1982. *Memorial Stones: A Study of Their Origin, Significance and Variety*. Dharwad: Institute of Indian Art History, Karnatak University.

Sewell, Robert. 1900. *A Forgotten Empire (Vijayanagar): A Contribution to the History of India*. London: Swan Sonnenschein & Co., Ltd.
Shamba Joshi. 1999. *Śaṃbā Kṛti Saṃpuṭa*. 6 Vols. (In Kannada). Edited by Mallepuram Venkatesha. Bangalore: Kannada Book Authority.
Sharma, R.S. 1987. *Urban Decay in India: c.300-c.1000*. New Delhi: Munshiram Manoharlal.
_________. 2007. *Material Culture and Social Formations in Ancient India*. Second edition. New Delhi: Macmillan.
Sheik Ali, B. 1976. *History of the Western Gangas*. Mysore: University of Mysore.
Shivanna, K.S. 1992. *The Agrarian System of Karnataka (1336-1761)*. Mysore: Prasaranga, University of Mysore.
Shivaprakash, H.S. (trans). 2010. *I Keep Vigil of Rudra*. New Delhi: Penguin.
Shulman, David (ed). 1995. *Syllables of Sky: Studies in South Indian Civilization in Honour of Velcheru Narayana Rao*. New Delhi: Oxford University Press.
_________. 2001. *The Wisdom of Poets: Studies in Tamil, Telugu, and Sanskrit*. New Delhi: Oxford University Press.
_________. 2012. *More Than Real: A History of the Imagination in South India*. Cambridge, Massachusetts and London: Harvard University Press.
Siddharama Swami, S.J.F. 2002 [nd]. *Śirahaṭṭiya Śrī Jagadguru Fakīrēśvara Caritre*. Shirahatti: Shri Fakeereshwaramath.
Simmons, Caleb. 2014. "The Goddess and Vaiṣṇavism in Search of Regional Supremacy: Woḍeyar Devotional Traditions During the Reign of Rāja Woḍeyar (1578-1617 CE) *Indian History*, 1, pp. 27-46.
Sinopoli, Carla M and Kathleen D. Morrison. 1995. "Dimensions of Imperial Control: The Vijayanagara Empire". *American Anthropologist* (New Series), 97 (1): 83-96.
Sinha, A.J. 1996. "Architectural Invention in Sacred Structures: The Case of Vesara Temples of Southern India". *The Journal of the Society of Architectural Historians*, 55 (4): 382-399.
Smith, Wilfred Cantwell. 1997. "A Human View of Truth". In John W. Burbridge (ed), *Modern Culture from a Comparative Perspective*. Albany: State University of New York Press, pp. 99-119.
Soppimath, Basavalinga. 1995. *Koḍēkallu Basavaṇṇa: Ondu Adhyayana*. (In Kannada). Kodekallu: Kodekallu Basaveshwara Adhyayana Samsthe.
_________ (ed). 1998. *Koḍēkalla Vacanavākya*, Vol. 1. (In Kannada). Hampi: Prasaranga, Kannada University.
Srikantaya, S. 1938. *The Founders of Vijayanagar*. Bangalore: The Mythic Society.
Srinivasachari, P.N. 1943. *The Philosophy of Viśistādvaita*. Adyar: The Adyar Library.
Stein, Burton. 1980. *Peasant State and Society in Medieval South India*. New Delhi: Oxford University Press.
_________. 1989. *Vijayanagara*. Cambridge: Cambridge University Press.
Subbarayalu, Y. 1973. *The Political Geography of the Chola Country*. Madras: Tamilnadu State Department of Archaeology.
_________. 1982. "The Cola State". *Studies in History* (new series), 4 (2): 265-306.
Subrahmanyam, Sanjay. 1990. *The Political Economy of Commerce: Southern India 1500-1650*. Cambridge: Cambridge University Press.
_________. 2004a. *Explorations in Connected History: From the Tagus to the Ganges*. New Delhi: Oxford University Press.
_________. 2004b. *Explorations in Connected History: Mughals and Franks*. New Delhi: Oxford University Press.
Sundaram, K. 1968. *Studies in Economic and Social Conditions of Medeival Andhra (1000-1600)*. Madras: Triveni Publications.
Talbot, Cynthia. 1991. "Temples, Donors, and Gifts: Patterns of Patronage in Thirteenth-Century South India". *Journal of Asian Studies*, 50 (2): 308-340.

_________. 2001. *Precolonial India in Practice: Society, Region, and Identity in Medieval Andhra*. New Delhi: Oxford University Press.

Tambiah, Stanley J. 1976. *World Conqueror and World Renouncer: A Study of Buddhism and Polity in Thailand against a Historical Background*. Cambridge: Cambridge University Press.

Tarikere, Rahamat. 1998. *Karnāṭakada Sūfigaḷu*. (In Kannada). Hampi: Prasaranga, Kannada University.

Thapar, Romila. 2000a. “Dissent and Protest in Early Indian Tradition”. In Idem. *Cultural Pasts: Essays in Early Indian History*. New Delhi: Oxford University Press, pp. 213-234.

_________. 2000b. “Renunciation: The Making of a Counter-culture?” In Idem. *Cultural Pasts: Essays in Early Indian History*. New Delhi: Oxford University Press, pp. 876-913.

_________. 2000c. “The Householder and the Renouncer in the Brahmanical and Buddhist Traditions”. In Idem. *Cultural Pasts: Essays in Early Indian History*. New Delhi: Oxford University Press, pp. 914-945.

Tharakeshwar, V.B. 2003. “Translating Nationalism: The Politics of Language and Community.” *Journal of Karnataka Studies*, 1 (1): 5-59.

Thimmappayya, Muliya. 1977. *Nāḍōja Paṃpa*, second revised edition. (in Kannada). Edited by M. Keshava Bhat. Mysore: Geetha Book House.

Trautmann, Thomas R. 1997. *Aryans and British India: New Perspectives on Indian Pasts*. Berkeley: University of California Press.

Varadarajarao, G. 1987 [1973]. *Śrīpādarājara Kṛtigaḷu*. (in Kannada). Mysore: Institute of Kannada Studies, University of Mysore.

Veluthat, Kesavan. 1990. “The Role of Nāḍu in the Socio-Political Structure of South India (AD c. 600-1200)”. In H.V. Sreenivasa Murthy, B. Surendra Rao, Kesavan Veluthat and S.A. Bari (eds), *Essays on Indian History and Culture: Felicitation Volume in Honour of Professor B. Sheik Ali*. New Delhi: Mittal Publications, pp. 85-98.

_________. 2009. *The Early Medieval in South India*. New Delhi: Oxford Univeristy Press.

_________. 2012. *The Political Structure of Early Medieval South India*. second edition. New Delhi: Orient Blackswan.

_________. 2013. *Brahman Settlements in Kerala: Historical Studies*. revised and enlarged edition. Thrissur: Cosmo Books.

Venkataramanayya, N. 1935. *Studies in the History of the Third Dynasty of Vijayanagara*. Madras: University of Madras.

Vidyashankar, S. 2013-14. *Vīraśaiva Sāhitya Caritre*, in 4 Volumes. (In Kannada). Bangalore: Priyadarshini Prakashana.

Viraktamath, Shivananda S. 2005. *Amarakalyāṇa*. (In Kannada). Hospet: Nudi Prakashana.

Wagoner, Philip B. 1996. “‘Sultan Among Hindu Kings’: Dress, Titles, and the Islamicization of Hindu Culture at Vijayanagara”. *Journal of Asian Studies*, 55 (4): 851–880.

_________. 2000. “Harihara, Bukka, and the Sultan: The Delhi Sultanate in the Political Imagination of Vijayanagara”. In David Gilmartin and Bruce B. Lawrence (eds), *Beyond Turk and Hindu: Rethinking Religious Identities in Islamicate South Asia*. Gainesville: University Press of Florida, pp. 300-326.

_________. 2014. “Money Use in the Deccan, c. 1350-1687: The Role of Vijayanagara *Hons* in the Bahmani Currency System”. *Indian Economic and Social History Review*, 51 (4): 457-480.

Weber, Max. 1958. *The Religion of India: The Sociology of Hinduism and Buddhism*. Translated by Hans H. Gerth and Don Martindale. Glencoe, Illinois: The Free Press.

Wink, André. 1986. *Land and Sovereignty in India: Agrarian Society and Politics under the Eighteenth-Century Maratha Svarajya*. Cambridge: Cambridge University Press.

Yocum, Glenn E. 1973. “Shrines, Shamanism and Love Poetry: Elements in the Emergence of Popular Tamil Bhakti”. *Journal of the American Academy of Religion*, 41 (1): 3-17.

Younger, Paul. 1995. *The Home of the Dancing Sivan: Traditions of the Hindu Temple in Citamparam*. New York: Oxford University Press.
Yogeeshwarappa, D.N. 1999. *Hagalavadi Nayakaru*. (in Kannada). Hampi: Prasaranga, Kannada University.
Zaehner, R.C. 1962. *Hinduism*. Oxford: Oxford University Press.

List of Tables

Index

www.ingramcontent.com/pod-product-compliance
Lightning Source LLC
Chambersburg PA
CBHW050359110426
42812CB00006BA/1744
* 9 7 8 3 1 1 0 5 1 7 3 6 1 *